Arthur C. Coxe

Institutes of Christian History

an introduction to historic reading and study

Arthur C. Coxe

Institutes of Christian History
an introduction to historic reading and study

ISBN/EAN: 9783337262716

Printed in Europe, USA, Canada, Australia, Japan

Cover: Foto ©Lupo / pixelio.de

More available books at **www.hansebooks.com**

The Baldwin Lectures, 1886

INSTITUTES

OF

CHRISTIAN HISTORY

An Introduction

TO

HISTORIC READING AND STUDY

BY A. CLEVELAND COXE

BISHOP OF WESTERN NEW YORK

I do but prompt the age to quit their clogs. — MILTON

CHICAGO
A. C. McCLURG AND COMPANY
1887

TO

SIBYL AUGUSTA,

WIFE OF HENRY PORTER BALDWIN,

Sometime Governor of the State of Michigan, and subsequently a Senator of the United States.

MADAM,
    It was your happy privilege to associate yourself with your distinguished husband in the endowment of the Baldwin Lectures, following the example of illustrious women in the Mother Church and furnishing an example which I trust will be imitated by Christian women in America in time to come. I count it a great honour to have received the first appointment as Baldwin Lecturer under the judicious provisions of the foundation. Suffer me to inscribe these first-fruits of the project to you, as a tribute to yourself and to my beloved friend, "the Governor," as his fellow citizens still delight to call him, even now when he has withdrawn himself from public life.

The far-seeing and gifted prelate who presides over the diocese of Michigan has endeared himself to the Church at large by the establishment of the HOBART GUILD *at the seat of the State University, for the promotion of Christian work in that seat of learning. And greatly is he to be congratulated upon the sympathy and co-operation with which you and Governor Baldwin have so promptly and so effi-*

ciently sustained his effort. Without lay helpers what can an American bishop do? And where innumerable works for developing and sustaining Christianity in the Republic ought to be set on foot vigorously and without delay, how good it is that there are not wanting some to lend the eloquence of their practical beneficence to the appeals of their fathers in God!

May you and your husband, even in this life, enjoy great recompense in seeing the rich results which are sure to spring from your good works. In the better life to come, what blessed promises of God's Word assure you, through the Redeemer's merits, of rewards unspeakable and full of glory!

Let me remain, dear madam,

Your faithful and grateful friend,

A. CLEVELAND COXE,
Bishop of Western New York.

LEACOTE,
RHINEBECK-ON-HUDSON,
September, 1887.

PREFACE.

THE foundation of the "HOBART GUILD," and therewith of the "BALDWIN LECTURES," in the University of Michigan, has directed the attention of the Church to a new and wise policy with reference to our State schools and colleges. The instrument which fully expounds this movement will be found in another page of this book.[1] We owe these foundations to the enlightened wisdom and foresight of the Right Reverend prelate, who, with such great advantage to the Church at large, now presides over the Diocese of Michigan. But he would hardly forgive me should I neglect to add, that in the munificence of Governor Baldwin and his accomplished wife he has found that sort of encouragement and help without which the ablest and most zealous bishop is impotent to effect what his heart and head may prompt him to propose as due alike to the Republic and to the Church of Christ.

[1] See "Deed of Trust," p. 299.

This book would have been more promptly issued from the press, had not many important practical questions demanded prudent delays in a publication designed to be the first of a series. Such a series must be uniform in size and appearance; and what should be the form and cost? The choice of a publisher to whom, probably, many future volumes must be intrusted in the progress of the successive annual courses, and many subordinate considerations, were also to be decided. It was our deliberate conclusion, that a judicious medium between cost and cheapness must be accepted to secure the widest possible circulation for the series; and we trust the "make-up" of this book will be regarded as justifying a conclusion of great practical importance. A Western University, it was also thought, should not look eastward for a publishing house, while the great book business and admirable publishing facilities of Chicago invited us to the great midland metropolis.

Those who listened to the Lectures last autumn will find a rearrangement of some of the lectures, and some transpositions of material. This grows out of the fact, that, in the arrangement of the course, the more important matters were grouped, less logically, with reference to the evenings of the week most free from other work in the University, and hence most likely to secure the larger audiences. I have also taken the liberty, even at the sacrifice of material which seemed on the whole less important, to enlarge upon some points which I was forced to slight in oral lecturing. In this I was partly guided by kind inquiries and suggestions of friends who attended the entire course. I must be allowed to express my sense of obligation to the President and Professors of the University, who afforded me so much encouragement, and by whose influence, no doubt, I was able to secure, for so many evenings, one of the largest, and, including the youth whom I considered so interesting a class in themselves, one of the most intelligent and inspiring auditories, which it was ever my happiness to address.

A. C. C.

LEACOTE,
RHINEBECK-ON-HUDSON,
September 10, 1887.

CONTENTS.

LECTURE I.

INTRODUCTORY.

		PAGE
1.	Truth	9
2.	Humanity	9
3.	History and its Study	10
4.	The Use of Lectures	12
5.	The Heritage of the Ages	13
6.	Christian History	14
7.	The Pivot	15
8.	Empirical History	16
9.	Conventional Ideas	17
10.	An Underestimated Epoch	18
11.	The Ruts of Habit	19
12.	Another Example	21
13.	Tokens of a New Era	22
14.	A Brilliant Work that just misses a Prize	24
15.	Scientific History	25
16.	The Mother of Theology	25
17.	Institutes	26
18.	Truth, Old and New	28
19.	Catholicity	29
20.	A Comparison	31
21.	Bacon and his Idols	31
22.	Dates of Anchorage	33
23.	The Great Epochs	34
24.	A Practical Plan	35
25.	The Survey	37
26.	A Practical Use of Historic Science	38

LECTURE II.

THE APOSTOLIC FATHERS AND NEXT AGES.

1. Antioch 40
2. A Contrast . . 41
3. An Inquiry 42
4. The Portraiture of Antioch . . . 42
5. The Populace 45
6. The Jewish Element 47
7. The Church in Antioch 48
8. The Exceptional Apostolate 49
9. Apostolic Institutions 50
10. Apostolic Fathers. — Ignatius . . . 52
11. Justin Martyr 53
12. The Persecutions . . . 55
13. Polycarp 55
14. Primitive Schools. — Alexandria . . 57
15. Many Doctors. — Athanasius 58
16. The Punic School. — Tertullian and Cyprian . . 59
17. Arnobius and Lactantius 61
18. Maxims of Lactantius 62
19. Harmony of Theologians 62
20. The Roman Diocese 63
21. Irenæus, — his Place in the West . . . 64
22. Roman Receptivity 66
23. The Nascent Patriarchate 67
24. Hippolytus 69
25. Caius and Novatian 70
26. The Gallicans 71
27. Chronic Persecutions 71
28. Growth of the Church 73
29. Conversion of the Empire 74
30. Cæsars conquered by Martyrs . . . 75

LECTURE III.

THE SYNODICAL PERIOD.

1. The Conversion of Constantine 77
2. Reserve and Moderation 78

3. The Celibate . . . 78
4. Other Immediate Results 79
5. Disadvantages 82
6. Lasting Results . . 83
7. Primitive Councils . 83
8. A Nursing Father . 85
9. The Temporal Bishopric . 86
10. A General Council . . . 87
11. Nicæa 88
12. The Opening . 89
13. Significant Facts . . 91
14. Results of the Council . . 92
15. The Paschal Letters . 93
16. The Patriarchates . 95
17. The Great Councils . 96
18. The Second Council 97
19. The Council of Ephesus . . 98
20. The Fourth Council . . 99
21. Chalcedon 100
22. Eutyches 102
23. Leo, Patriarch of Old Rome . . 102
24. Immutable Catholicity . . 104
25. Two Supplementary Councils . . 105
26. Ratifications 106
27. The Final Judgment . . . 107
28. Who are Catholics 108

LECTURE IV.

THE CREATION OF A WESTERN EMPIRE.

1. The Breaking up of Old Rome . . 110
2. The Goths, Vandals, and Huns . . . 111
3. Retrospect 112
4. Minor Councils 113
5. Irene 114
6. A Counter Council 115
7. The Rule of Faith 116
8. The Maxim of Vincent 116
9. The Council of Frankfort 117
10. Alcuin 119

11. Universities, and their Origin 119
12. The Caroline Books 121
13. The Degeneracy of the East 123
14. Mohammed 124
15. Successes of Mohammed 125
16. Isnik and Dan 126
17. Frankfort once more 127
18. The Blessed Results 128
19. Charlemagne 129
20. Christmas Day, A. D. 800 130
21. What it meant 131
22. Widely Different Effects 132
23. The Holy Roman Empire 133
24. Insulation of England 134
25. Distinctions 135
26. Formation of the Paparchy 136
27. Conditions Precedent 138
28. My Position 139
29. Nicholas and the Decretals 140
30. An Illustration 143

LECTURE V.

THE MIDDLE AGES.

1. Dark Ages 145
2. Maitland's Elucidation 146
3. A Glance at the East 146
4. The Decretals in Operation 148
5. How it looked in English Eyes 151
6. The Latin Churches 151
7. Gallicanism 152
8. St. Bernard 154
9. The Patristic Period 156
10. The Scholastics 157
11. Relations with Modern Thought 158
12. The Crusades 159
13. Barbarism 161
14. Expiry of the Dark Ages 162
15. The Cinque-Cento 164

16. The Medici	166
17. Gothic Architecture	167
18. The New Christian Architecture .	169
19. Navigation	170
20. Printing	171
21. Great Movements	172
22. The Fall of Constantinople	174
23. Light out of Darkness	175

LECTURE VI.

THE CHURCH OF OUR FOREFATHERS.

1. Identity and Continuity . . .	177
2. Origin of the Church in Britain	178
3. Periods	179
4. The Primitive Period	179
5. Groans of the Britons	180
6. Conversion of the English	181
7. The Early English	182
8. Consequences	183
9. Relations to the Apostolic See	183
10. A Discovery	184
11. The Other Side of the Case . .	185
12. A Conference	186
13. And Another	186
14. Iona and its Missions	188
15. Counsels of Unity	189
16. The Mission of Theodore	190
17. Perilous Innovations	191
18. Compromises	192
19. What its First Archbishop had made of the Anglican Church	193
20. The Venerable Bede	194
21. First English Missions	194
22. The Later Period	195
23. Alfred, the Head of our Race . . .	196
24. Taking our Bearings	197
25. The Anglo-Norman Period	198
26. The New *Episcopus ab Extra* . .	199

27. The Foreign Archbishops . . 200
28. The Great Lanfranc . . . 201
29. Old Landmarks 201
30. An Anglican Primate . . . 202
31. Cypriote Autonomy 204
32. Anglican Liberties asserted . . 205
33. The Great Anselm . . . 206
34. Intrusion of Legates 207
35. Where we stand . . . 209

LECTURE VII.

THE ELEMENTS OF RESTORATION.

1. The Transition yet Incomplete . . 211
2. The Plantagenets 212
3. The Submission 214
4. Two Forces 215
5. Three Classes involved . . . 216
6. Innocent III. . . 217
7. The Ebb of the Normans . . 218
8. Archbishop Langton 219
9. England a Fief of Rome . . . 221
10. Magna Charta . . 222
11. Henry the Third . . 222
12. Two Edwards . . . 224
13. The Third Edward 225
14. Spiritual Progress 227
15. Oxford Men 229
16. Greathead . . 230
17. Wiclif 231
18. The English Language . . 231
16. The Popes of Avignon . . . 232
20. Wiclif's Antecedents . . . 233
21. The Good Parliament . . . 234
22. The First Citation 235
23. The Second Citation . . . 235
24. Lambeth 236
25. The Friars 237
26. Wiclif's Death and Character . . 239

27. An Estimate of Wiclif's Work . . . 241
28. Mistakes 241
29. The Good Things 243
30. A Period of Delays . . 244
31. Our Great Benefactors . . . 245
32. The Epoch of Wolsey 246
33. Restored Rights 248
34. Who did this? 249
35. Another Step 251
36. How it looked in France 251
37. The Sequel 252
38. The Bloody Queen 253
39. The Martyrs 254

LECTURE VIII.

A CATHOLIC VIEW OF CHRISTENDOM.

1. The Accession of Elizabeth 256
2. The Marian Schism 256
3. The Restored Autonomy 258
4. The Articles 259
5. Their Catholic Core 261
6. The Formation of the Trentine Church 261
7. Retrospect 264
8. The Mistake of Gerson 265
9. School Grudges 267
10. Pisa 268
11. Sigismund visits England 269
12. The English Embassy to Constance 270
13. Huss as a Reformer 270
14. Constance 271
15. The Martyrs of Constance 272
16. The Infamy of Constance 273
17. One Vote and the Consequences 274
18. The Council of Basle 275
19. Two Points set Right 276
20. Political Protestantism 278
21. Reflections 278
22. Recent Reaction 281

23. The Contrast 282
24. The Fall of the Papal Throne 284
25. Survey of Christendom 285
26. Nicene Constitutions Imperishable 286
27. Practical Unities 288
28. The Parable of Patmos 289
29. Perils of the Republic 291
30. The Constructive Forces of the American Church . . 293
31. An Appeal to Youth 295
32. Conclusion 296

GENERAL NOTE. — DEED OF TRUST . . . 299
MISCELLANEOUS NOTES 303

INSTITUTES

OF

CHRISTIAN HISTORY.

LECTURE I.

INTRODUCTORY.

1. TRUTH.

TRUTH, like her divine Author, is despised and rejected of men. Bleeding between malefactors, it sheds out of its great heart streams of mercy for mankind. It often seems wounded beyond all hope of resurrection; but, as one has happily said, "Not always shall Christ hang between two thieves; there shall yet be a resurrection for crucified Truth."

2. HUMANITY.

In a day like ours, when millions whom Christianity has lifted out of Paganism, and blessed at least with civilization and mental enlightenment, recognize no obligations to the source of human welfare, it is ignoble indeed to belong to a herd of the ungrateful and unbelieving. Yet, while we come out from among them and separate ourselves from their corrupt society, let us reflect, as our Master has taught us, that "they know not what they do." Let us treat humanity, even in its most offensive forms of degradation, with veneration and with tenderness. Christ has bought it with His blood, and clothed its ulcers with the imperial purple of His cross. How dear mankind should be to those who glory in that sign! In a materialized generation, let us rebuke with no scornful words, but by a pure example and by practical love, those who persecute what we adore, — "shooting out their arrows, even bitter words." Let us bear our testimony to the eternal verities which must soon vindicate themselves. While, all around us, the people of the epoch live to eat and drink, and, above all, to be amused, — to trifle and chase butterflies, — to quarrel about sordid things and disquiet themselves with low and transient interests of the earth, — let us live like sons of God and heirs of immortality. Let us assert the lofty mission of witnesses for truth; let us tenderly expostulate with the multitudes who are rebels to the dictates of experience, and blind alike to the lessons of history and the sunlight of revelation.

3. HISTORY AND ITS STUDY.

If history be "philosophy teaching by example," who does not see that it is the noblest study to which we can devote ourselves? It is the study of humanity, illustrated by innumerable specimens, and enriched by the lives and teachings of the masters of human thought in all ages. Let us beware, however, of mistaking for history the fables which often claim the title. Let us feel the vital importance of discovering historic truth. Let us reflect that in every investigation we have been furnished with a guide to the real and the unfeigned in the only perfect history,— that of which it is written, "Thy word is truth." I hesitate not to say, that, in the search of historic truth, he who begins not with the inspired narratives has no education that prepares him for his task. It is the blessed prerogative of faith in God to gather from His word the great secret of history, as something directed by Providence, always at unity with itself, proceeding from one Author and tending to one result. He who stupidly deals with events as if they were a random product of undirected human caprices and of men's undisciplined instincts, may be an annalist, a chronologist, a collector of details, but he cannot be, in the highest sense, a genuine historian. The lofty intelligence, akin to military genius, which marshals, combines, analyzes, and co-ordinates facts, showing their mutual relations, and their bearings on human progress and on the revealed plans of the Most High, is essential to the philosophic historian. Not less is something of the same kind essential to the student of history,— to us, young gentlemen, who are mere recipients, economizing the lives and labours of the world's benefactors, in order that we in turn may not be wholly wanting in our life-work and in our appointed place among men.

4. THE USE OF LECTURES.

He who outlines truth in the form of popular lectures has, indeed, the distasteful prospect of producing only momentary impressions. In spite of this, my effort shall find encouragement in the fact that I address myself to youth, — to young men of liberal pursuits and zealous to be directed to the sources of real knowledge and sound principle. To the growing mind that thirsts for information supported by evidence, the lecturer who brings truths that will bear investigation has a cheering mission. History gives us many examples of disciples, fired by earnest teachers, who long outlived their masters and greatly surpassed them. A word, an expression, a turn of thought, may quicken in some young brain impulses which shall give direction to all the future labours of a noble and successful life.

Long after I am dead and forgotten, some of you may live to say with effect what I can only enforce with earnest conviction. After the chastisements which a foolish age is bringing upon itself, you may live to be welcomed by a wiser generation. You will find your appointed task at another epoch. In your faces I seem to salute the twentieth century. As for us who must soon pass away, *Morituri vos salutamus !* The future belongs to you. Prepare yourselves to be its masters. But be sure you cannot be such save as you accept the lessons of human experience from the venerable past. Under the idea of progress, our times are chasing a mere will-o'-the-wisp;

a light engendered from decay, "that leads to bewilder and dazzles to blind." True progress always takes up the winnowed harvests of the ages, and scatters the seed of all that must be food for the ages to come. Instead of having "no past at your back," the youth of this Republic start with the manifold treasures of all time, of all arts and sciences, of all that man has done, warned by the failures and mistakes of old countries and of unpractical theorists. You are here in America to build up a nation by the maxims of tried wisdom, and to establish its institutions upon the rock of God's word.

5. THE HERITAGE OF THE AGES.

You are heirs of the ages; and it shall be my endeavour to make you great collectors of its lessons, its morals, its warnings. Under my own observation, a few shells given to a boy, by a friend who encouraged him to add to the little stock of smooth and many-coloured toys, created for the boy his life employment, made him a naturalist, and enabled him to amass from all the seas and oceans of the globe a museum of conchology, and to classify and expound his treasures as a philosopher. So I have known others to be made botanists, or enthusiasts in geology or chemistry, or passionate collectors of gems and coins. All such scientific pursuits are ennobling. Even the "dried beetle with a pin stuck through him" may be full of instruction to a careful observer; and under the microscope what miracles of creative wisdom are unfolded to the student of an insect's eye or wing! But I claim for the student of historic truth a nobler sphere, and the faculty of bringing together a sublimer collection for ends unspeakably more practical and beneficial to the world. You collect portraits and pictures out of every age and clime, and furnish the chambers of your imagination with all that is most beautiful and precious in the results of human life. The philosopher whose department is biography and history makes his mind —

> "A mansion for all lovely forms,
> His memory to be a dwelling-place
> For all sweet sounds and harmonies."

The whole world is a mine for his research, and all times are the fields of his exploration. From the Pyramids to the Catacombs; from the ruins of Egypt or Assyria to the mysterious remains of the Aztecs; under the arches and monuments of ancient Rome; amid the more splendid relics of Greek art and munificent ostentation; and passing thence to the wealth of the Rhineland, of the Louvre or the British Museum, — everywhere among men, he finds his material, his work, and his elevated enjoyments as well. The master of historic truth is the master of contemporaneous thought, in proportion as he instructs his age or contends with it. To such ennobling pursuits I now invite you.

6. CHRISTIAN HISTORY.

You know the difference between "anatomy" and "comparative anatomy" in the schools of the surgeon. The latter is a science which extracts auxiliary knowledge from the bones and muscles of brutes, while the anatomist *par excellence* deals with the physical frame of man. In calling your attention to Christian history, I remind you that the history of Pagans and Barbarians is but comparative history, — a useful auxiliary merely. But the history of Christendom is the history of man as very man, the image of his Maker. Christian history is the history of civilization; Christianity alone is the civilizer of the human animal. At best, the race beyond its pale exhibits only here and there a specimen of true manhood. It is only as enlightened from the manger of Bethlehem and the cross of Calvary that the race ceases to be savage.

Reflect that Christianity is as old as the world. Among the patriarchs and under Moses it worked only in element. "Ye are the light of the world," said the Master to the Galilean fishermen; and so it has proved. Not where the Gospel is merely named, but in proportion as it penetrates the life of a nation, this is realized. It needs no elaborate argument. One scorns to argue that sunlight makes the day. Look at mankind, look at the nations. The character of the true woman is the influence that refines, and where is the true woman, the wife, the mother, the home, apart from Christianity? In a word, Christianity is civilization.

7. THE PIVOT.

The world's history turns, as on a pivot, upon the Mount of Olives, and upon the great mission,

"Go ye into all the world, and preach the Gospel." The Old Testament shows us how all preceding history was its prelude, and every succeeding generation establishes the fundamental truth, that the people and nation that will not be taught of Christ must perish. Adequate ideas of the world's history can be gained, if this be true, by him only who surveys the world from this standpoint.

8. EMPIRICAL HISTORY.

It is a curious thing in literature, that popular historians have been to so great an extent inspired by an unnatural enthusiasm against the Gospel. Such a perverted genius as that of Gibbon has unfortunately controlled the fancies of others, and our libraries are filled with elaborate distortions of historic fact, one book begotten of another, and all conveying the most confused and inadequate ideas of the world's progress. What a splendid opportunity was lost by Gibbon, when he resolved to leave out from his narrative the story of the apostles and martyrs, ignoring the unquestionable base of all he undertook to tell! The stubborn facts could not be overlooked; but, as far as possible, he gropes on with Paganism under the Antonines, without reference to realities which he only reaches in his fifteenth chapter, and of which he then condescends to take notice as "a very essential part of the history of the Roman Empire." Ah, indeed! Hamlet a very interesting part of the drama! The entire chapter reflects disgrace upon its author, alike by its place in his ponderous work, and by the spirit with which he struggles to assign the origin and progress of the Gospel to every cause but the true one, — to every auxiliary influence, forgetting those which are primary and fundamental. It is as if an historian of the United States of America should begin with the great exhibition of industries which took place in Philadelphia at our late Centennial Celebration of Independence, and then, after a volume about the activity and enterprise of the American people, should devote a chapter to prove that Washington and his contemporaries deserved a retrospective glance, as having in a remarkable manner fallen in with times and circumstances and mingled some wisdom and more mistake in their influences upon succeeding times and manners.

9. CONVENTIONAL IDEAS.

A better class of historians, such as Robertson, and Ranke, and Dean Milman, have been unable to divest themselves of conventional ideas and habits in their valuable works. They adhere to traditional notions and misleading phrases, even where they demonstrate the fallacy of such forms of thought and speech. Thus, while they tell us about the exploded Decretals, and other fables of the mediæval period, they still adopt the old raiment of language which puzzles the student. They speak of Roman pontificates, as if there had been such things in the days of Clement or Hippolytus, and give us tables of "the Popes" beginning with St. Peter! In the very same pages they demonstrate that St. Peter was never at Rome except to be beheaded, and that it is about as sensible to call Sylvester a Pope as it would be to date the Empire from the first consulate, to speak of the "Emperor Cincinnatus," or to paint him at his plough in imperial purple.

10. AN UNDERESTIMATED EPOCH.

The transfer of the Roman capital to Byzantium, for example, is evidence of overwhelming significance, as to the workings of Christianity before Constantine, as to the predominance of the East in its origin and progress for three centuries, and as to the leavening influences in Roman politics, which, in spite of Diocletian and the persecutors before him, had made such an astounding revolution possible, if not inevitable. Christianity had made no assault upon the Cæsars; but the upsetting of their throne upon the seven hills, and the removal of their capital to the Thracian Bosporus, was a mere index of what it had been doing while it fought with the rabble of Olympus and mocked the shameful superstitions of mythology. Yet this most consummate of all the changes and revolutions in history has been wellnigh overlooked, or only treated as a curious incident. Like the Chinese, who survey the universe each one from his own habitation as its focus, our historians have thought and written as Occidentals. They have not condescended to observe that the original seat of Christianity was the Orient; that its triumph was the triumph of Greek thought over the less intellectual Latin races; that this truth was the magnet that drew the Empire eastward, that diminished the influence and dignity of old Rome, and that dictated to it from the Œcumenical Synods, — all Eastern in geography, all Greek in language — in their idiomatic expression of dogma. How comes it, when to state these admitted facts is to prove the conclusions to which I point you, — how comes it that all our popular histories, and most of those which aim to be scientific, chronicle these truths indeed, and then go on to ignore them? They treat of Christianity as if it were generated in Italy, and as if its first doctors and missionaries had been commissioned from the Vatican, in the same pages that enable us to prove the essentially Grecian origin and character of the Church.

II. THE RUTS OF HABIT.

The human mind is slow to turn out of the ruts of habit; it prefers the beaten way, even when it makes them plod in a thoroughfare imprinted only by the hoofs of asses. A noteworthy example presents itself in the condescension of transcendent genius to the trammels of conventional expression. Milton flourished more than a century after the true theory of the universe had been taught by the presbyter Copernicus; he had himself conversed with Galileo, who crowned the system of Copernicus with the glory of irrefragable demonstration. Milton understood the heliocentric structure of the solar system, and the rotations of the earth, diurnal and annual. Now it is most curious, that, although his great poem would have gained immensely by adopting this philosophy, and placing Uriel in a central sun, he yet stuck to the conventional ideas of the poets, and so commensurately degraded the ground plan of his immortal epic. The critical student of that scheme may recall the explorations of Lucifer, as he passed through Chaos and at last discovered our universe, enclosed in a spherical shell and pendent from the resplendent gates of Heaven. When he gained the surface of this shell, and looked down upon the stellar worlds enclosed within, how admirably it would have suited the poet's purpose to have conducted him to our solar system, by a discovery of its real nature,— the glorious sun illuminating the planets, and our earth, with its little moon, in its true relations with all the rest. But no: even the gigantic genius of Milton must fall into the dull routine of untruthful science, and disfigure his work with the rubbish of the outworn Ptolemaic theory; that incomparable monument of the genius and plausibility with which mankind can embellish what is false, and make "the worse appear the better reason." Take a specimen of the consequences: —

> "They pass the planets seven, and pass the fix'd,
> And that crystalline sphere whose balance weighs
> The trepidation talk'd, and that first moved."

Here is neither rhyme nor reason; but it illustrates my point, namely, the disposition even of noble minds to adopt the idols of the market-place, to express themselves in phrases of vulgar thought, and to sacrifice truth to popular ignorance for momentary convenience.[1]

12. ANOTHER EXAMPLE.

Take a notable example. Canon Hussey in his valuable work, "The Rise of the Papal Power," demonstrates that this enormous system was the product of multiplied abuses, beginning with harmless incidents and accidents, and growing by slow accretions into the arrogant claims of the Middle Ages. A schoolboy's snowball becomes an avalanche, in like manner, when it falls from his hand and rolls down the mountain. It was not the avalanche, however, while it was the plaything. Yet this learned author confounds his own plan of tracing the "*Rise* of the Papal Power," by talking of the "supremacy" (which was never universally admitted or enforced even in the Roman communion until our own times) as if it existed from the fourth century. He confounds it with the "primacy"; and while he shows that the whole fabric grew out of a harmless function conferred only for the West by a provincial council, and probably by an abuse of that, he yet speaks of "the supremacy" as if it had been born at this council, where, as he proves clearly enough, such a thing was not even conceived.[2] Going back of this, however, he calls good Sylvester "Pope Sylvester"; whereas if he was a Pope in the Nicene age, there was no "*Rise* of the Papal

[1] See Note A.   [2] See Note B.

Power." Why do men go on proving by facts what they seem to refute in words? If a scholar undertakes to show how and when Bishops of Rome became "Popes," why does he confound his pupil by calling them "popes" ages before a *pope* was dreamed of? To recur to my illustration: all this misleads and mystifies, as when the Ptolemaic system is adopted in practice, while the Copernican verities are theoretically proved.

13. TOKENS OF A NEW ERA.

There are gratifying tokens of an approaching era of investigation, and of historiography based on demonstrated truth and fact. Several recent writers have just fallen short of making themselves leaders in this coming era of scientific history. In a mere sentence Milman records a fact, which, had he seen its importance, would have led him to construct his history of Latin Christianity on fresh and original bases. Such work would have immortalized him. I refer to his brief but all important statement that the local Roman church was for three hundred years a mere colony of Greek Christianity, and that the Church's roots and matrices were wholly Oriental.[1] Dean Stanley enlarges on this in his "Eastern Church," but just misses the bearings of his facts. Had he based his attractive work upon them, it would have risen to the rank of a grand epoch-maker, a genuine work of genius. Take, for example, the passage I will cite, and observe how it revolutionizes con-

[1] See Note C.

ventional ideas of the antiquity of the Paparchy, or of Rome as the "mother of churches." He says:—

"The Greek Church reminds us of the time when the tongue, not of Rome, but of Greece, was the sacred language of Christendom. It was a striking remark of the Emperor Napoleon, that the introduction of Christianity itself was, in a certain sense, the triumph of Greece over Rome; the last and most signal instance of the maxim of Horace, *Græcia capta ferum victorem cepit.* The early Roman church was but a colony of Greek Christians or Grecized Jews. The earliest Fathers of the Western Church wrote in Greek. The early *popes* were not Italians, but Greeks. The name of *pope* is not Latin, but Greek, the common and now despised name of every pastor in the Eastern Church. . . . *She is the mother,* and Rome the daughter. It is her privilege to claim a direct continuity of speech with the earliest times; to boast of reading the whole code of Scripture, Old as well as New, in the language in which it was read and spoken by the Apostles. The humblest peasant who reads his Septuagint or Greek Testament in his own mother tongue on the hills of Bœotia may proudly feel that he has access to the original oracles of divine truth which pope and cardinal reach by a barbarous and imperfect translation; that he has a key of knowledge which in the West is only to be found in the hands of the learned classes."[1]

All this is true, but the author fails to see what it carries with it. *E pur si muove,* said Galileo; but if that was true, the whole system of the universe was to be reformed, as it existed in the schools and in the inveterate habits of human thought. "The East is the mother, and Rome the

[1] See Note D.

daughter," says the Dean; but if this be true, the entire structure of scholastic theology, the Paparchy, and the Council of Trent, are swept away with the fallacy that assumes the reverse. Dean Stanley's work should have proceeded on this fundamental fact of history, and his history of the East should have been illustrated in its true relations to the original constitutions of Christendom.

14. A BRILLIANT WORK THAT JUST MISSES A PRIZE.

But the saddest specimen of collapse is the framework of a book which would have revolutionized Western thought about one of the grandest of historical themes, had it been true to the very facts which it proceeds to make evident. I refer to Bryce's "Holy Roman Empire," a most valuable work, and one which betokens the coming era, but only as a foggy morning is often the harbinger of a brilliant day. How could the writer have missed the opportunity of identifying the rise of the "Holy Roman Empire" with the formation of the Paparchy, which never existed till Charlemagne had created the possibility of a new œcumenical theory for the Church by creating a new *Œcumenc*, or Imperial basis, for its development. Bryce fails to economize this truth. It is a pity that so good a monograph must be written over again. Its faults are as glaring as its merits are great; and that is saying much in a single phrase.[1]

[1] See Note E.

15. SCIENTIFIC HISTORY.

Now the new era of scientific history will be created just as soon as some able and original genius shall be raised up to apply, in historiography, the principles which our age has inexorably demanded in other scientific work. The law of such a movement is simply that of sweeping away demonstrated falsehood and fable, and of proceeding at every step upon the rock foundation of fact. If the East gave to Christianity its historic form and shape, its creed and doctrine, its whole cast and visible outline before the world, why not proceed accordingly? Yes, why not? A thousand myths disappear from the Western mind when once these truths are worked out and made manifest. No more haggling about the popes of controvertists. The entire Papal theory perishes as soon as we find where Rome stood at first, and how absolutely inconsiderable was her place in the early founding and teaching of churches.

16. THE MOTHER OF THEOLOGY.

He who examines the true history of the ages before Constantine is forced to find in Alexandria all with which popes and schoolmen have credited old Rome. After Antioch, the see of St. Mark was the nurse, if not the mother, of the churches, and if not their mistress, yet their schoolmaster.[1] It formed their mind and speech. Latin Christianity itself rose out of Alexandria, the head and brain

[1] See Note F.

of original Christendom. It was formed in Africa and in Carthage, not in Rome. Entire independence of Rome was steadily maintained under the founders of Latin theology,— Tertullian, Minucius Felix, Cyprian, Lactantius, Arnobius, and Augustine. Rome had no voice, in her own tongue, till the heretic Novatian first spoke in her and for her. From Clement to Hippolytus, and later, her few writers thought in Greek, wrote in Greek, and submitted their work to the maternal churches of the East, as filial and loyal sons. To exhibit these facts is to dismiss the whole system of the Latin schools, based on unhistoric myths and fables, all as baseless as the "Donation of Constantine," and all as recent in their fabrication.

17. INSTITUTES.

In presenting these Institutes, then, to my young pupils in this University, I undertake to proceed upon a rigidly scientific plan, of which I have tried to explain the scientific grounds. I adopt the old word *institutes* to signify elementary instructions. They present, in outline, certain predominant features of history, which will guide to just conclusions in the further studies to which they introduce the learner. And now let me fortify my positions by citing the language of a man of science, who speaks for other purposes and with a different intent, upon the very matter which underlies my plan. He, too, gives token of the new era as at hand.[1] Could any one have expected from the

---
[1] See Note G.

apologist of Huxley and Darwin such a tribute to primitive Christianity as John Fiske has given us in the following passages? He says:—

"It is interesting to observe the characteristics of the idea of God as conceived by the three great Fathers of the Greek Church, Clement of Alexandria, Origen, and Athanasius. The philosophy of these profound and vigorous thinkers was, in large measure, derived from the Stoics," etc.

"The views of Clement's disciple, Origen, are much like those of his master. Athanasius ventured much further into the bewildering regions of metaphysics. Yet in his doctrine of the Trinity . . . he proceeded upon the lines which Clement had marked out."

"It is instructive to note how closely Athanasius approaches the confines of modern scientific thought, simply through his fundamental conception of God as the indwelling life of the universe."

Now, without pausing to correct some possible misconceptions of this great matter, I ask you to observe the phenomenon of this mind struggling out of "modern thought" towards what modern thought has affected to ignore, and finding himself met where he stands by these ancient Fathers of Christendom. Two reflections suggest themselves as pertinent to my subject: (1) It is to primitive Christianity that modern science must recur to find its "guide, philosopher, and friend"; and (2) It is to the East, and to Alexandria as the fountainhead, that the inquirer into the origin of Christian thought and dogma must have recourse.

18. TRUTH, OLD AND NEW.

Another suggestion, I trust, will arrest the attention of all who hear me. In guiding your thoughts towards primitive antiquity, I am preparing you for a wise and healthful investigation of recent research and discovery in scientific matters. How often you hear of these old Fathers as mere fossils; and of the Church of Christ as behind the age. Listen again to John Fiske, as he works his way through philosophy to Theism.[1] He says: —

"One has only to adopt the higher Theism of Clement and Athanasius, and the alleged antagonism between science and theology, by which so many hearts have been saddened, so many minds darkened, *vanishes forever*."

And now mark what he says of the dawn of Christianity, in the period illuminated by the Septuagint, and also what he adds of Ante-Nicene Christianity in Alexandria: —

"The intellectual atmosphere of Alexandria for two centuries before and *three centuries after* the time of Christ was more modern than anything that followed, down to the days of Bacon and Descartes. . . . The system of Christian Theism was the work of some of the loftiest minds that have ever appeared on the earth."

Staking off these five centuries accordingly, during which the thought of Christendom was formed under Clement and his forerunners, reflect that between the two centuries of preparation for Christ and the three that ushered in the Great

[1] See Note H.

Council of Nicæa, our ultimate limit, stands the noble figure of Apollos, — " eloquent and mighty in the Scriptures," — a monument of the Gospel in its power to unite the Jew and the Greek, and not less of the Church, to speak from her ancient throne to the hearts and minds of thinking men in our own distracted times.

19. CATHOLICITY.

Here observe a most important point. The centuries which a disinterested thinker has thus characterized, without a thought of aiding the position of the Christian, are precisely those to which the great Anglican doctors have appealed in their noble work of restoration. For the Anglican reformers were restorers rather; they brought back the primitive simplicity and the unadulterated catholicity of Nicæa, — the catholicity which is covered by its own appeal to "ancient usages," and by the formula of the Nicæno-Constantinopolitan Creed. Of course there can be no other. For there cannot be two catholic churches nor two catholic theologies. But in this country and in England two antagonist systems claim to be catholic; which is most harmonious with the catholicity of Nicæa? If it be true that the first three centuries were in spirit, not *mediæval*, but *modern*, the answer is apparent. If they correspond with Bacon and Descartes rather than with Aristotle and the Schoolmen, then the Anglican reformation is vindicated. The "Syllabus," which refuses all commerce with modern thought, shows itself equally at war with Christian antiquity. The present venerable pontiff, a scholar and a most respectable character in all his personal qualities, has accepted the Syllabus of his unlettered predecessor, which denounces all that freemen hold dear, while, to give his thinking subjects something to do, he commands them to study St. Thomas Aquinas. That is, they must revert to the Middle Ages for all the thinking they are allowed to exercise. Precisely so. He rules out the masculine thought of genuine antiquity as modern. He thus convicts his theology of its mediæval origin, while we appeal primarily to the primitive Fathers, — to Clement of Alexandria, and to Athanasius, not undervaluing Aquinas so far as he agrees with antiquity. It is not difficult, then, to decide where catholicity is to be found, if the apostolic ages and the primitive Fathers supply the criterion. Ours is the old religion, because it is identified with the oldest. We appeal to the Holy Scriptures interpreted by the whole undivided Church at Nicæa.[1] Leo XIII. appeals to Aquinas [2] and to the systems of a divided Christendom, — to the West and to the twelfth century with those that followed, down to the Trent Council. And this was a council of the West only, and of the sixteenth century, composed chiefly of Italians, and engineered by the Jesuits, who had just been created, and whose conduct excited the indignant remonstrances of all the abler theologians there assembled. Which, then, is the catholic system, — ours or theirs? [3]

[1] A. D. 325. [2] A. D. 1274. [3] See Note I.

Note, also, that there can no more be two *catholic* churches in Christendom, than there can be two universal physical systems in the same universe. But the "Roman Catholic" scheme of catholicity accepts only the Western churches, and excludes the more ancient churches of the East, while ours includes just what the Nicene Creed includes; that is to say, all the Greek and Latin churches, and all other churches which preserve an apostolic episcopate and the Nicene faith. We recognize the Latin churches as part of the Catholic Church; "the *Roman* Catholic Church is a fiction, derived from the "Holy *Roman* Empire," which called itself the *œcumene*, and hence considered its established church *œcumenical*. Analyze this artificial system and you find it made up of ancient national churches which are all catholic in organic form, but orthodox just so far as they adhere to the primitive theology, and no further. With all her blemishes and failings, the Anglican Church is ready to be judged by this rule, and it is a rule which utterly destroys all claims of catholicity for those Latins who adhere to the modern Council of Trent, and the yet more modern — nay, the recent — additions of Pius IX., which reduce their creed to a thing of yesterday.[1]

21. BACON AND HIS IDOLS.

How comes it that many gifted men fail to see what is so evident when once set in the light of

[1] See Note J.

facts and of common sense? I have spoken of the ruts of habit; let me refer to Bacon's forcible postulates concerning "Idols." That great inciter of all genuine "modern thought" threw down the idols of the Schoolmen which dominated in the realms of physical science; but even to our own times their idols have largely stultified the domain of theology and corrupted historic truth. He was himself an illustration of the sway of idols over the human intellect, for he remained a slave to the Ptolemaic astronomy, in spite of his emancipation from so much that clouded and fettered intellect in his times. He calls these idols, images, or, as we should name them, illusions, "the deepest fallacies of the human mind;" and he adds, "They do not deceive in particulars, as do other fallacies, which cloud and ensnare the judgment, . . . but they are imposed upon the understanding (1) by the *general* nature of the human race, or (2) by the *particular* nature of every several man, or (3) by words, or *communicative* nature." To expose, in some degree, the influence of a corrupt use of words in producing the confusions of historical authors and of popular thought is part of my plan. For the idols of the market-place, which still maintain themselves in our day are almost ineradicable and supremely mischievous. Words as understood in the streets and used by the vulgar, when adopted by the learned in all their ambiguity, are instruments for distilling nightshade alike inebriating and fatal to intelligence.[1]

[1] See Note K.

22. DATES OF ANCHORAGE.

Such idols have too long neutralized the penetrating and generative sunlight of historic truth, as icebergs and fogs hinder the advance of spring. Let me present an outline of the points to be illustrated in these Lectures, which will be an effort to confute idols. For I pursue a practical plan, and am willing to let historic facts speak for themselves. But to be felt in all their force, let them be presented with method. What Ruskin[1] has called "dates of anchorage" are essential to the student of history, who would grasp and retain great facts and epochs, on which others turn as upon pivots or hinges. Geography and chronology are the eyes of historical science. Skeleton maps must be hung up before the mental eyesight, and they must be bordered with cardinal dates of the world's annals, — the epoch-marking dates, that is, or those which have created eras in history. An epoch is a point of time; an era is a period developed from it, as a line is generated in geometry. He who seizes these pivots, hinges, or "dates of anchorage," becomes master of the art. Minor dates and epochs marshal themselves naturally about these heights of command, which afford the soldier a masterly survey of fields where he may meet an enemy. Take, for illustration, some notable examples.

The most convenient and sharp-cut date in Christian history is that of Charlemagne's creation of the Latin Empire; he was crowned, or virtually

[1] See Note L.

crowned himself, on Christmas day, A. D. 800. Nobody can forget such a date as this; and you observe that it divides modern history very equally, if we confine ancient history, as we should, to the periods before the Light of the World appeared. And note its commanding character: it marks the era of Western history, as distinct from that of the East. It is the index of Latin Christianity left to itself; severed from its parent stem; developing into something alien to catholicity; creating the Paparchy; involving the Latin churches in functional schism; defiling them with novelties; darkening their atmosphere with the mists of fable; disfiguring the worship of God with idolatries; inventing new theologies, and condemning the West to centuries of ignorance and superstition, not inappropriately called the "Dark Ages." Not that Charlemagne promoted this directly or intentionally. The reverse is eminently true. But his policy created the Paparchy, which had no existence before his time, nor while he lived; and to the Paparchy, based on the imposture of the Decretals, we owe the Dark Ages, which include the whole period from A. D. 900 to 1400. The Middle Ages include this period, and stretch from the eighth century to the sixteenth, from the imperial crowning of Charlemagne to the birth of Charles-Quint.

23. THE GREAT EPOCHS.

Observe other "dates of anchorage," in dealing with Western history, to which we shall be necessarily limited in these Lectures when once we touch the era of Charlemagne. After the nativity of our Divine Lord, the great epoch of Constantine and the Council of Nice (A. D. 325) marks the close of the martyr ages and the subjection of the Cæsars to the cross. The period which closes with Charlemagne is that of Catholic unity, under the Synodical Constitutions. From Charlemagne to Charles-Quint, we have seven hundred years of Western schism, the Paparchy and the inferior epochs of Imperial and Papal strifes, the Crusades and the Scholastics. From A. D. 1500, the epoch of Charles the Fifth, we date the increase of learning, the struggles for popular freedom, the Continental Reformers, the Anglican Restoration, and the creation of the "Roman Catholic Church," — which, as such, is a modern organization, more recent than Lutheranism itself.

24. A PRACTICAL PLAN.

In establishing this reformed syllabus of historical science, my scheme is less bold than at first sight might appear. It pretends to no original discoveries as to matters of fact: every point on which the scheme depends has been proved, elucidated, overwhelmingly established, by learned writers, — as well among those who have retained communion with Rome, like Erasmus, Bossuet, and the Jansenists, as by the Continental Reformed and the grand old Caroline theologians of England. My only innovations are found in accepting the demonstrations of these authorities, and constructing a harmonious system accordingly, giving facts their place, enforcing their value, and calling things by their right names. For example, the unparalleled imposture of the Decretals is admitted by Jesuits and Gallicans; they are laughed out of court by the Ultramontanes themselves.[1] Yet these "idols of the market-place" impose on Protestants generally. For they go on calling things by the fabulous terms and phrases which the Decretals created. They ignore the East and the constitutions of Catholicity, and give to the *parvenu* system of Trent the old Nicene title of "the Catholic Church." They speak of the Roman pontiffs as "successors of St. Peter"; they dishonour the apostle's memory, by speaking of the criminal throne of the Vatican as the "chair of St. Peter"; they surrender history to the fabulists, by making the early Bishops of Rome into a succession of "Popes," created by Christ himself, and they confound the canonical "primacy," conferred by the Councils of Nice and Constantinople, with an usurped "supremacy," which, had it existed, would have made the action of all councils equally superfluous and impertinent.[2] Modern "Protestantism" clings to its name all the more stoutly because it has ceased to protest. It believes in God with all its heart, but, after all, feels very charitably about the Devil. It glorifies Martin Luther, but cannot but think he went a little too far when he burnt the Pope's bull. It adopts Galileo's conviction that the earth moves, but would not wholly censure the Roman court for putting him to torture and making him abjure it as heresy. In short, it always holds with

[1] See Note M.   [2] See Note N.

the hare, but prefers to run with the hounds, especially if it be in a question of politics. It accepts the Messiah, and feels the force of *Ecce homo!* but its sympathies are always with poor Pilate, except when even Pilate ceased to be a politician, and said, "What I have written I have written."

25. THE SURVEY.

On the principles I have thus illustrated, and exposing the illusions I have mentioned to a searching comparison with facts, I invite you, then, to survey with me the outlines of Christian history, in its majestic sweep through the ages which we owe to the light of the Gospel. This survey will prepare you for many departments of study, and will give you a delight in the ennobling researches to which it is an introduction. Open your eyes, young men, and if you would know the world you have so lately entered, ask how it came to be what you see it, and then trace its progress upward through the ages before you, till your familiarity with past times gives you mastery over your own. The lives of the world's benefactors will inspire your life career. The fatal mistakes and failures so sadly marking the pages of biography will warn you off from shoals and quicksands which have proved so fatal to your predecessors. You will be philosophers from the start; the experiments of others will make your career a success. You will go "from strength to strength," and age itself will find you invested with immortal youth in the prospect of eternity.

26. A PRACTICAL USE OF HISTORIC SCIENCE.

When you begin your travels, my beloved young friends, recall "the dates of anchorage" to which I have endeavored to introduce you. On the *Via Sacra* of old Rome, take your stand beneath the Arch of Titus: it marks[1] the close of the generation which crucified the Son of God, and verifies his prediction of the consequent downfall of Jerusalem and the dispersion of the Jews. Turn then to the stupendous Coliseum, which, reared in large measure by the captive Jews, was the scene of the martyrdom of Ignatius, and stands an imperishable memorial of the ages of heroic suffering which saw the Church in conflict with the princes of this world. Hard by rises the Arch of Constantine, — a memorial of the Nicene age, and of the triumph of the cross over Paganism. The Column of Phocas, on the other hand, beyond the Arch of Titus and under the Capitol, marks the decline of the Synodical Period, and reminds us of two clouds, not bigger than a man's hand, that became visible just at that epoch: one was the cloud of Islam in the East, and the other that of a Papacy in the West. Cross the Alps and stand beneath the cathedral domes of Aix-la-Chapelle; under your feet is the sepulchre of Charlemagne, with whom the Middle Ages began, and there was crowned Charles the Fifth, his successor with whom the Middle Ages expired. Last of all you reach Paris, and survey that arch of vanity which lifts its majestic bulk on the crown of the Champs Elysées.

[1] A. D. 70.

It stands for the close of the eighteenth century and the extinction of "the Holy Roman Empire," so called. It marks the end of just one thousand years between Charlemagne and Napoleon. These are the landmarks of these Institutes; they indicate our "dates of anchorage." Blind must he be, and dull beyond comparison, who sees not in the precision of these periods, in the characters and the events that created them, and even in these monuments which Providence has allowed proud men to rear, and which Providence only has preserved, tokens of an overruling Hand in history, which the wise and true of heart must recognize and understand.

LECTURE II.

THE APOSTOLIC FATHERS AND NEXT AGES.

1. ANTIOCH.

THE disciples were called Christians first at Antioch, says St. Luke. Justly have the antecedents of St. Paul been noted as providentially shaping him into the vessel of election for mankind: not sufficiently have the specialties of Antioch been regarded as forming that marvellous capital to be the cradle of the infant Church. Strange indeed that so dissolute a city should become the source of human regeneration, but even in this paradox we discover a divine plan. The good physician attacks disease at its seat, and pestilence must be stayed at its source. Our Lord had promised that his disciples should do greater works than his own; and surely, when the Church, in all her virgin glory, rose up in Antioch and issued from its port bearing the new life to a world "lying in the Evil One," there was a greater miracle than when Lazarus obeyed the command of Jesus, and came forth from his dank grave, a putrid corpse made whole. Here was a dead man revived: but from Antioch began the resurrection of nations that lay festering in moral darkness, bound with grave-clothes, smelling to heaven with corruption, and powerless to help themselves as the dry bones in Ezekiel's valley of vision. Antioch itself was the epitome of such a world.

2. A CONTRAST.

The Augustan age had glorified Rome with marbles for its bricks, and with the golden lyres of poets for its legions of iron, yet left it more debased than ever before. Horace had just died, and Herod was rivalling Augustus in his Roman extravagance by making the very pavement of Antioch of solid marble, when the Galilean maiden sang her *Magnificat* in obscure and despised Nazareth, and gave the first hymn of Redemption to those who looked for the Messiah. Nazareth and Antioch! behold the contrast. But note the meek virgin in her cot, and all the powers of the world in their forts and palaces: hear her sweet song, the first strain of Christian poesy, the germ of liturgies and prayers for evangelized tribes and peoples of the earth, and contrast it with the frantic rites of the bacchanal, the sensual orgies, the licentious dances, and the reeking wickedness of that city on the Orontes, which was so absolute a type of all that stretched away from its port to Greece and Italy, to the barbarians of Germany and Gaul, and to the ancient seats of our own race in Jutland and Britain. Truly hath God chosen "the weak things of the world to confound the mighty," and, as we shall soon observe, "things which are despised hath God chosen, yea and things which are not, to bring to naught things that are."

3. AN INQUIRY.

But why was Antioch rather than Jerusalem made the capital of the new empire of Messiah? Among other reasons this will afford an answer: the Prince of Peace came not to the Jews only. "In Him shall the Gentiles trust," was the promise He has so richly fulfilled. Now Antioch was "a mart of nations"; it was, in type, Gentilism itself. Jerusalem could not be made the metropolis of Catholicity; it was the stronghold of Judaism. The rod of the new power was to "*go forth* from Jerusalem." To have kept it there would have been to fortify and perpetuate those intense prejudices of the Circumcision, which in the case of St. Paul himself were the most formidable of all obstacles to his work. "New bottles for new wine." He who had broken down the Jewish wall of separation, and made the new temple walls to unite Jew and Gentile in Himself as the corner-stone, brought both walls together in Antioch. It was "the foolishness of God, wiser than men," to economize the moral rubbish of the Seleucid capital, as he took a hill of refuse from the Jebusites when he created Zion the stronghold of the typical Church.

4. THE PORTRAITURE OF ANTIOCH.

The unhappy genius of Renan has so ably depicted this ancient Paris, borrowing his colours from the modern one which inflames his imagination and has debased his pen, that it would be folly for me not to adopt the vivid picture with which he has anticipated the tasks of all who would hereafter undertake to describe it. I shall therefore freely translate his brilliant rhetoric, amplifying or abridging it as may best suit my purpose, but making it my own by the very injury I must inflict on such splendid work by my attempt to infuse its spirit into English words.

According to Renan,[1] the metropolis of the Orient was a city of more than five hundred thousand souls. Before its recent extension Paris itself was hardly larger. Its site was one of the most picturesque of the whole earth, made of the space between the Orontes and the slopes of Silpius. Unrivalled were the beauty and the abundance of its waters. Nature had fortified it as by a masterpiece of military art, surrounded as it was by lofty rocks, which crowned it with a radiating circlet of peaks. Thence were afforded surprising perspectives: one beheld within the walls hills not less than seven hundred feet high, great rocks bristling with spires, precipices, inaccessible caves, torrents and cascades rushing into deep ravines, where delicious gardens nestled. Here were dense thickets of myrtles, of flowering box, of laurels and evergreens, of which the verdure was most tender, and rocks embroidered with pinks, hyacinths, and cyclamens, which gave their savage summits the effect of hanging gardens. Such was the Antioch of Libanius, of Julian, of Chrysostom.

[1] See Note O.

Here the imperial legate of Syria kept his court. The Seleucid kings raised it from nothing, and like the growth of a single night, to a lofty pitch of splendour, but the Roman occupation had glorified it even more. The Seleucids had indeed set the example of decorating cities with theatrical effect, multiplying baths, basilicas, aqueducts, and temples. The streets, more symmetrical and regular than elsewhere, were bordered with colonnades, and at their intersections adorned with statues. Antiochus Epiphanes had carried through the city, stretching three miles from end to end, a superb *Corso*, ornamented by columns, in four rows, which made covered galleries on both sides, with the broad avenue between. But, besides its huge constructions of public utility, Antioch was distinguished above other Syrian cities by its possession of masterpieces of Greek art, — admirable statues, and delicate specimens of classic taste, of which at this epoch the refined perfections could no longer be imitated. Into this region of the Orontes, the Macedonians, transplanted by Seleucus Nicator from Antigonia, had brought the worship and the territorial names of their own land, lasting memorials of their attachment to Pæonia and Pieria, and to "the fair humanities" adored at Castaly and in the Vale of Tempe. Thus the Greek myths gained a new creation and new seats of worship in Syria. Phœbus and the Muses were part of the population of the city, — in mute marble, it is true, but seeming to live and breathe, as in fact they inspired the surrounding masses of flesh and blood. As a retreat from the bustling market,

Daphne opened to its inhabitants an enchanting grove where the most charming fictions of the Greek poets were brought to the minds of the Orientals. Here the wretched Julian was destined long afterwards to make a last desperate effort to heal the death-wound of idolatry. The spot was a practical plagiarism; counterfeiting a plan of the nomadic tribes, who originally brought names to Berecyntia, Ida, and Olympus. Altogether, the fables of outworn heathenism made up for the place a religion hardly more serious than the Metamorphoses of Ovid. Girdled by the river, Mount Casius lifted to the skies altars and idols, the graver relics of indigenous superstition. This spot was doomed to retain its hold on local enthusiasm when surrounding idols should give way before the Light, and to smoke with the last faint whiffs of incense that symbolized expiring Paganism. In short, the Syrian frivolity, Babylonian quackery, and all the impostures of Asia, muddled and confused at this meeting-point of two worlds, had made of Antioch a sewer of infamies. It was the metropolis of Lies.

5. THE POPULACE.

The Syrian tongue was yet to be heard among its aborigines, infesting its *faubourgs* and forming the suburban population of a vast vicinity. By a law of Seleucus, all resident aliens were made citizens, and by intermarriages with Greeks his capital at the close of three centuries and a half was the place of all the world in which the human race seemed most effectually hybridized. The consequent debasement of minds was frightful. In such a process, divers races lead downward to a common estate of moral putrefaction. Hardly do we find a parallel corruption in the basest of those Levantine marts, which we see given over to ideas the most base and selfish, and tied hand and foot by the intrigues of tyranny. It was an incredible jumble of buffoons and quacks, drolls and tricksters, wonder-workers, sorcerers, and juggling priests, — a bazaar of races and ballet-dances, pomps and processions, Saturnalian feasts and Bacchanalian orgies, of luxury and lust unbridled, of fanatical outrages and superstitions the most pestilent, — in a word, of all the follies of the Oriental world. Obsequious to servility and then again basely ungrateful, at times cowards and then impudently rebellious, the population was thoroughly a specimen of hordes enslaved to Cæsarism, with no name to preserve or lose, without family character, without nationality, without country. Its grand *Corso* was a circus, through which flowed all day long the foul tides of a brute populace, light, volatile, always ready for an outbreak, sometimes clever enough, however, to be absorbed by diversions of music, by harlequins and their farces, by ambiguities, jokes, and impertinences of every sort. Cicero affects to credit them with a literary spirit, but it was a mere literature of spurious rhetoricians. The public shows were curious. The entire spectacle was made palatable to such a crowd by exhibitions of nudity; naked girls sharing in all the performances, with a mere fillet on their shameless foreheads. St. Chrysostom has denounced their favorite *Maï-*

ouma, where troops of prostitutes showed themselves swimming in nakedness, with wanton display, in vast reservoirs filled with crystal waters. It was an inebriation of debauch, a revery of Sardanapalus, where all manner of indecencies, the worse for a certain simulation of refinement, were tumbled together pell-mell, in voluptuous contempt of ordinary pretences to propriety. Such was the Antioch which Juvenal, perhaps justly, accuses as the source of Roman degeneracy, — of those abominations which he deplores; which St. Paul, on widely different grounds, bewails, and to which, with inimitable condensation, he administers his scathing rebuke. Yes, indeed, says the satirist,[1]

"The Syrian Orontes, at last, makes the Tiber the mouth of its vomit;
Here comes, with its flutes and its strings, a jargon of tongues with all evils."

"The valley of the Orontes," says Renan, " opening to the west, gives the neighbouring lake an outlet to the sea; or, to be more exact, enables the city to communicate with the vast world beyond, where the Mediterranean lies embedded, and where, through all the ages, it has afforded to the surrounding nations a neutral highway, and a bond of federal unity as well."

6. THE JEWISH ELEMENT.

To approach my subject, and to illustrate the decisive fact which fitted Antioch to become, through the Mediterranean, the starting-point for Christian

[1] See Note P.

missions, I must strictly translate from Renan, and borrow his condensed and most suggestive paragraph about the Jews.

"They were among the most numerous of those colonies which the liberal policy of the Seleucids attracted to their metropolis. Their immigration started with Seleucus Nicator's grant of equal privileges with the Greeks. They had an ethnarch of their own, but not less were their relations very intimate with their Gentile co-citizens. Here, as at Alexandria, it is true, these relations were occasionally interrupted by strifes and mutual aggressions; but, on the other hand, they afforded a base for proselyting, which the Jews knew how to make very lively. More and more was polytheism proving itself unsatisfactory to all reflecting minds, and Greek philosophy in common with Judaism was attractive to those incapable of resting in the empty pomps of an effete mythology. The number of Jewish proselytes was considerable. Nicolas, a proselyte of Antioch, was enrolled among the seven deacons. Here were the germs of a harvest, which waited only for the day-beams of grace to blossom and bring forth fruits more beautiful than mankind had ever seen before."[1]

One recognizes here the hand of God in the mission and work of Alexander: Antioch, with its Jewish colony and its traffic with the West through Asia Minor and Greece, as well as Alexandria with its library and its schools, had been fashioned beforehand for the Evangelists and Apostles.

7. THE CHURCH IN ANTIOCH.

In the spring of A. D. 43, just ten years after the Light of the World had been despised and rejected

[1] See Note Q.

of men, all things were ready for a fresh outpouring of the Spirit. Barnabas found Saul at Tarsus, and brought him from his native shores to this Antioch, where the little church was sheltered, in its obscurity and feebleness, in a poor quarter under the hill *Stavrin*, and near a gate which sustains the Christian tradition by its time-honoured name of St. Paul's gate. It was " in Singon Street hard by the Pantheon." Among the believers here, fulfilling their local mission against such frightful odds of evil in the very citadel of Satan, imagine the effect of the appearance of these twins, Barnabas and Saul: the one with those massive and majestic traits which led the heathen to suppose him Zeus; the other with that light and active motion and electrifying voice which the same rustic idolaters could only identify with Hermes. They came to make the lily of gospel purity spring forth and shed its fragrance over the world out of a dunghill of pollution.

8. THE EXCEPTIONAL APOSTOLATE.

The exceptional addition to the choir of original Apostles of these twain, born out of due time, deserves a passing note of explanation. St. Paul was created an Apostle by Christ himself in person; Barnabas, by Christ, through his Vicar, the Holy Ghost. To confer their " Mission " and attest their apostleship to the churches was yet a logical necessity; but had even this been done by other apostles, they might seem to have been commissioned, if not " by men," yet at least " through men ";

they would have been, not founders of the Apostolic Succession, but only its earliest recipients. Certain inspired prophets were therefore, by an oracle of the Holy Ghost, directed to do for Barnabas and Saul what the fiery tongues of Pentecost had done for Matthias. By an exceptional laying on of hands they conferred, not the "order" of apostles, but the "mission" to which their apostolic work was designated. The ordinals of Apostolic Churches have preserved this distinction: first orders and then jurisdiction are conferred in the rites of ordination. Barnabas seems to have been made St. Paul's coadjutor; but the pupil of Gamaliel was sent out with the world for his field. This mission of the Spirit was afterwards accepted by James, Peter, and John, when they "gave to Paul and Barnabas the right hand of fellowship,"[1] and recognized the several jurisdictions proper to St. Peter and to St. Paul: the former restricted in mission to the Circumcision, while to the latter was assigned an unbounded mission to the Gentiles. And it is most instructive to observe how strictly St. Paul adhered to this "canon,"[2] as he calls it, in all his ministrations.

9. APOSTOLIC INSTITUTIONS.

To the inspired narrative of events at Antioch I must refer you for further subjects of great interest touching the early institutions and constitutions of Christianity. But it remains to note them as reflected in this school after the Apostles had

[1] Gal. ii. 9.   [2] 2 Cor. x. 13-16.

fallen asleep. When the Council of Nice cited "the ancient customs" as the normal example of the Catholic Church, Antioch was the great original to which their testimony necessarily reverted. Happily, we possess in our day a wealth of material for deciding what this primitive school received and taught, such as has never before been enjoyed for many centuries. The brilliant light which has been concentrated upon it by the learning and genius of Lightfoot has closed a long period of controversies excited by the interests which all modern schools feel to be at stake when their tenets and teachings are referred to it as a test. Its great martyr bishop, Ignatius, had seen St. John; in all probability had been his disciple. Under Trajan he was thrown to the lions in the Flavian Amphitheatre. His Epistles, sifted to the bran in a prolonged and unparalleled controversy, are now in our hands in their genuine form, and furnish us with a mirror of the virgin Church in its manners, its ordinances, and its doctrines. Nobody is fit to discuss the principles of unity and catholicity who has not studied the Scriptures in the reflected light of what Ignatius shows to have been the ordinances of inspired wisdom. But his practical maxims are like "the goads and nails" of Solomon himself. Some of them lose little by translation, so pungent are they and so sententious. To Polycarp he bequeaths his mantle, like another Elijah going up in a fiery car and dropping his raiment on Elisha. "The times demand *thee*," he says to his successor, "as pilots seek the haven." Would God we more nearly resembled Ignatius and his faithful contemporaries, among whom Polycarp is chief, in their zeal for truth, their sanctity of life, and their fidelity even unto death to our Master, Christ; but, so far as the conformities of the Anglican Church to an apostolic original are concerned, we may rejoice indeed that the church of Antioch, as Ignatius portrays it, is the triumphant vindication of our Anglican reformers and their work of restoration in the sixteenth century.

10. APOSTOLIC FATHERS. — IGNATIUS.

Though it is much later that Antioch assumes a leading place as a school, we associate it with the lead in Christian literature, as the source of "the Apostolic Fathers." Of Melito and Clement of Rome, the earliest of whom we have genuine remains, I shall speak by and by. The venerable Ignatius, on his way to martyrdom at Rome, and all the way "fighting with beasts," as he describes it, with reference to the rude soldiers that guarded him, wrote letters to the churches, and also to Polycarp, "angel of the church of Smyrna," his compeer and coeval in the school of the Apostles, which are among the choicest treasures of antiquity. To think of such a good thing coming so early out of Antioch! In vain may we search all heathen moralists for the lofty, unselfish philosophy which breathes in every sentiment of Ignatius, and inspires those inimitable maxims. Here are specimens, taken chiefly from the single epistle to Polycarp: 1. "Consider the times, but look to

Him who is above time." 2. "A Christian is not his own master, but waits upon God." 3. "Slight not the slaves and the maid-servants." 4. "Find time to pray without ceasing." 5. "The crown is immortality." 6. "Stand like a beaten anvil; it is the part of a good athlete to be bruised, and to prevail."[1] His subsequent suffering in the Coliseum, under the persecution which disgraces the name of Trajan, whetted the appetite of the Roman populace for Christian blood. It begot the common outcry of the amphitheatre, *Christianos ad leones!* Under Hadrian and the Antonines the chronic sacrifices of Christians called forth a new form of patristic literature known as the "Apologies," of which the earlier specimens have perished, but of which we have examples in the precious writings of Justin Martyr.

II. JUSTIN MARTYR.

He was a native of Samaria, though a Greek and a philosopher; but Jacob's well was near his native town, and he seems to have drawn his inspiration as a Christian from the water of life that has never ceased to flow ever since the weary Jesus sat by it and discoursed with the woman. This appears in his "Dialogues with Trypho," a Jew whom he laboured to convert; but not less conspicuously in his Apologies, addressed to the sons of Hadrian. These princes were professed philosophers, and Justin addressed them as one who had a right to be heard. He had been a

[1] See Note R.

student of the Athenian schools, and his pure
eclecticism had made him a Platonist. One wonders who may have been that unknown saint of
meek and reverend aspect whom he met walking
by the sea-side, and who first taught him the better
philosophy of Him who is the Light of the World.
Unknown as he is, he lives in the illustrious pupil
whom he led to Jesus, and who wore his philosopher's *pallium* not the less when he became a
disciple of what he had discovered to be the only
philosophy worth professing. In his writings, we
become acquainted with the Christians of the first
post-apostolic age, and blessed be their pure example. The philosopher addressed his first Apology
to Antoninus Pius (A. D. 150), whose reputation
is not unstained by the wanton effusion of Christian blood;[1] his second, to "the good Aurelius,"
as Pope styles him, — brutal stoic though he was,
and author of a general persecution which raged
through the Empire from the Tigris to the Rhone,
desolating the churches, and delivering men, women,
and children to wild beasts, to the sword, and to
the flames, in every imaginable form of cruelty
and torture. Under Aurelius, Justin earned his
noble surname of the Martyr, and soon after him
suffered Melito, Bishop of Sardis, of whose works
a valuable fragment remains.[2]

---

[1] See Lightfoot, Apost. Fathers, II., vol. i. p. 440.
[2] Lightfoot, Ibid., pp. 445, 446.

12. THE PERSECUTIONS.

Behold, young men, what the Church means by "the noble army of martyrs." This was the fourth persecution, and six more must be; though in fact the first three centuries are one protracted period of war against the followers of the Crucified, which began with Herod's slaughter of the Innocents, and stayed not till the Arch of Constantine was set up to commemorate the first peace. The Apologists imply the martyrs. Their blood was "the seed of the Church"; but

> "Their ashes flew
> No marble tells us whither; with their names
> No bard embalms and sanctifies his song,
> And history, so warm on meaner themes,
> Is cold on this."

The fury of their adversaries drove the sufferers like "conies to the stony rocks," to the deserts, to the catacombs. They were scorned for burrowing like the marmot, and were derided as "shunners of daylight." Light-shunning yet light-shedding; to them the ages and the nations that call themselves enlightened owe all their illumination. They were the victims of those who made "Philosophy" their boast.

13. POLYCARP.

The hoary and holy Polycarp suffered under that paragon of "philosophic" princes, the elder Antonine.[1] He was the disciple of St. John, and was

[1] A. D. 155. See Lightfoot's elaborate evidence, and his somewhat successful relief of Hadrian's reputation. Ibid., pp. 440, 492, and 628–702.

probably the Bishop of Smyrna to whom our Divine Master sends his prophetic promise of the martyr's crown in the Apocalypse. His pupil, Irenæus, tells us how he used to speak of the beloved disciple, and of "others who had seen the Lord."

We must reflect that while St. John survived, after his return from exile, Ephesus was temporarily the focus of apostolic illumination. If "old wives' fables" were to be heeded, the obscure Evaristus, Bishop of Rome, was St. John's superior, and had settled "who should be greatest," as Christ himself did not, by claiming from St. Peter a principality over the glorious survivor of Zebedee's children! Nothing of the kind disgraces the true history of Evaristus. Down to the first or second year of the second century the beloved disciple "tarried," as his Master had said, prolonging the age of the Messiah, and sealing the canon of the New Testament. Nor while Polycarp survived, to whom Christ himself had spoken in his message to the churches, could the apostolic age be regarded as ended. To him Anicetus deferred, and rendered homage at Rome. The date of his martyrdom closes the period which, in strict reckoning, is that of the Apostolic Fathers. As a school, the see of Antioch comes subsequently into view, and its consummate flower is Chrysostom, the great primate of Constantinople, the golden-mouthed John.

14. PRIMITIVE SCHOOLS.—ALEXANDRIA.

Of the primitive schools the see of Alexandria was the first, and stands without rival, or even one that can pretend to be its second. It may owe its foundation to the catechetical classes of Apollos;[1] Theophilus may not improbably have received his first instructions there; it ceased not to shed over the Christendom of three centuries the all-animating inspiration of its theology; and to it we owe the master spirit of that great Council of Nicæa, Athanasius, its burning and shining light. Here we find the genius of Clement, and the untiring toil of Origen, and the labours of others not unworthy to be named with them, who for centuries maintained a divine mastery over Christian thought applied to the exposition of the Scriptures. We must reflect that its early relations with Antioch were intimate, and pupils of Polycarp were probably enrolled in its schools;[2] while, not unreasonably, we may admit that St. Mark was its first bishop, and made it "the Evangelical See." It framed the primitive testimony into literature, and gave it symbolic and liturgic idioms. From voices attuned in her choirs sounds forth the organ-music of the Great Confession, — that anthem-like roll and swell of the successive utterances of the Nicene Creed. That "clothing of wrought gold" which adorns the Bride of the Lamb was wrought, as in a loom, at the feet of her Gamaliels. Truly, if "a mother and mistress of churches" ever existed, we must find in

[1] My reasons may be seen in Ante-Nicene Fathers, vol. vi. p. 236.
[2] Ibid., vol. ii. p. 166, and vol. viii. p. 796.

Alexandria the only see to which antiquity makes any such award. When it comes into notice, under Pantænus, it is already a Christian university. He is called "the Sicilian bee," and, lured by the scent of flowers sweeter than those of Enna, he flew from its fair fields to the Alexandrian storehouse where honey was dropping from the comb. Under him it became a beehive indeed, and, if it be not overworking the metaphor, it had no drones; all were workers and soldiers, among whom Truth was queen and mother both. Its cells were stored with scriptural nectar, and its great doctor, Clement, has immortalized its spirit in the wit by which he spake. His sayings, to pursue the figure merrily, are specimens alike of sweets and of stings. How uncloying the flavour of his words about Jesus! how keen and pungent his conflict with false philosophy and untruth! They writhe and perish like summer moths, pierced by his winged words and fanned by their airy impulse into oblivion.[1]

15. MANY DOCTORS.—ATHANASIUS.

I have time only to name the bright succession of doctors who adorned the see of St. Mark, like those apocalyptic stars which Christ held in his own right hand. To Pantænus, and Clement, and the colossal figure of Origen, succeed Gregory Thaumaturgus, Heraclas, Dionysius the Great, Julius Africanus, Anatolius, and Alexander of Cappadocia, with whom the sub-apostolic period expired in the Decian persecution. Theognostus, a pupil of

[1] See Note S.

Origen, and Pierius, who is called "Origen Junior" by St. Jerome, with Theonas, Phileas, Pamphilus, Peter the Canonist, and Alexander, the patron of Athanasius, carry on the brilliant succession. And these illustrious names, every one, have planetary lustres revolving about them; while, all together, they shine as the firmament, till the day dawns and the sunlight of the Gospel breaks over all the world. Then appears Athanasius, "clothed with the sun," — he who afterwards stood "against the world," — Athanasius, in whose great heart the Catholic faith found shelter for a moment while others forsook it and fled, — but only to break forth, when "the fire kindled and he spake with his tongue" the "truths that wake to perish never." Even in our own vain and self-asserting times, it has been conceded that the treasures of Alexandrian Christianity are a forecast of modern thought, and must still continue to enrich the universe.[1]

16. THE PUNIC SCHOOL. — TERTULLIAN AND CYPRIAN.

Carthage, like a candlestick of many branches, borrows its lustre from the Alexandrian Pharos. This appears in Tertullian, who teaches in crabbed Latin, but with original force and perspicuity, what he learned in Greek. Here begins "Latin Christianity"; here first we find a "Western theology," which became anthropology rather, and which lives on and works yet, and ever will work among men, in the master spirit of Augustine. To Ter-

[1] See Note T.

tullian, erratic genius as he was, must be attributed this marvellous creation, the illustrious Punic school. But it took shape under Cyprian, who recognized his obligations to his masterly predecessor, delighted to pay him honour as the autocrat of his thought, and rectified his mistakes, throwing a mantle over his faults. To Cyprian must be attributed the clearest exposition of the primitive polity to be found in history. He builds up the system of Ignatius, as Ignatius reflects it from the Scriptures. To him we owe the ideal of the Episcopate, as the primitive Christians had received it; and through all his writings breathes the spirit of St. Peter, imploring the clergy not to make themselves "lords over God's heritage." Intrepid in vindicating his order, uncompromising in maintaining the autonomy of national churches, this noble confessor and martyr is yet the text-book of the laity who wish to know their place and privileges in the Church. I love his free spirit; the great synodical features of Catholic polity of which he is the champion; the maxims which he has left to Christendom. He is the great "Anglican" of antiquity, if I may anachronize so boldly. To his system, rightly understood, we of the Anglican communion may boldly refer our cause, as against Pope and Puritan. I love St. Cyprian. He finds a modern counterpart in our own Bishop Bull. Must I merely mention the noble names that are entwined with his in the creation of Latin thought? Study for yourselves the works of Minucius Felix, of Commodian, of Arnobius and Lactantius.

17. ARNOBIUS AND LACTANTIUS.

Nor let any accept the unjust judgment of Coleridge about Arnobius, in whom we have a great layman, like himself, not half as faulty, and quite as praiseworthy.[1] His scornful rhetoric was privileged to chase the hosts of heathenism, already conquered, and to put them to an ignominious rout. He mocks them, like another Elijah dealing with Baalim; he pursues them with the artillery of his genius, as they flee before him, —

"Chased on their night-steeds by the star of day."

And so we reach Lactantius, — dear Lactantius! I feel as if I had known him personally. He emerges, with the persecuted Church, from the Diocletian persecution, like gold tried in the fire. In him, we meet the earliest Christian who has leisure to cultivate his style. He adorns the court of Constantine; he wins the title of the Christian Cicero; he closes the blessed march of the Ante-Nicene legions, and his flourish of trumpets is not of "sounding brass." We hear the silver trumpets of the angels in his notes of triumph. Less harmonious than his other writings is his account of the persecutors and their retributive deaths. Gibbon, indeed, affects to doubt if it be his; but the fascination of those pages is created, not by their style, but by the downright honest words, in which they give the testimony of one who seems to say, —

"All which I saw, and part of which I was."

[1] See Note U.

18. MAXIMS OF LACTANTIUS.

Let me add, young gentlemen, if you would know why I speak so warmly of Lactantius, two of his maxims which became dear to me in early life: would that I might transfer them to you, to make a better use of them than I have done. I can only atone for my failure by urging you to catch from them the inspiration of a future which you may render tributary to God's glory and to the good of mankind. "If life is to be desired by a wise man," says this charming instructor, "truly for no other reason could I wish to live than to effect something worthy of a lifetime." Again, he says: "I shall judge myself to have lived satisfactorily, and to have fulfilled the duty of manhood, if only my efforts may liberate some from error, and direct them into the heavenly way."

19. HARMONY OF THEOLOGIANS.

And so must end my insufficient testimony to the school of Carthage, while I point you forward to its noblest example, in the imperial genius of Augustine. Vainly have recent writers tried to set him over against Athanasius, as an antagonist, not a helper.[1] Brain and heart, heart and brain: do they conflict, or harmonize, because their functions are so diverse? In the attempts of the West to fathom the mystery of the Human, we find the complement of what the East had done to illustrate the Divine. The Alexandrians understood,

[1] See Note V.

however, that the Infinite was past finding out: the genius of the great Bishop of Hippo shrank from no investigation of humanity, felt no similar restraints. He paused, indeed, to take breath, and went no further; but just there the remorseless genius of Calvin found his task incomplete, and scrupled not to give it a logical conclusion. It was a test of strength and courage not inferior to Samson's; it was on a larger scale, and involved even more terrible consequences, than "the wreck of matter and the crush of worlds." Warned by this experiment, we may accept Augustine, while we reject the Epimetheus that ventured further. To Augustine we owe the true exposition of the doctrines of grace, though the Church has only accepted it filtered from the lees. In his immortal works and the immense literature they have created, Carthage still asserts her moral grandeur, though bats and owls infest and hoot where Marius once sat among her ruins.

20. THE ROMAN DIOCESE.

If I have not yet noted among Christian schools even in the West that see which claims to be "the mother and mistress of churches," it is only because the facts compel me to say nothing where nothing can be said. Her first bishop, St. Clement, indeed, leads the noble array of the Apostolic Fathers; but he writes in Greek, not in Latin, and is himself a striking witness to the colonial and dependent character of the church in Rome, of which I have spoken. In his time, this colony of

Jewish converts, and their faithful Gentile brethren, had lost nothing of the faith which was said by St. Paul to be "spoken of throughout the world." But it was a church of works, not words;[1] of noble suffering, not of study and teaching. Her children, always exposed to fierce eyes that glared upon them from the Palatine, lived in daily expectation of being thrown to the jaws that gaped for them in the Coliseum. Their circumstances were little favourable to the cultivation of letters, and even their bishops, though generally pious men, were taken from a class greatly inferior to that of their Eastern brethren. A pleasing picture of the age of the first Bishop of Rome, who bore the name of Pius, comes to us in the pages of the "Shepherd" of Hermas, who was the brother of that prelate. Little interesting as this allegory is in our day, it illustrates the simple piety and habits of the primitive Romans, their character as "a Greek colony," and their gentle efforts to repel heresy by persuasion rather than by anathemas.

21. IRENÆUS,—HIS PLACE IN THE WEST.[2]

How it came to pass that such depraved and ignorant creatures as Zephyrinus and Callistus are found at an early period in the Roman succession, is to be accounted for, perhaps, by their personal history, which suggests that they were ambitious to fill a place not coveted by better men, because they meant to betray their brethren and save themselves while making gain their godliness.

[1] See Note W.   [2] See Note X.

Of these I shall soon speak more particularly, but must now mention the illustrious name of Irenæus as the great light of Western Europe, in whom we find the teaching of Polycarp transferred from the Orient to Gaul, and thence echoed back to Rome, to supply her lack of knowledge and of wisdom. He was, spiritually, the grandson of St. John, as the disciple of Polycarp, and twice did his gentle interposition, in the spirit of the beloved disciple, save Rome from peril of schism and heresy. When Eleutherus was patronizing Montanism, and when Victor was violating the sacred compact which Anicetus had accepted from Polycarp, the voice of Irenæus sounded forth from the Rhone, and restored truth and peace to the church upon the Tiber. Pacific, as his name implies, he was yet, like St. John himself, "a son of thunder" when he confronted the great army of heretics who stole the Christian name, in early times, only to corrupt and trade upon it, after the example of Simon Magus. When the sun rises upon a pestilent marsh, its very light and warmth breed fogs and evil exhalations, and it was not possible that many in a population like that of Antioch, when it was smitten by the glory of the Gospel, should fail to borrow its lustre to set off their false philosophies and monstrous superstitions. These they strove to make at once a snare to the faithful, and a palatable bait to ungodly men for accepting themselves instead of Christ as teachers and masters. Irenæus, in an elaborate treatise, exposes their artifices and their base counterfeits of Christian gold; and his great work, of which only a small part comes to us in the original Greek, entitles him to the honours of a prince among the writers of Western Europe, where he became the founder, in fact, of a distinct school, and of those traditions which long afterwards were stigmatized as "Gallicanism," though supported by nearly all the illustrious names, clerical and lay, of Christian France.

22. ROMAN RECEPTIVITY.[1]

And here let me note a memorable passage, in which he explains the relations of Rome in his day to other churches of the West. His own history sufficiently illustrates its meaning, though in the Latin translation by which we know it there is a possibility of making it somewhat ambiguous; and artful commentators have not been wanting to read into it their own modern views of what it ought to mean. To keep it free from any colouring of mine, I quote it as rendered by a Roman Catholic writer of the more liberal class.[2] He gives it as follows: —

"To this church, on account of more potent principality, it is necessary that every church (that is, those who on every side are faithful) resort; in which church, ever, *by those who are on every side*, has been preserved that tradition which is from the Apostles."

I do not know how words, even in this clumsy rendering, could more clearly define the receptive character of Rome, and her dependence upon other churches for her knowledge of the faith. The

[1] See Note Y.
[2] Waterworth, "Faith of Catholics," vol. ii. p. 3.

apostolic tradition, he says, is preserved in her " by those who are on every side," resorting to her, as was necessary, because of her civil pre-eminence in the Empire. In other words, Rome had no school or teaching of her own, but, because she sat at the corners where all roads met, and where all travellers must come, she gathered from them the concurrent testimony of all other churches, and hence was able to reflect the faith everywhere received. Her " more potent principality " was defined at Nice and Constantinople, in the Great Councils, as purely that of the Imperial Capitol; not a word in Irenæus or the language of the canons suggests any other idea; yet the passage quoted has been made ambiguous by assuming that an ecclesiastical principality was intended, and by transforming the words " necessary to resort unto " into the phrase " necessary to agree with." Had this been his idea, Irenæus must have gone on to say: " For there the doctrine of the Apostles Peter and Paul is preserved by the infallible authority of its bishop." But he says just the reverse: " There the tradition of the Apostles is preserved by the contributions of the faithful *from other churches*, each bringing to it what he has learned in his particular church, and so establishing a Catholic consent."

23. THE NASCENT PATRIARCHATE.

It is easy to see how this very position of the only Apostolic See of the West became instrumental in stretching her influence over Western Europe. Travellers from Gaul and Britain resorted thither, and there learned in Latin what Rome had been taught in Greek. The development of a Patriarchate, without the name as yet, was the immediate consequence; but the Council of Nice, which first recognized this name for all the greater sees, recognized the limits of this patriarchal jurisdiction as quite restricted.[1] Not only Gaul, but the territory over which Milan began to tower with commanding dignity, was far beyond the limits. It was not a Patriarchate of the West in any other sense than that it was in the West. And just how its "suburbicarian" influence operated, and in turn was often checked and overruled, is powerfully illustrated in the history of Zephyrinus and Callistus, two Bishops of Rome contemporary with Hippolytus whose influence with their diocesan synods not only reduced their judgments to insignificance, but rescued the Roman Church at this early date from an ignominious apostasy. Here, too, we observe the force of the maxims of Irenæus we have just considered. Hippolytus was his disciple, and with his fellow suffragans, as they would now be called, he resisted the heretical teaching of those patriarchs. Gathering and bringing into Rome the testimony of the Catholic churches, East and West, they convicted Zephyrinus and Callistus of heresy, and made them retract. "They confessed their errors for a short period," says Hippolytus, "but after a little, they wallow again in the same mire."[2]

[1] See Note Z.   [2] See Note A'.

24. HIPPOLYTUS.

When you visit the Vatican, be sure to note the statue of Hippolytus.[1] It gives us the clearest idea of the appearance of a primitive bishop. Over the tunic he wears the pallium; modest vestments, well represented by the Anglican rochet and chimere. He sits in his episcopal chair, in mild majesty, a noble figure: high forehead and features composed but resolute; slightly bearded; one hand placed on his heart, while the other hand grasps a book, the arm crossing his breast to reach it. Thank God for such testimony as his, brought to light in our own times, and for the Providence that placed this statue in the Vatican to remind the degenerate Church of "Old Rome" of its fallibility even from the primitive day, and, as it were, to repeat those warnings of St. Paul: "Be not high-minded, but fear: for if God spared not the natural branches, take heed lest He also spare not thee. Behold therefore the goodness and severity of God: . . . toward thee goodness, if thou continue in goodness: *otherwise thou also shalt* be cut off."[2] These words were addressed to the virgin Church of Rome, while yet her pure "faith was spoken of throughout the whole world."[3] And by them those marble lips of Hippolytus, seated in his truly apostolic chair, seem to repeat the warning, as it were for the last time.

This history, then, shows where Rome stands in the primitive period, just a hundred years before the Council of Nicæa. Neither a school nor a teach-

[1] See a picture in Bunsen's "Hippolytus," vol. i.
[2] Rom. xi. 20–22.   [3] Rom. i. 8.

ing see, she was still a Greek colony or daughter church, which had not given a single page to Latin Christianity, now coming to light in Africa. Thus we see her saved by the Greek doctor Hippolytus from the unfathomable infamy and self-destruction which must have resulted had her faithful listened to their own bishops. In Hippolytus, with his co-bishops of the Roman province, Irenæus speaks again, and puts a practical comment upon the often distorted words which I have quoted from that great Father.

25. CAIUS AND NOVATIAN.

Contemporary with Hippolytus was the Roman presbyter Caius, who also wrote in Greek, and in whom Hippolytus, no doubt, found an able helper against the heretic bishops. He has left us a valuable testimony as to the books of the New Testament which were received at Rome in his day, from which it appears that Rome yet waited upon the East for the Canon. The Epistle to the Hebrews she had not as yet accepted, and of the Apocalypse Caius says, "Some among us will not have it read in the church." They knew of no infallibility in Zephyrinus and Callistus to settle this matter, and were still divided about it in the Roman presbytery. The Eastern patriarchs were Rome's arbiter. In Caius the Greek succession of Roman authors comes to its close, and the Latin series begins (A. D. 280) with Novatian "On the Trinity." Though an able defender of truth in this treatise, this author unhappily fell away and became a titular bishop, claiming to be "Bishop of Rome." This grievously defective claim was denounced by Cyprian, and he closed his melancholy career with the reputation of schism and heresy together. Such and so little was the venerable see of Clement, down to good Sylvester and the first Œcumenical Council.

26. THE GALLICANS.

Truly might the Gallican Church, if she were yet faithful to her history and traditions, assert her splendid character in the primitive age as the mother of Catholic orthodoxy in Western Europe. This is her true position through Irenæus and his disciples. Not only does Gaul owe everything to the illumination of his genius, but through him the churches of Britain, and so also the Church of England, derived not a little of that Greek type of orthodoxy which has always distinguished their history. Of the development of Gallicanism we shall learn more by and by. But here we must pause, with a brief glance at the spread of the Gospel down to the times of Constantine.

27. CHRONIC PERSECUTIONS.

From the days when St. Stephen fell asleep in the stony hail-storm, to the days when the rage of Diocletian had left the Universal Church apparently in desolation and in ruins, the faithful soldiers of Christ fought their good fight with unflagging zeal, patience, and intrepidity. Efforts have been made to minimize the extent of the ten persecutions, — their atrocities, the numbers of those who perished, and the mystery of the uninterrupted increase of the Church. But the writings of the Apologists, and those of Tertullian and Cyprian, with the final testimony of Lactantius, are sufficient to prove that persecution was the chronic estate of the primitive Church. It was looked upon as the normal condition of Christian life. The Church's children accepted their profession as that of "dying daily"; they looked for the coming of Christ as near at hand, but they seem not to have anticipated before His appearing any relief from their lot of "laying down their lives for His sake." The unaffected language of the Apologists and later writers is evidence of this: nor is it to be accounted for, if the persecutions were, at worst, only what such writers as Gibbon are willing to concede. Truly, were the Master's words fulfilled, — " Ye shall be hated of all men for my name's sake." Yet how gloriously did the martyrs copy the blessed example of their Master in praying for their murderers! At the stake they chanted the psalms, or lifted up their voices in the Christian hymns, — in the *Gloria in Excelsis* at daybreak, or in their even-song for the sunset, or "the lighting of the lamps."[1] In the Coliseum whole families were thrown to the wild beasts, refusing to save their lives by throwing a grain of incense on the brazier that glowed before an idol. Tender women clasped their husband's necks, entreating them not to surrender, and little children, clinging to their fathers' knees, or the white raiment of their mothers,

[1] See Note B'.

cried out, "We shall all sup with Jesus; let the lions come on." From the martyrdoms of Antioch to those of Lyons and Vienne, — from those of Proconsular Asia and Northern Africa to those of our forefathers at St. Alban's, — the blood of the martyrs became the seed of the Church. But —

"How that red rain did make the harvest grow!"

28. GROWTH OF THE CHURCH.

They have tried, also, to minimize the blessed result; but the testimony of our Christian authors is unequivocal, nor could they have hazarded such language as they habitually used had their statements been such as their adversaries could deny. Of this the crowning evidence is the submission of Constantine. The conversion of the Empire, which was its immediate consequence, and which Julian might have very readily suppressed had it rested on any other than the solid base of a defeated Paganism, is the pyramid of evidence which none can overthrow.

It is noteworthy how often, in a great moral revolution, reactionary periods have been allowed to defeat themselves, and to give the last clinching blows that confirmed the change with the very hammer lifted to destroy it. Julian's apostasy drove the last nail into the coffin of Paganism, a word which, coming into vogue at this epoch, proved that Christianity had become predominant everywhere save among rustics and barbarians in uncivilized villages (*pagi*), even Julian himself with his adherents treating the old myths as a creed outworn, and striving to give it a new base of poetical and philosophical theory. Note, too, what the admissions of his apostasy imply. His own new and theoretical heathenism demonstrates the extinction of the old idolatries; the apostate borrows from Alexandria the ideas of Clement and of Athanasius, who had made learning, and not ignorance, the handmaid of religion. From the Church, too, he catches the ennobling principle that a lofty moral system must sustain the new augurs and priests of his reformed mythology; they must rival the clergy at least in outward respectability. Note, too, what a tribute he pays to Christianity, in closing the Christian schools, and trying to throw education, even in grammar and rhetoric, into the hands of his philosophers. From first to last, his effort to supplant the work of Constantine demonstrates the superior statesmanship of the latter, whose sagacity discovered that nothing remained of Numa's priestcraft but a hollow shell. Even if his dying lips are not to be credited with the words, we may say with truth that his bitter convictions must have been, as he bit the dust in death, "O Galilean! thou hast conquered."

29. CONVERSION OF THE EMPIRE.

Thus this most wonderful revolution of institutions, laws, and manners which the world has ever seen, was proved to be the outcome of a popular conviction so general as to furnish it with a firm support. It had become a necessity. This is the only logical way of accounting for the conduct of the soldiery, who hailed the accession of Jovian, and who restored the cross to their ensigns, never again to be dishonoured. Look at this dilemma of unbelief. If the Christians were not numerous, if the cross had not won its triumph, then all the greater the miracle. Then Constantine supplanted the Roman eagles on the Imperial standards while yet the cross was infamy and all but universally abhorred. Who can credit this? But more, on such a theory, he substituted churches for idol temples, and removed the capital itself from the immemorial seat of empire to adorn the first Christian city, none presuming to remonstrate, while Christians were yet inconsiderable in numbers and in the influence of their characters. Is this to be credited? But be it so! Then is the miracle all the greater: all the stronger the right hand, all the more manifest the stretched-out arm of the Crucified, in giving his churches rest. Have it as you will: here is the fulfilment of the promises, but only in part. The ages of persecution have demonstrated the fact that the gates of hell cannot prevail: they have made the heathen feel that the chariots of salvation cannot be stayed in their career of conquest and of universal dominion. Nay, more, they have made the princes of this world to feel that "they come to naught."

30. CÆSARS CONQUERED BY MARTYRS.

Yes, and still further, they have taught kings and Cæsars that, as Christ can triumph in spite of them, so too can He reign without them. Come then, ye Cæsars,[1] if ye choose to be wise at last; now when this humbling lesson has been forced upon you, so

See Note C'.

that all mankind must see it, — now you may do your part, if ye are ready to " kiss the Son." Take your place as servants, if ye will, and so become "nursing fathers" to His kingdom; but "know yourselves to be but men," and ascribe nothing to yourselves which Christ may permit you to do by His grace. Abolish the brutal manners of the heathen; throw down their fœtid altars; destroy their hateful slavery and gladiatorial shows; reform the morals and the times; give men Christian wives, and mothers, and families; give them the day of the Lord; make Christian laws to sustain human rights; build churches; restore the Christian schools; endow hospitals, enlarge charities, send forth missions; emblazon the cross on your standards, set it on your sceptres, your orbs and crowns; but know that Christ needs not your patronage, much less your control. Think of the millions of martyrs and confessors your cruel edicts have made; think of the deserts and the catacombs, the wilds and caves of the earth, to which you have driven them; think of the humble and the poor whom ye have been impotent to bribe or to terrify; reflect that, without carnal weapons, these have overcome your legions. Behold the Cæsars vanquished by old men and women, by youth unarmed, by babes and virgins: "Not by might, not by power, but by my Spirit, saith the Lord of Hosts." Own it, and be sure of the rest. The Nazarene must reign for ever and ever; the kingdoms of this world are to be the kingdom of our God and of His Christ. He has gone forth conquering and to conquer; He is "King of kings and Lord of lords."

LECTURE III.

THE SYNODICAL PERIOD.

1. THE CONVERSION OF CONSTANTINE.

THE conversion of the Emperor introduced the Church to new trials and temptations, and these were, in some respects, more formidable perils than those of the preceding centuries. I have noted the influence of the persecutions, protracted through ten generations of believers, in producing among Christians a habit of thought, most natural in the circumstances, identifying the Christian profession with their actual experiences. To be a Christian was to be persecuted of course. This was accepted as a fact, and grew into a principle. The estate of outward prosperity was ignobly selfish, if not absolutely unlawful, for the faithful. The glories of martyrdom were naturally exaggerated; confessorship assumed the forms of voluntary exile, of the celibate, of ascetic life in the desert, in the catacombs, in caves of the earth, and finally of monasticism. All these varieties of cross-bearing, honourable and sanctified as they were in themselves, were yet liable to beget extreme opinions as to their merits, and fanciful views of the life (as if less godly and consistent) of those who served the Lord in the holy estate of matrimony, reared families, and created the Christian home.

2. RESERVE AND MODERATION.

It is noteworthy that the new state of things under Constantine was received by the Church with little exultation.[1] No doubt it was, to Christians, incredible that it should continue. The Emperor was unbaptized; there was no disposition to shorten his time as a catechumen; there was evident distrust of him, as well might be, considering the untamed paganism of his manners. He might at any time relapse; and then they foresaw a reaction, and could not be sure of his successors. A wise and prudent reserve is the temper of the times almost universally; but, even in accepting it as a fact that the Empire was to be Christian, the Church seems to have adapted herself with consummate caution to the novelty of the circumstances.

3. THE CELIBATE.

There was no haste to marry and to give in marriage, on the part of those born Christians, but rather, as there was now no immediate prospect of martyrdom, it became a favourite idea to prove one's deadness to the world by following St. Anthony into the sort of life which was subsequently developed into monasticism. Oriental in its origin, it afterwards assumed distinct types in the West; and, pure and useful as it was at first, the institution

[1] See Note D'.

rapidly degenerated, and, with many noble exceptions, became, in the East and West alike, a mere anachronism; unsuited to the real wants of the ages that followed those of the great Councils.[1] In after times the urgent necessity of reforms was met by the creation of new orders, and these, in turn, becoming as salt devoid of savour, there arose in the West the new form of "Friars," aiming to restore an evangelical poverty and simplicity. But these again, in their rapid degeneracy and greed of riches, rendering the system hateful alike to the powers of Church and State, invited spoliation and suppression; and conflicting, as they did, with the divine institution of the Episcopate, from allegiance to which they always contrived to release themselves, they have been everywhere abolished, or reduced to the shadows of their originally gigantic proportions.

4. OTHER IMMEDIATE RESULTS.

Of other immediate effects of the great revolution, some were beneficial and some quite the reverse.[2] Let me rapidly glance at them in outline. (1.) The close of three centuries of fiery persecution was of itself a gain to civilization, and in many ways promoted the growth of the Church. To repair the desolations of many generations; to rebuild the churches destroyed by Diocletian, to found new ones, and little by little to turn pagan temples into Christian basilicas, — all this was great gain. (2.) To enable the cowardly and ignorant

[1] See Note E'. [2] See Note F'.

masses to hear the gospel, and to embrace it, with impunity, was yet a greater benefit. (3.) The blow given at once to idols and their shrines, and the contempt into which they fell immediately, was a leap out of the shadow of death into the dawn of day, an unspeakable blessing to the souls of men, and not less an emancipation of the human intellect. (4.) But the reformation of laws, which in some degree was an instantaneous consequence of the change, cannot be regarded by any candid mind without exultation. The edict for observing the Day of the Lord (A. D. 312) was of itself a restoration of one of the primal endowments of mankind by the benevolent Father of the race, and the speedy reform of laws affecting marriage and divorce concurred with the recognition of Sunday as a day of rest to endow the converted heathen with the purified institution of the family, and with the gift of the Christian home. (5.) Upon these followed the erection of Christian society, in marked contrast with Paganism, by its benevolent provisions for the sick and needy, by its care for the widow and the orphan, by suppressing open profligacy and licentiousness, by ameliorating the public burdens of the poor, by discouragement of gladiatorial shows, and softening the hardships of slavery, which it gradually destroyed. (6.) The laws, moreover, were tempered by mercies unknown before, in the mitigation of Draconian penalties, and in the protection of the poorer sort, who were encouraged to appeal against official abuses and maladministration; while the germinal principle of the *habeas corpus* was also interposed for the relief of all classes. (7.) If these benefits softened the manners and elevated the morals of the masses, it cannot be denied that indirectly they favoured science and the domestic arts, if not as yet the fine arts and the cultivation of letters, which had fallen so low under the brutalized successors of the Antonines. (8.) The founding of a Christian city on the Bosporus, and the transfer of the capital, were marks of a lofty genius in Constantine, and this effort was not unfavourable to the development of Christian culture in other respects. If the movement failed to arrest the decline of the Roman Empire, as such, it may be doubted whether anything else contributed in the same degree to its perpetuity under its new forms and conditions. In the East, the direct line of the Cæsars perished not till after the middle of the fifteenth century; and in the West, at least the shadow of its name vanished only with the earlier years of our own. (9.) But, greatest of all, the immediate result of the conversion of the Empire was the development of catholic unity by the gathering of the Universal Episcopate at Nicæa for synodical action, and the opening of that great synodical period which defined the Faith and the Constitutions of Christendom. It laid the groundwork of all the free Constitutions that have been since developed; the spirit of the Gospel has been the seed of growth and progress wherever it has been disseminated in its purity. (10.) "There was a time," says Bishop Horne, "when a Christian could travel through the civilized world, with letters from his bishop, finding in every city a welcome and a home among his fellow Christians." The stranger, whose very name was equivalent to that of enemy, thus became a guest, and humanity received a new charter from man, in the name of God. Such was the new bond of society, the "fellowship of nations," the brotherhood of the human family in the Fatherhood of God.

5. DISADVANTAGES.

Certain temporary disadvantages may indeed be cited by the pessimist, and worldly philosophers may dwell on the weakening of the Empire as a primary and fatal consequence. But, on the other hand, even this may be doubted; for the policy of Diocletian in partitioning the Empire among titular Cæsars had already diminished the grandeur of the Imperial crown, had divided the strength of the Empire, and introduced such intestine feuds as would probably have much sooner dismembered it and reduced it to fragmentary sovereignties, had not some elements of new life been infused by the bold and hazardous experiment. Far more grievous is the unquestionable evil which was so soon obvious in the court Christianity, in the worldly religion made fashionable by the revolution. The Church became political almost inevitably, and men whose "kingdom was wholly of this world" began to exercise authority in her sacred name. "Whence hath it tares?" "The Enemy had done this," as the Master had predicted; and the net to which he had likened His kingdom began to enclose "a multitude of fishes, both good and bad."

6. LASTING RESULTS.

The Church Militant here on earth must feel the Enemy, and at times his grip is terrible. Yet who can fail to see that, in these reprisals, he was revenging, as he could, a tremendous convulsion, that had rent into fragments the hold he had kept for ages, like a "strong man armed." It was the fury of Satan, dispossessed by one destined to crush his head; he had been made to feel that the eleven Galilean fishermen were stronger than himself, in the might of that One. In spite of all he did then, and has been doing ever since, as the war goes on to its glorious conclusion, we must not fail to recognize the truth, that most substantial gains to the cause of Christ were the fruit of Constantine's mighty revolution. It greatly contributed to scatter far and wide the seeds of evangelization, of civilization, of human progress; and while it threw down the horrible despotism of heathenism from the throne of the world, it enthroned in its stead, as a law that cannot be broken, the love of Christ to the world of men. Under this law, it gathered people out of all nations into one spiritual kingdom, and substituted for a universal bondage of despair the catholic ties of faith, hope, and charity, and of a common destiny in life beyond the grave.

7. PRIMITIVE COUNCILS.

"He who shall introduce into public affairs the principles of primitive Christianity will change the face of the world." Such was the sagacious aphorism of Franklin, recognizing a truth not sufficiently affirmed by Christians: for those principles did change the face of the world.[1] By departing from them, Christian nations relapse into the former barbarism satirized by Juvenal and scourged by St. Paul. It is only where and so far as those principles are restored, that man is a man, and the brotherhood of humanity is maintained. Free governments find their original in the combinations of law and liberty which were first seen in the primitive synods. These were first developed in the East, like everything else that is Christian. They found their model and their warrant in the Council of Jerusalem, when the "apostles, presbyters, and brethren" came together to deliberate, and in its results which were published in the name of "the whole Church." But we find councils naturalized in Italy in the days of Hippolytus, when the suburbicarian bishops confronted and humbled the bishop who presided over them, in the free spirit of their Master's maxim, "All ye are brethren." But unquestionably the grand expounder of the primitive synodical system is Cyprian, the martyr Bishop of Carthage, who would do nothing without the approval of his presbytery,—*omni plebe adstante*,—the laity also having their place and their voice. Note also, that while, after Ignatius in the East, we find no one so strenuously maintaining the principle of episcopacy as Cyprian, it is not less true that he is equally energetic in asserting the rights of priests and deacons, and of the whole

[1] See Note G'.

people, — the faithful in Christ, as he loved to call them.¹ So then, even during the martyr ages, the synodical features of the Church's polity became a precedent. Early Christians believed in the presence of Christ, by His Vicar Spirit, wherever two or three were gathered in His name. They believed in His promise concerning the *agreement* of the disciples in anything to be prayed for. They considered the plural form, "*Our* Father," as embodying the great law of the communion of saints; that is, of all Christians in one spiritual family. Moreover, they understood that "where the Spirit of the Lord is, there is liberty." It is surprising how instinctively, when they were no longer a persecuted flock, this spirit showed itself in the general demand for an Œcumenical Council.

8. A NURSING FATHER.

Here, it is true, a new idea was generated with a strange unanimity, illustrative, indeed, of the loyal and dutiful spirit of Christians under the tyranny of persecutors, but now taking a filial and loving form toward the Emperor, as "a nursing father" of the Church.² With wonder, and gratitude to God, they not merely saw in Constantine the fulfilment of this promise, but they naturally classed him with those potentates whom God had raised up in divers ages to serve and to succour His people. If even Nero was "the minister of God to them for good," as St. Paul had taught, how much more was the believing Cæsar another Cyrus, to whom

¹ See Note H'.   ² See Note I'.

God himself was saying, "Thou art my shepherd"! Hence, the easy transition to a mild and loyal "Cæsarism," perilous indeed beyond all they could then conceive, and destined to make mischief in after times; but most conspicuous at this epoch, making emphatic the entire absence of any papal ideas or claims, and rebuking, as it were beforehand, the arrogance and worldliness with which pontiffs afterwards struggled, as they do even in our day, for earthly crowns and for a temporal supremacy over nations and their rulers.

The sovereign was but a catechumen, but then Cyrus was uncircumcised. As "God's ordinance," they had no doubt he was in God's hand, and called to "perform all His pleasure." His was the only voice that could reach to every corner of the *œcumene*, and his the only bounty that could provide for the cost of an *œcumenical* synod. No human being doubting, — no bishop preferring any claim to be the authority for a call of brother bishops, — all acquiesced in the natural course of things, and while a Cæsar voiced the wishes of the whole Church, it was apparently the voice of Cæsar only that was heard. Again was seen that which was foreshadowed at the nativity: "A decree went forth from Cæsar Augustus that all the world should be enrolled."

9. THE TEMPORAL BISHOPRIC.

So now began that view of the relations between Church and State which God overruled for so much good, but which, in its developed form, has been so very bad for Church and State alike. In the primitive age the *internal* affairs of the Church were not subject to any state interference: the Church was self-governing. But her *external* concerns and interests were largely intrusted to Cæsar, who began to be esteemed a sort of "bishop," or overseer of its temporalities. Hence the common concession to sovereign princes, in later times, of the *Episcopate ab extra*. The Gallicans called their kings *evêques au dehors*.[1] The German Emperors often maintained this position against the pontiffs with a strong hand; and the Anglicans restored to Henry VIII. nothing more nor less than pontiffs themselves had over and over again recognized in the Heinrichs and the Othos. It was the undoubted position of Alfred and of William the Norman. We shall have occasion to recur to this matter when I come to Charlemagne.

10. A GENERAL COUNCIL.

As early as A. D. 313, Constantine convoked a local council at Rome in the affair of the Donatists; but it settled nothing, though the Bishop of Rome presided in it, and an appeal to the Emperor led him, in the succeeding year, to call together a more general Council of the West, at Arles, in Gaul. Bishops from Africa came thither; and what is more interesting to us, there were present also, three bishops from Britain, who subscribed to its decrees, viz. *Eborius* of York, *Restitutus* of London, and *Adelfius*, possibly of Lincoln, though

[1] See Note J'.

his signature is ambiguous. When, eleven years afterwards, the great see of Alexandria was shaken by the innovations in doctrine of the unhappy Arius, and when it was observed that the time had come for the regulation of the paschal usages, which were still diverse in the West from those of the East, the sublime thought of an Œcumenical Synod took shape spontaneously, and the Cæsar called it to assemble at Nicæa, in Bithynia.

11. NICÆA.

Let us pause for a minute to get some idea of a spot so sacred in associations. The modern traveller finds it a wretched site of hovels, under the name *Isnik*, where, amid majestic relics, are huddled together some thirty Turkish families and about as many Christians. Great is the desolation, but superb even yet are the ruins of what was once the opulent and beautiful Nicæa, named from the wife of Lysimachus at her own suggestion. Antigonus, his predecessor, was its founder, and he aspired to give it his own name. Its position and importance as a centre of commerce, with roads radiating thence in every direction, made it a convenient place for those coming to southern ports, from Antioch and Alexandria, or to those arriving from the West, and landing at Ephesus or Smyrna. Its twofold circuit of walls, with lofty towers and gates sublime, still announces its departed splendours. Lake Ascanius lies near, in quiet beauty, surrounded by hills and groves, and thence the land stretches upward to the Bebrycian

Olympus, whose glistening domes of snow are visible in the horizon. As an emblem of what was done to desecrate the spot in the eighth century under the infamous Irene, pestilence bred of stagnating puddles has succeeded its once delicious and healthful climate.

Here then came the Christians. Of many tongues they were, and from many climes. Constantine himself was a native of Britain, born at York. But all recognized the language of the New Testament as the catholic language, and the East as the native seat of the Church. Hosius, Bishop of Corduba, in Spain, had lately been to Alexandria, and it is not doubted that the Emperor was moved to this great measure by him and by the Alexandrian church. Here, then, "the Holy Catholic Church" rose up before all the world in its unity. Decius and Diocletian had made havoc of the fathers, but "instead of the fathers were the children." They said, "Here we are." The gates of hell had not prevailed.

12. THE OPENING.

Then was seen the fruit of that little "handful of corn" that Christ had left upon Olivet, and the hills round about Jerusalem, when he went up on high. How "green it was in all the earth"! how truly it " shook like Lebanon"! The "eleven" and "the hundred and twenty," — they had become "the Holy Church throughout all the world," and now their bishops came to testify that "always, everywhere, and by all" it had acknowledged "the

Everlasting Son of the Father Everlasting." Over these Roman roads that stretched from the Capitol, like the threads of the spider's web, to Gaul and Britain, to Persia on the east, and by Spain to ports that opened to Africa, the Emperor had multiplied vehicles like the wagons which Joseph sent out of Egypt for his father and his brethren. They came from all lands where they had published the Gospel of Peace, many of them men of literary attainments, eloquence, and great piety; others of them venerable confessors, relics of Diocletian's cruelty, maimed in their banishment to dark mines, — branded in the flesh, one deprived of an eye, another "halting on his thigh," another bowed down with age and infirmities, — "bearing in their bodies the marks of the Lord Jesus." What a spectacle for angels and men! Bishops, 318, like the number of Abraham's household, they enjoyed this association with the Father of the Faithful. In divers preliminary conferences, "like our committees of the whole," held in a church or oratory with solemnities of worship, not only presbyters took part, but also lay-brethren. The Council itself was strictly a "house of bishops." Yet Athanasius was there as a deacon, attending his bishop, Alexander, who soon after left to this marvellous youth his great patriarchal see and the defence of the faith. Hosius was called to the presidency, but was assisted probably by Eusebius. When all were gathered in a great hall of the palace, the Cæsar appeared in imperial purple and glittering ornaments of state, like Saul for his stature, and stately in his pace. He blushed as he stood face to face with his fathers in God, passing from the end of the hall to his throne, while they stood to meet him in rows on either side. What must have been their reflections? What were his? Surely there was a shaking among the shades in Hades. If the dead were stirred up at that moment; if Pilate, if Nero, if Aurelius, if Decius, if Diocletian, saw their heroic successor there among Christ's servants, standing modestly till they begged him to be seated, — surely they must have anticipated Julian in the outcry, " O Galilean! thou hast conquered." For the moral sublime, I can hardly recall any like moment in mere human history to be compared with it; its impressions upon the imagination and the thoughtful intellect are beyond comparison overwhelming and elevating, at once tender and majestic. Blessed martyrs! from your repose in paradise were ye permitted to behold, and to exclaim, " What hath God wrought?"

13. SIGNIFICANT FACTS.

Here two facts are to be noted. (1.) The holy Gospels were set on a throne in the old councils [1] as the symbol of the Holy Ghost. Above the bishops and their presidents — above Cæsar — O how far! — God's holy word was supreme. The rule of faith was the word of God. Councils were only to bear testimony to the universal interpretation handed down in the churches. (2.) The regimen and polity of all the churches were the same, — those of Ignatius and of Cyprian.[2] Not a hint was

[1] See Note K'. [2] See Note L'.

there of any difference; from the Persian Gulf to the *Ultima Thule* of the Northwest, " the ancient customs " and traditions of Christians in this respect were a unit. Now, if these were a departure from what apostles had ordained in all the churches, when and how was the universal innovation established? We have the history of conflicts and schisms, starting from very trifling novelties. How comes it to pass, if the Episcopate was an afterthought, an innovation, a usurpation, that no convulsion followed, — no primitive witnesses recorded their protest? How, since human nature is always the same, were there none among the presbyters to maintain their order against a universal invasion? How is it — when in all the presbyteries of the universe, respectively, some one man rose up claiming to preside over them by a divine call, and to be something which they were not — that not a voice was heard to remonstrate, and to testify that it was not so in the days of Polycarp, and of the holy men who had seen the apostles and others who had seen the Lord?

14. RESULTS OF THE COUNCIL.

The results of the Nicene Council are not left to the fossilized past; they are universally felt to this day. Arius, whose heresy it condemned, finally stickled only for an *iota:* insert this least of all letters between two *omicrons*, and he would subscribe. But on the field of Waterloo the surrender of a single bar in a farm-yard gate would have been more fatal to Europe than the betrayal of

Gibraltar. So the compromise of truth by one jot or tittle added or taken away, would have proved the triumph of Antichrist. Not the *homoiousion*, but the *homoousion* was the truth of God. Christ is not of *like* substance with the Father; He *is* the Father, "of one substance" with Him of whom he could say, " I and my Father are one "; "He that hath seen me hath seen the Father." Such is and ever was the catholic faith. Further, the first pages of the Common Prayer, after the tables of lessons, embody the Easter Canons of Nicæa; its sublime symbol is recited liturgically in all the churches; in the Ordinal is to be found a strict conformity to its laws for preserving the succession of apostolic bishops. Its great canon, recognizing the patriarchates under the law of already existing usage, but admitting no inequality among them, except for convenience of order, has never been repealed. It makes the two capitals, "Old Rome" and "New Rome," as equals, first and second on the roll, but simply because they were the chief seats of empire; and this great canon is the law of the Church to this day, and as such defines those Westerns who refuse to obey it to be, not catholic, but schismatical.

15. THE PASCHAL LETTERS.

To Alexandria the council assigned a practical *hegemony* of the churches.[1] Its bishop was to send forth annually the computation for Easter, which was thenceforth to be observed everywhere, by

[1] See Note M'.

the Nicene canon, on the Lord's day after the full moon following the vernal equinox, and from his decision there was to be no appeal. Bishops on the Tiber took their law from the Nile. The *Pope* of Alexandria, for so its bishop is called to this day, exercised no pontifical powers, but only the canonical powers granted by the synod; yet if there was any shadow of a "papacy" at this period, it was not at Rome. Gregory Nazianzen, himself one of the primates of Christendom as Bishop of Constantinople, said justly of his brother patriarch, "The head of the Alexandrian church is the head of the world." At a later period, Justinian's rescript also recognizes Constantinople as the head of all the churches.

The traditional cultivation of astronomical studies in Egypt was thus invested with fresh interest and utility. To the Church belongs the glory of giving to science a revived and vigorous life in this sublime department. Men of science had kept her fettered to the Ptolemaic system, their marvellous invention. For two thousand years they had sworn by it, against Pythagoras. The Court of Rome only acted for them when it blindly imprisoned Galileo. But the Court of Rome is not the Church, nor has Christianity any responsibility for its follies. And let us never forget that it was a Christian presbyter who taught to scientists the true system of the universe. Copernicus was the forerunner of Newton, and a herald of the Reformation.

16. THE PATRIARCHATES.

Before passing to the other Œcumenical Councils, let us pause a moment to consider these patriarchal dignities, and what their name imports. Tertullian tells us of the natural influence exerted by the great centres upon surrounding churches; and, apart from civil centres, he notes the importance of those churches which had been founded by the apostles themselves, and which were known as "Apostolic Sees." In days when books were few and intelligence was transmitted with difficulty, the bishops and clergy were constantly forced to resort to these strongholds of testimony, for the solution of practical difficulties and for studying the Holy Scriptures. Those who were near to Corinth repaired to that city; and so others went to Ephesus, Jerusalem, or Cæsarea. In the West, Rome, being the only Apostolic See, had a larger *clientèle*. But for the preservation of order, the consecration of bishops, the enforcement of canons, and such matters, the great centres of Antioch, Alexandria, and Rome had gained, by force of custom and convenience, a pre-eminence which the Nicene Council now made canonical. The *parvenu* capital called New Rome, lifted, *ipso facto*, as the seat of empire into equality with Old Rome, was made superior, in order of mention, to the older sees of the East. To Old Rome was conceded a primacy of honour, both as the ancient capital and as an Apostolic See, which Byzantium was not; but in other respects the new capital was made its equal, and owed it no obedience whatever. A vast jurisdiction was adjudged to Alexandria, and a very restricted one to Rome, because "ancient usages" were strictly recognized in defining these jurisdictions. The subsequent Councils of Constantinople and Chalcedon still more closely limited the Roman jurisdiction, and defined it as a canonical grant, and by no means an apostolical bequest. All these facts must be borne in mind with reference to future discussions; but I need not speak here of the minor patriarchates, nor of the honorary distinction of Jerusalem as the "mother of all churches." I have already shown why she was not invested with any corresponding powers.[1] It is only necessary to note that Cyprus was pronounced *autocephalous*, having no dependency even upon Antioch, its natural centre; while, for like reason, all insular churches were rendered equally independent of the patriarchs. By this fundamental law, the Anglican Church reasserted her independence, of which she had never been deprived by any canonical authority.[2]

17. THE GREAT COUNCILS.

The Councils truly Œcumenical, not including the normal Council of Jerusalem, were six. There never has been an Œcumenical Council since the division of the West from its Eastern mother. Nor in the nature of things could there be. How can any council be universal, in which the Orientals are not heard, and with which they have not consented? But of the six which are truly Cath-

[1] Lecture II. § 3. [2] See Note N'.

olic, four are conspicuously the Great Councils; and these Gregory, Patriarch of Rome, reckoned next to the Four Gospels. The fifth and sixth, like the codicils of a will, are the supplement of the foregoing; unlike codicils, they took nothing away from their originals. They enacted no canons. Such Councils only confirm and adjust more specifically and minutely what their originals established.

18. THE SECOND COUNCIL.

The Second Great Synod was held (A. D. 381) under Theodosius, to confirm the Nicene faith and to complete the Great Symbol, bearing testimony against the " Macedonians," who were teaching a new doctrine about the Holy Spirit. The Nicene Creed, as left by the Council, did not touch this subject, which we must infer was left to usage indifferently; the West probably closing the Confession with the language of the Apostles' Creed, and the East reciting that of the Creed of Jerusalem, so called. The Second Council now adopted the latter, slightly expounded it, and set it forth as the unalterable creed of Christendom. So, when we speak precisely, we call it the Nicæno-Constantinopolitan Creed; commonly, to say "the Nicene Creed" is sufficiently correct.[1]

This council forbade all bishops to meddle with churches beyond their jurisdiction, and it reaffirmed the Nicene decrees as to Alexandria and Antioch, and also as to "New Rome." It was

[1] See Note O'.

very numerously attended by the bishops of the East, and was made Œcumenical afterwards by its universal acceptance in the West. It is noteworthy that Theodosius, who was now Cæsar, had carried on the work of Constantine so effectually as to make the Christianity of the Empire a fixed fact. Paganism was abolished, and temples and basilicas were turned into churches; but, like snow-drifts behind walls and fences, that linger in April, while the harvests are green in the blade about them, Paganism had its lurking places. And far down, till the Goths came, among the rustics of *Magna Græcia*, one might have come upon a group of pagans, wreathing a goat or a lamb for sacrifice before some altar of the old idolatry, concealed by a grove, or hidden amid masses of projecting rock; but as for their deities,

"They lived no longer in the faith of reason,"

and another Julian was impossible.

19. THE COUNCIL OF EPHESUS.

In A. D. 431 met the Third Council, at Ephesus. Theodosius was still Emperor. It settled the dispute which Nestorius had raised about the two natures of Him who is "perfect God and perfect man," and it justified the expression *Theotokos* as applicable to the mother of the God-man. This is not literally rendered "Mother of God," which is an awkward rendering into English of a word delicately compounded in the Greek. I prefer the beautiful Latin *Deipara*, or even the Greek word reduced to the form *Theotoce*, the God-bearer. It means just what was said by Elizabeth, when she saluted the Virgin as " the Mother of her Lord."

20. THE FOURTH COUNCIL.

The Fourth Council was that of Chalcedon, A. D. 451. Marcian was Emperor, and Leo I. was Bishop of Rome. He wanted to be something more than the canons had made him. He honestly felt his want of power. The Western churches needed his influence and support. Had he been a "pope," a mere Gallican papacy would have been a good thing for the moment. A great man he was, but not a little peevish about the departing dignity of his see. Naturally he looked with some surprise upon its upstart rival; upon a new Rome where no apostolic foot had ever been planted; and naturally enough he began to boast about St. Peter, and to rest his dignity on the apostolic antiquity of the genuine Rome, so cruelly stripped of its ancient headship. Yet he could not influence the Easterns to look at it just so. They reverenced the older seat of empire, but there was a glory in the Christian city which had supplanted it, and which held its unrivalled site on the Bosporus as a trophy of the cross. Besides, the Easterns regarded Antioch, rather than Rome, as the great Apostolic See, where St. Peter had preached and ministered, where St. Paul and St. Barnabas had begun their world-wide mission; where, while Rome was yet without a clergy, apostles and martyrs had been moved by the Holy Ghost, in Pentecostal oracles, to send missionaries to the West.

Doubtless Old Rome had its dignities, but if Antioch and Alexandria could yield their apostolic honours to the new Rome, so also must Leo. Such, as we shall see, was the spirit of this Council, which ratified anew what had been done at Nicæa and Constantinople, assigning to Old Rome, in presence of Leo's representatives and in spite of its distasteful features, the permanent and indelible character of one among many apostolic sees. In no respect was it superior to its more ancient sisters, but it merited a primacy of honour, not by any divine right, but by concession of its sister churches, because it was the ancient capital. It was not any more than divers other apostolic cities associated with St. Peter. It had never been his see, for his mission was limited to Jewish Christians, and St. Paul had the earlier claim to be its founder, with his larger jurisdiction as the "Apostle of the Gentiles." Such was the thrice uttered voice of the Catholic Church, in her holy and Œcumenical Synods. The seal and final ratification were set at Chalcedon.

21. CHALCEDON.

This city was called the "City of the Blind," because they who founded it had overlooked the more eligible site of Byzantium. But if theirs was the modest ambition to enjoy rather than to traffic, to satisfy taste and not commercial greed, we must own that they were wise in their generation. Lying over against Byzantium, like Birkenhead to Liverpool, or Jersey City to New York, but on a more lofty site, Chalcedon was pre-eminently a city for those who have eyes. Like Scutari to modern travellers, they who preferred seeing the "Golden Horn" to being enclosed within its walls found it the spot where the eyesight might best be regaled. Let me quote Evagrius, who adorns his account of the Fourth Council by a rhetorical portrait of its advantages; and you must let me quote it in full, as evidence of that delight in landscape which the Gospel has incidentally done so much to develop, among all Christian people. The church of St. Euphemia, in the suburbs, was the appointed place of the council, and thus speaks the historian: [1] —

"Directly opposite is Constantinople, and the charms of the sacred precinct are heightened by the view of so great a city. The site of the church is a beautiful spot, of easy access to those who climb, and so far concealed that before they are prepared for it they find themselves in the holy enclosure. Here are three vast fabrics, one open to the sky, — a spacious court, adorned with colonnades, that surround it. From this one enters a similar area, embellished in like manner, but covered by a roof. To the north of this, and facing the east, is the martyr's sepulchre, under a dome surmounting its circular walls and decorative columns. They who have mounted to this site survey the level meads beneath them, green with herbage or undulating harvests, and adorned with trees in great variety. The range of their view takes in as well the wooded mountains, towering in cliffs, or swelling uplands that approach them. They survey the sea besides; here, sheltered from the breezes, the quiet waters with their dark blue tint softly courting the beach and breaking

[1] Eccl. Hist., Book II. cap. 3.

upon it with gentle crispings; or there, fiercely swelling under the winds, and with refluent waves throwing back the petty scallops and the sea-weed that line the shore. The place of meeting was this sacred precinct of Euphemia."

22. EUTYCHES.

Former councils had set forth the faith of ages in the Great Symbol, and had cleared it from the ambiguous interpretations of Nestorius. It had now become necessary to protect it from the reactionary interpretations of Eutyches, who acknowledged only a single nature in the Incarnate God, so that he was of a mixed nature, and not "perfect God and perfect man." A scandalous assembly, which has always been known as "a rabble of robbers,"[1] had elevated the teaching of Eutyches into a public scandal; hence this Fourth Council had become a necessity.

23. LEO, PATRIARCH OF OLD ROME.

Leo, the Bishop of Rome, had wished it might be called in Italy, but the traditional East was adhered to, in place and in language. He then tried to delay the meeting, and with good show of reason, for Attila and his terrible Huns had invaded Gaul, and was ravaging the fair seats of the Gallican Church: the Western bishops, obviously, could not be expected to attend. But Marcian, "with pious zeal," would not brook delay. Leo had a just position as against Eutyches, and he was now made the rather popular and more hon-

[1] Latrocinium.

ourable, because Dioscorus of Alexandria had rashly excommunicated him. Though he did not appear personally, he sent presbyters to represent him, as good Sylvester and other predecessors had done. In the earliest instance, the age and infirmities of the Roman bishop had justified this course; that the precedent was followed in order to draw councils to the West, is a surmise which Leo's conduct tends to make highly probable.

Out of sympathy, no doubt, Leo's desire that he might virtually preside in the Council was complied with. With others, his envoys sat as co-presidents. It seemed but just, and balanced the account with Dioscorus, who had excommunicated him after presiding over the *Latrocinium*. The "Fourth Œcumenical Synod" condemned Eutyches and closed the grand series of the Four Synods, which correspond with the Four Gospels. But we are chiefly to note its spirit in these two particulars: (1.) By enthroning the Gospels, as at Ephesus,[1] we find its testimony to the supremacy of the Scriptures maintained as from the beginning, with unalterable fidelity, in the noon of the fifth century. (2.) It reiterated, and in spite of all Leo's efforts, in spite of his genius and his orthodoxy, forever fixed the relations of the Roman see to Catholic Christendom, in unambiguous and conclusive words, as follows: —

" We, following in all things the decisions of the holy fathers, and acknowledging the canon of the *one hundred and fifty* bishops which has just been read, do also *determine and decree the same things*, touching the privileges

[1] See Note P'.

of the most sacred city of Constantinople, the New Rome. For the fathers justly *gave the primacy* to the elder Rome, *because that was the Imperial city;* and the (150) bishops, moved with the same purpose *gave equal privileges* to the most sacred throne of the New Rome : judging, with reason, that the city which was honoured with the sovereignty and senate, and which enjoyed equal privileges with the elder princely Rome, should be also magnified, like her, in ecclesiastical matters, and be second after her."

24 IMMUTABLE CATHOLICITY.

Nothing could be more clear. If ever there was a moment when the Catholic Church was tempted to create a Papacy, it was this. Great and good was Leo, though censurable in his ambition; the crisis was grave; the Western churches were threatened with extinction. But no! The Church knew nothing about St. Peter's *supremacy ;* nothing about any succession even to his *primacy.* The primacy was one of honour purely, and granted absolutely to both cities *on civil grounds alone.* Leo's envoys themselves made no claim to any divine primacy, much less to any *supremacy;* they only made a feeble appeal to the sixth canon of Nicæa, of which they produced an interpolated copy. This forgery aimed to neutralize the synodical *gift* of the primacy to Rome, and made it a recognition of aboriginal institution. A bishop refuted them by producing the genuine canon, — "Let the ancient customs prevail," etc. They were silenced with ignominy. Another affirmed, that when at Rome he had read the genuine text to Leo himself, and that Leo approved it. He must not be blamed, therefore, for the act of his envoys. After inquiry whether the additional canon was unanimous, there was an outcry, "We all adhere to this decision." The Roman envoys yet pressed their remonstrance; they were answered, "What we have said has been approved by the whole Council." With this truly Roman reply, *Quod scripsi scripsi*, the Catholic Church was adjudged to have no supreme bishop, and not even an honorary primacy, except by a synodical concession yielded on purely civil considerations. These considerations are now obsolete, and hence the primacy itself might be awarded to Jerusalem or to Antioch, most wisely, should a restoration of Catholic unity be granted by the Holy Ghost, before the return of the Son of God to complete His triumph over the Evil One and the present evil world.

25. TWO SUPPLEMENTARY COUNCILS.

Our review of the Synodical Period is not completed until the two supplementary Councils, the *Fifth* and *Sixth*, are at least briefly noted. They are of a purely interpretative character, expounding and limiting the work of the *Third* and *Fourth* Councils. In the *Fifth Council* (A. D. 553), under the Emperor Justinian, the "Monophysite" aggressions of a century received a partial settlement. It assembled in Constantinople in the month of May, and, as it confirmed the preceding Councils, it is an important witness to the universality of their reception, in spite of a hundred years of agitations, all hateful in themselves, all working for truth in the result, and verifying St. Paul's language about heresies. But it required another Council to throw out the bane of "Monothelite" refinements upon the now inveterate heresy of Eutyches. The Sixth and last General Council assembled (November 7, A. D. 680) in the "Trullus," or dome-crowned hall of the palace, in New Rome. Constantine the Bearded was Emperor, and presided in person with dignity. It is gratifying to find that far down in the seventh century the Easterns still led the whole Church, and were able to close the period of Œcumenical Synods with entire fidelity to the spirit of Nicæa. Their testimony settled the Messianic controversies forever. Sifted to the bran, the Scriptures were found to have given no uncertain sound. The Christ of the Gospels was the God-man, perfect in his divine nature and perfect in his human nature; our "elder brother," and yet the Father's Consubstantial and Co-eternal Son.

26. RATIFICATIONS.

But, as bearing on subsequent histories, these auxiliary Councils yield an emphasis to the action of the entire synodical series, which is invaluable to the Catholic of our ages, who is called to resist the heretical system of Trent, and of its flagrant successor, the late "Council of Sacristans,"[1] and the decrees of Pius IX. Observe that a hundred years after the ambitious theory of Leo had been dismissed with ignominy at Chalcedon, Catholicity

[1] The late Archbishop of Paris (Darboy) gave it this name.

knew nothing of it in doctrine or discipline. Rome herself had repeatedly ratified and confirmed all that had been done in spite of her, and now she was forced to set her seal, with final and conclusive force, against the Leonine assumptions. At this date, then, there was no Papacy. But note the clinching facts which follow.

The Fifth Council was called, not only without reference to any authority of the Bishop of Rome, but against his sullen and stubborn remonstrance. Vigilius, by name, was censured in its acts, and died soon after in disgrace; but not before he had humbly subscribed to its decisions, and ascribed his own previous opposition to the instigation of Satan. The unprincipled Pelagius, who had been his accomplice, and very discreditably became his successor, also subscribed to the Council, and enforced its acceptance; but he too died soon after, and has left a name stained with the taint of an unlawful intrusion into his office. Both were Bishops of Rome, but it is evident they were not Popes.

27. THE FINAL JUDGMENT.

And now comes the final judgment of the Catholic Church as to the Bishops of Rome. This Trullan Council, called without any warrant from Old Rome, and presided over by the Emperor with universal approbation, closed its work by a memorable act, of which even Bossuet and the Gallicans have recognized the vast significance. Honorius, Bishop of Rome, had patronized and defended the Monothelite heresy, but his successors had tried to cover up his errors and to make out an apology for his course. This made matters serious. The Council had to examine his letters, and their final decision was, that "in all things Honorius has followed the opinions of Sergius, and has sanctioned his impious (Monothelite) teachings." His letters were ignominiously burned, his name was subjected to perpetual anathema, and Leo II., his successor (A. D. 682), not only ratified this solemn testimony, but added his own, condemning Honorius because, instead of "purifying his apostolic see by the doctrine of apostolic tradition, he had yielded its purity to defilement by a profane betrayal of the faith." Over and over again have the Bishops of Rome ratified this anathema, as required by the forms of the *Liber Diurnus*, which every pontiff was for ages obliged to sign on his election. There is no escape from the conclusion; and with this one fact before us down falls the entire system of Trent, and all that has been based upon it since, more especially in the decrees of the late Pope addressed to his "Vatican Council." To impute any "supremacy," or "infallibility," to the Bishops of Rome, is to destroy the whole Catholic system, and to justify all the heresies and schisms they have taught, including those which the Church, in her Great Synods, has so mightily rebuked.[1]

28. WHO ARE CATHOLICS.

"When shall we see the Church," said St. Bernard, "as it was in the ancient days?" Should

[1] See Note Q'.

Rome herself return to catholic unity, and to unfeigned love of truth and right, who would grudge to her the old canonical primacy? Let her Bishops follow St. Peter's example and humility, — who would deny to them anything that St. Peter himself ever received in the way of honour and filial affection? Not I, for one. But so long as the recent *Latrocinium* of the Vatican presumes to enforce a creed which the fathers never knew, and to rend the Church with new divisions, followed up by anathemas most impious and profane, " let us hold fast the profession of our faith without wavering." We are the Catholics, — we who accept no innovations, — we who cry out with the Nicene fathers, " Let the ancient customs prevail." The great contemporary exponent of the Four Councils is Vincent of Lerins. His " Commonitory " is the voice of the fifth century as to the rule of faith, and the echo of the Synodical Period. It shows that he only is the Catholic who maintains the truth as professed from the beginning, " always, everywhere, and by all." No matter how few in number, if they stand by antiquity. A hundred and twenty souls once made up Catholicity. Such was Athanasius when " all forsook him and fled,"— when he stood against the world.

LECTURE IV.

THE CREATION OF A WESTERN EMPIRE.

1. THE BREAKING UP OF OLD ROME.

PURPOSELY I have avoided choking my subject with the intensely interesting, but mystifying, details of the breaking up of the Roman Empire in the West. Hardly was the Christian metropolis founded on the Bosporus, when the Goths and Vandals began to make their terrible names known to the Empire, and to receive their momentary repulse from Constantine. The inundations of barbarism were stayed till the great Theodosius had left a divided sway to his sons. The triumphant siege and pillage of Rome by Alaric begins a new period of history for the world. Augustine trembled in Africa before the downfall of an imperial system long supposed to be eternal, — the last development of law for mankind. He composed his "City of God" to illustrate the only durable empire, and to disprove the outcries of the heathen remnant in the West, that the contempt of Numa's gods had occasioned the disasters of the age.

2. THE GOTHS, VANDALS, AND HUNS.

The Goths were Christians of a sort: they professed Arianism, and their conquests were somehow capable of being harmonized with the Imperial power of New Rome. But had they made themselves permanent masters of the West, Arianism, which the Council of Nicæa had proved to be at war with the catholic faith of Scripture, must have overspread the West. It pleased God to subject Rome to fresh humiliations under the savages of Genseric, who also ravaged Northern Africa and its primitive seats of Latin Christianity. Then came the onset of Attila, "the Scourge of God," more general in its sweep of flame than all that had devoured before. The Goths and Ostrogoths, however, who enjoyed a temporary occupation of Italy for two generations, made themselves a satrapy of the Empire, and after the extinction of Augustulus somewhat prolonged the Imperial fiction in the West.

Meantime, God was raising up the Franks. They became a Christian race under *Clovis*, in whose name we recognize that of *Louis*, familiarized to us by subsequent history. If one considers the changes brought upon Europe by the invasions of Italy, Gothic and Teutonic, — by the overflow upon Spain, from all sides, of Goths, Moors, Franks, and nameless hordes brought with them and after them, — as also the corresponding movements along the Rhine and through all Germany and ancient Belgium, — the rise of such a creature and creator as could mass them and give shape to their destinies must be recognized as proof of a God who rules and overrules the universe. Referring you to the usual sources of information upon this meagre outline of the grand movements of Providence for developing Modern Europe, we now come to the dread and imposing career of Charlemagne. It was his to reconstruct after devastation, to regulate after nomadic chaos, and to prepare the way for forms of civilization which are perpetuated even in our own times.

3. RETROSPECT.

Let us return for a moment to the period of the Councils, and trace the hand of Providence in putting an effectual close to it by what is called the Disunion of East and West. Since that "disunion" — the mild word for a schism, which suspends *functional* unity, but does not destroy *organic* life and spiritual communion — it is manifest that no œcumenical or catholic council has been possible. The Greeks might meet in Eastern synods, or the West in Occidental ones; but no catholic action is possible without the free and united consent of Greeks and Latins. The old patriarchates of the East must be heard in any synod truly œcumenical; but even they cannot make any canons or customs for Christendom without the free acceptance of all the Western churches. The patriarchate of Rome never was allowed to consent in the name of the entire West, for the Catholic Church restricted its jurisdiction to Lower Italy and adjacent islands; if, indeed, the "suburbicarian" limits included so great a range as this.

Bearing this in mind, we must take a retrospective glance at certain provincial councils, ambitious of the œcumenical name, in which the Synodical Period found its limits; like a majestic river, losing itself at last amid marshes and lagoons, in petty mouths and friths, which leave undistinguishable the unity of its current, or the point where the name of the river belongs to any one division of its tides.

4. MINOR COUNCILS.

The Fifth and Sixth Councils failed to enact canons, and hence a council (A. D. 692) which aimed to supply this defect is called the *Quini-Sext*, to indicate its supplementary character, as a sequel to both. It was held in Constantinople. The Latins, however, would not accept it. It displeased Rome, because it maintained the old canonical equality of New Rome, and also the rights of the married clergy, which Rome was trying to suppress in Italy. Early in the next century, the walls of churches in the East and West alike had become disfigured by wretched caricatures of our Lord and of the saints, known as *Icons;* not graven or molten images, but miserable daubs with tinsel decorations; bits of tinfoil silvered or gilded, often covering all but the face and hands of the absurd figures. Against these objects all the canons of good taste cried out; but every page of the early fathers which assailed the heathen images not less bore witness that Christianity abhorred such things. It is disgraceful to reflect, however, that it was left to a semi-barbarian Emperor to imitate the zeal of Epiphanius, who had torn to shreds the first thing of the kind of which we hear in history. Leo III., the Isaurian, issued his edict (A. D. 724) against them. It caused him endless confusions and distresses to sustain this policy, till he died, in A. D. 741. The excesses of his zeal, not always according to knowledge, had rendered the name of "the Iconoclasts" not a little odious, when his very able but unfortunate son and successor, Constantine V., to whom clings the scornful name *Copronymus*, called a council to settle the matter. It was attended by more than three hundred Eastern bishops, who condemned the *Icons*, with unquestionable fidelity to antiquity. This council has no claim to œcumenical character; but when, not long afterwards, the Western churches bore precisely the same testimony in one of the most memorable of Western councils, we have irrefragable evidence, putting both together, that such was the unbiassed testimony of the Catholic Church in the eighth century, and long after its close.

5. IRENE.

Leo IV., the feeble son of the fifth Constantine, was the "husband of his wife," the Athenian Irene, who did not wait till he died to "reign in his stead." When he died, under a dose administered by her, she became regent for her son, and with a taste for art quite feminine, but hardly Attic, she made herself the fanatical patroness of pictures which Zeuxis would have laughed at. Beautiful, but infamous, the poisoner of her husband afterwards slew her son, the boy Emperor, usurping his throne and making herself the first Empress in the line of the Cæsars. She bewitched the court, and was able to carry all before her by corrupting many of the clergy and banishing powerful nobles. At one time she had a scheme to marry the great King of the Franks; but, Bluebeard as he was with his nine wives, he had tastes and schemes of his own, and did not care to be poisoned. Her name means *peace*, but Alecto and her sister furies all seemed incarnate in her. This was the Jezebel whom Adrian, the Roman patriarch, forgetting the warnings of the Apocalypse, encouraged and patronized in mingling her cup of fornications. Thank God, our English Alcuin rebuked her for presuming to teach in the church, against the inspired command of St. Paul. This wicked woman convened a council at Nicæa (A. D. 787), which except in its name has no claim to any association with the great Nicene Synod. Just as " Romulus-Augustus" was the name of the poor creature in whom Old Rome perished ignominiously, so the council called with solemn irony *Deutero-Nicene* overruled the second commandment and all Christian antiquity, and established image-worship.

6. A COUNTER COUNCIL.

The Roman patriarch accepted it, and officially proclaimed its acceptance in the West; but Adrian had a master beyond the Alps, and the great West was soon able to speak for itself in a free council. It was called by Charles, King of the Franks, and assembled at Frankfort, A. D. 794. It overruled Adrian and his officious pretensions, refuting Irene's council, — corroborating, in fact, the testimony of the previous council of Constantine the Fifth. Of all councils not œcumenical, Frankfort comes nearest to being such; and it worthily and nobly brings to a close the period of the synodical testimony of the whole undivided Church.

7. THE RULE OF FAITH.

What then was the rule of faith recognized and established by all the Œcumenical Councils? The answer comes to us, as from that lofty seat on which the Gospels were enthroned at Ephesus and at Chalcedon, when Vincent of Lerins replies, "The Holy Scriptures." But when we come to interpretation, What is the rule? he answers, "What from the beginning has been received always, everywhere, and by all."

8. THE MAXIM OF VINCENT.

Such is the great principle established by Tertullian, in his "Prescription against Heretics." But, as I reminded you, it is convenient to quote it in the aphorism of Vincent; his test of catholicity being so terse in statement, so clear in application, and so conclusive in its force. It comes to us just at the epoch that closed the Four Great Councils, and certifies us as to the whole spirit of their legislation in words that are "nails and goads." Observe then, (1) negatively, that no one bishop or see was of any decisive weight in the definition of doctrine. "No," says Vincent, quoting St. Paul, "nor an angel from heaven, should he teach anything that was not from the beginning." But (2) positively, catholic doctrine must be that which has been "always held"; (3) and that not merely in one church, see, or patriarchate, but "everywhere"; and (4) not merely everywhere, by some individual doctor, speaking his private opinion, or presuming to speak for others, but "by all,"—that is to say, with the *Amen* of the whole Church ratifying and confirming the same. Such was catholicity then, as understood by the undivided Catholic Church; and with this understanding we shall better comprehend the melancholy divisions we must soon consider.

9. THE COUNCIL OF FRANKFORT.

Let us dwell a little longer on the Council of Frankfort. It stands for the old landmark. I claim for it no secondary place in church history; it shows a far-reaching proleptical wisdom, of which God only could have been the author. Let it be praised for its invaluable testimony to the faith, as essentially unaltered at its date, and for its thunders of remonstrance against Irene's degenerate bishops: "We have no such custom, neither the churches of God."

It is gratifying to an Anglo-Catholic moreover, that he may identify in this epoch the first movement of the Church of England towards her present position in Christendom. Nobly had she earned her *hegemony* by the exceptional spirit of her history in this century so degenerate elsewhere. To her Winfrid, apostle and martyr of Saxony and the Rhineland, Charles knew that he and his Franks owed their origin as Christians. The "Low Countries" also, and their see of Utrecht, so honourably distinguished even in its decay, were the product of English missionary zeal and intrepidity. What Alexandria was at Nicæa, England was at Frankfort. What Athanasius was under Constantine, that our Alcuin was under Charlemagne. The council was called by this great King of the Franks, without any idea of waiting for a summons from Adrian, the Roman bishop. Nor did Adrian interpose any remonstrance, even when it overruled him and nullified his obsequious and heretical consent to Irene's dogma. This all-important fact proves that the Roman patriarch was not yet a "pope." Nobody dreamed that he alone could summon councils; none held that his approbation decided doctrine, or that communion with him was the test of Catholicity. Charles conducted himself in this business, from first to last, as the imperial bishop,— the *episcopus ab extra*, — doing what Constantine had done before him. But in things spiritual Alcuin led the council, under the Holy Spirit.

10. ALCUIN.

This great light of the eighth century was born at York, and nurtured in theology under Egbert, its learned and pious archbishop. Egbert is the link between Alcuin and Bede the Venerable, who seventy years previously had illuminated our Saxon forefathers with the sunbeams of his godliness and learning. A darker age was soon to follow; but Alcuin now did a work for England and for Christendom which enabled the immortal Alfred, in the succeeding century, to repel in some degree, by his own piety and genius, the ignorance and barbarism to which for a time his clergy were about to succumb. Alcuin had early attracted the admiration of Charles, who, while he yet signed " his mark " and could not write his name, invited him to the Frankish court, made him the preceptor of his household, learned all that he knew of science and theology under his mastership, and made him the conscience-keeper "whom the king delighted to honour." In defeating an attempt to revive Nestorianism he became conspicuously chief at Frankfort where for the second time he refuted the heresy of Felix, Bishop of Urgel. It is hardly to be doubted that Charles summoned the council at Alcuin's suggestion. And here let us note what more we owe to this illustrious light and glory of a degenerate age.

11. UNIVERSITIES, AND THEIR ORIGIN.

He was the parent of universities: he founded a school of learning in the palace at Aix-la-Chapelle, and by his influence similar academies were instituted in France and Italy. When he modestly retired from the court to Tours in France, he there established a school in the abbey of St. Martin; but he kept up his influence with Charles by a constant correspondence.

Let me quote one of his letters,[1] which throws a flood of light upon his work, upon his times, and upon the state of things among our ancestors in the England of that day. He says: —

"The employments of your Alcuin in his retirement are suited to his humble sphere, but they are neither ignoble nor useless. Here I spend my time in teaching the noble youths about me the mysteries of grammar, and inspiring them with a taste for the learning of antiquity. I explain to them the system and revolutions of the starry hosts in the heavenly vault, and to others I open the secrets of divine wisdom contained in the Holy Scriptures. I endeavour to suit my instructions to the capacities of my pupils, hoping to make them ornaments of your court and of the Church of God. In this work I find great lack of many things which I enjoyed in my native country; particularly of those excellent books which could there be had under the care and expense of Egbert, my great master. May it please your Majesty, therefore, to allow me to send some of my pupils into England to get the books we want, that so, animated by your own most ardent love of learning, we may transplant the flowers of Britain into France. Thus their fragrance shall no longer be confined to York, but may perfume the palaces of Tours."

And so chiefly to him we owe the subsequent learning of Europe. He is described as an orator,

[1] See Note R'.

mathematician, philosopher, and the greatest divine of his times. Young gentlemen, reflect that here, in Ann Arbor, where within the memory of living men stood the wigwams of savages, if you are able to pursue all the liberal arts and sciences with the accumulated advantages of modern attainments, it is because Alcuin flourished a thousand years ago, and by his genius, "like a light shining in a dark place," laid up, as in magazines against years of famine that were to follow, the harvests which he gathered like Joseph for the salvation of his brethren.

12. THE CAROLINE BOOKS.

At Frankfort, then, truth was rescued from its perils by this same master spirit. Four books, probably the work of Alcuin,[1] and known as "the Caroline books," were composed, under the direction of Charles, to sustain the second canon of Frankfort, which condemns the Deutero-Nicene Council and all worship of images. Thus Adrian himself was taught to obey the ancient constitutions by the unanimous and free testimony of the Gallican and Anglican bishops. "The Church of God doth altogether abominate the doctrine that images ought to be worshipped," says Roger Hoveden, an old English historian of the twelfth century; and Matthew of Westminster, in the thirteenth, praises Alcuin for writing against the new heresy, "fortified by the authority of the Holy Scriptures."

[1] See Note S'.

By all sorts of refinements and hair-splittings Roman theologians have subsequently defended Adrian and accepted the Council of Irene, pretending that Alcuin and his contemporaries did not understand the decrees they so indignantly rejected, and that they only objected to rendering *divine* worship to images. On the contrary, says a very learned authority, "Nothing can be stronger than the opposition of the Caroline Books to every act or appearance of worship as paid to images, even to bowing the head before them or burning lights." Alas! the Western churches, in their downfall under the Paparchy, have gone far beyond the Greeks in this species of corruption. To this day, the Greeks protest against graven images, and adhere only to the use of pictures, which they are learning to excuse as meant for ornament, and so to be respected and not profaned; while some of their theologians merely reject "Iconoclasm," or the wanton destruction of pictures, approaching very nearly to the limit of our own use of stained glass. For the Greeks there is some excuse: unlearned and groaning for centuries under the Turkish yoke, they have been little able to study their own Fathers or the Holy Scriptures. One wonders that they can be as enlightened and faithful as they are, compared with the Latins, who have done their utmost to make them as corrupt as themselves. But a better day is begun: let us pray for the venerable churches of the East, and repay them, as did the Roman matron, who bared her chaste bosom to her aged father in prison, and gave him fresh tides of life in requital of the life she owed to him.

13. THE DEGENERACY OF THE EAST.

Reflecting on Irene's fatal success, one wonders how the East could so far have forgotten herself as to descend in any councils from the high themes that had once agitated her glorious churches and the immortal doctors of her schools. Think of Athanasius, gravely asked to come down from his eagle-gaze upon the sunlight of God's throne to disputes about the homage due to counterfeits, — the portraits of players and prostitutes, often profanely called the Icons of Christ and his Virgin Mother! Nothing can excuse the degeneracy of which the *Pseudo-Nicene* Synod is a memorial, but perhaps we can explain it. I have already noted that there stands at Rome a landmark, which even in Lord Byron's day was only —

"A nameless column with a buried base."

Excavations have since unearthed that base, and disclosed the hateful name which it commemorates. It is the pillar of Phocas, — a creature with whom Irene may be properly paired as a twin. Two names in Christian history more infamous than these it would be hard to find, till we come to the century of the earliest Popes. Now that pillar of Phocas marks the beginning of two calamities unequalled in their effects upon all succeeding ages of the Church. (1.) The first was the appearance, under the patronage of Phocas, of a Roman bishop who did not tremble to bring upon himself the name of "the forerunner of Antichrist," which his predecessor, Gregory the Great, hardly cold in his grave, had bequeathed to any one who should accept the title of "Universal Bishop." (2.) The second was the rise of Mohammed, who just then was forging his Koran. These were possibly the horrible figures which revealed to St. John in Patmos the period of decay and corruptions of Christianity which were coming to pass.[1] He shuddered to record them, and well may we to read the fulfilment. If it were not for the Apocalypse, I should not be able to support my faith that the Church of God is still His Church; so long has she suffered iniquity to rule supreme where once her apostles and martyrs bore testimony to the Gospel in its power.

14. MOHAMMED.

Mohammed owed his abhorrence of idolatry to heretical Christians, who were his first instructors. The Nestorian monks, who had rejected the truth about "the God-bearing Mary," had seen a reactionary tendency among the orthodox to pay her an almost idolatrous homage. Hence their inflamed orthodoxy on this point, that "Mary is to be honoured, not worshipped." When her *Icons* began to be multiplied and derided by these, it was easy to infer that what heretic Nestorians denounced should be patronized by the orthodox; and when the Saracens began to despoil and overthrow Christian churches, destroying the *Icons* in obedience to Mohammed, it was human nature to fall into the opposite extreme, and to begin to adore what heretics and Mohammedans abhorred. Alas that Mohammed had felt what Christians began to

---

[1] Rev. xvii. 6, 7.

forget, the unspeakable degradation of humanity when it permits the mind of man to offer religious worship, on any pretext, to anything less than God Almighty! It seems to have been under a divine impulse that Islam came forth avenging the Decalogue, under a mission from the insulted Lord who makes "the wrath of man to praise Him."

15. SUCCESSES OF MOHAMMED.

Observe the marvellous sweep of the besom he wielded among the dim candlesticks of many an Eastern and Western Sardis or Laodicea. The year of the Hegira is A. D. 622, and ten years later the impostor perishes. One year afterwards Jerusalem had fallen before the terrible Caliph; Cæsarea and Antioch followed, and all Syria was mastered by Islam. In all history is there a scene more strikingly dramatic than that which narrates how the patriarch Sophronius confronted Omar, after fruitlessly defending the Holy City and being forced to capitulate. The venerable bishop met Omar in the gates, the barbarian entering in his raiment of camel's hide, followed by his locust hordes. "Truly," said the holy man, "I see the abomination that maketh desolate, as spoken of by Daniel the prophet, standing in the holy place." Truly, as never before, "Jerusalem was now trodden down by the Gentiles." Next, Alexandria is taken; her glorious candle is put out; the Alexandrian library perishes. On goes the devouring fire. For the present Constantinople is repeatedly assaulted in vain; but Northern Africa is devoured before it. Carthage and Hippo, already laid waste by Genseric, and all those ancient churches, are consumed. In A. D. 710, the Saracens land at Gibraltar; all Europe is threatened with desolation; Spain is overrun, and in A. D. 725 the hordes of Islam have penetrated into France and captured Autun. But here God raises up Charles Martel, who strikes the Saracens with a decisive blow at Tours, and finally, laud be to God! he drives them out of France. He dies in A. D. 741, but in the next year his grandson, whom we call Charlemagne, is born, destined to settle the Carolingian line of kings in France, and in many particulars to revolutionize Europe and the world. It is important to recall all these facts, if we would comprehend the degradation of the East, the epoch of the Council of Frankfort, and the blessings we owe to the Venerable Bede, to Egbert, and to Alcuin.

16. ISNIK AND DAN.

We see, perhaps, in this review, how it came to pass that Irene's clergy could yield to her corruptions. It was testifying against Mohammed and the Nestorians. But go now to miserable *Isnik*, that oncê was Nicæa, and see to what God has reduced her, just as, of old, he gave his temple to the flames, and to long years of ruin, under the Chaldeans. The tribe of Dan has lost its name in Israel because it introduced the contempt of the second commandment, and polluted truth with idols.[1] So Nicæa is blotted out.

[1] Compare Gen. xlix. 16, Rev. vii. 8, and Judges xviii. 30.

17. FRANKFORT ONCE MORE.

We may now come back to Frankfort. God is faithful to His promise: "When the enemy shall come in like a flood, the Spirit of the Lord shall lift up a standard against him." Surely, if ever there was a flood of iniquity and desolation, it was now poured out in fire and fury upon the churches. Alcuin and Frankfort were the standard of the Lord against Mohammed and against Adrian, as well as against Irene. But Frankfort is not immaculate. It admitted into the Nicene symbol those words, *and the Son,*—which, true as they are, are no part of the creed. Here the Easterns find, justly, a ground of complaint against us. At Nicæa, the fathers would not tolerate the introduction of an *iota* into their testimony. The Greeks complain that we owe to this innovation all the additions to the Creed which have been made by the Popes. Here is our mistake; "Ephraim shall yet say, What have I any more to do with idols?" till then "let not Ephraim envy Judah, nor Judah vex Ephraim." But for the rest, in the spirit of Alcuin, let us adopt the thrilling words of a modern Anglican, worthy to be named with Alcuin himself, the holy Bishop Ken. Hear his faithful testimony in his last will and testament:—

"As for my religion, I die in the Holy Catholic and Apostolical Faith professed by the whole Church before the disunion of East and West; more particularly I die in the communion of the Church of England, as it stands distinguished from all Papal and Puritan innovation, and as it adheres to the doctrine of the cross."

That is my standpoint, young gentlemen. It enables you to comprehend the entire spirit of these Lectures.

18. THE BLESSED RESULTS.

Note then as concerning Frankfort: (1.) It is an index of "the goodness and severity of God," in dealing with a degenerate Christendom. (2.) It is a token of His fidelity in "reserving to himself" many millions of men who "had not bowed the knee to Baal." (3.) It shows us just where the churches stood on the eve of the great disruption; how terribly the Latin churches had been diminished; how marvellously the Church of England had been raised to influence, and was permitted at this crisis to sow the seeds of her subsequent restoration, and to bear a testimony which she was destined to reclaim as her heritage forever. (4.) At the same time, it marks a great epoch in the ecclesiastical history of France; it proves that as yet Rome, however exaggerated her pretensions, was not the seat of a Paparchy; it renews the spirit of Irenæus and Hilary; it creates what was afterwards called Gallicanism. (5.) It enables us to comprehend the more modern Councils of Constance and of Basle, so far as they asserted what was true to antiquity. (6.) But especially should we note the hand of God, who thus closed up the period of Œcumenical Councils just when they were no longer likely to prove true to their charter in the Scriptures; when they had stooped down from the Gospels and the adorable Trinity to fables and to *Icons.* It was Divine fidelity to the promise that interposed and saved all subsequent corruptions of truth from any claim to catholic consent. And (7.) I cannot but add that we see the same hand in giving us of the West something to confess with shame, when we remonstrate with the Easterns. " *Tu quoque!*" they may reply; "there is a beam in your own eye."

19. CHARLEMAGNE.

When Charles Martel struck the Saracens, it was God who stayed the ravages of the enemy, and for a time said, " Thus far, but no further." How great he waxed, ruling the Franks under nominal kings of the long-haired race, — how his son Pepin the Short deposed them and reigned in their stead, and how Charles succeeded as king and founded the Carolingian line,— are not all these things written in school-books? But look at him with whose name the epithet "Great" has been so incorporated that it is all one word. At Aix-la-Chapelle I have seen a group of peasants singing their German hymns before daybreak, under the dome that once covered his remains. They stepped aside, and I read upon the slab which had been trodden by their rough shoes, CAROLUS MAGNUS. It was there that his remote successor, Barbarossa, opening the sepulchre three centuries after his burial, saw his gigantic skeleton sitting on a throne, crowned and decked in imperial robes, his falchion in his grasp, and the Gospels opened upon his knees. They still show one of the bones of his terrible arm: our measure called a *foot* is said to come from his giant foot, twelve inches long. Like Constantine, this Titan was one of those mysterious beings who perform all the Lord's good pleasure, while only seeking their own. Marvellous is this economizing of man's free will by the omnipotence of the All-wise and All-good. In such characters we are pretty sure to find evil and good mingled in vast proportions. This mysterious creature, who fascinates and astonishes and overawes, is yet, in some aspects, a ferocious barbarian, a moral monster.[1] Nevertheless, on the whole, he was a benefactor of the world. He seemed to forecast the destinies of Europe; he tamed barbarous tribes; he encouraged learning; he shaped the destinies of mankind for ages after him. As for his religion, like Jehu, he had a zeal for God, and he "drave furiously." The Church has felt his influence, for woe or weal, ever since he lived. It would be of no use to prejudge him; as to motives, no doubt they were mixed. If he was very cruel, not less so was Theodosius. Like Cyrus, like Alexander, he was an "arrow of the Lord's deliverance"; he was the saw and the hammer in the hand of the Almighty.

20. CHRISTMAS DAY, A.D. 800.

We have seen him helping the saintly Alcuin to humanize and Christianize the Franks, to tame the ambitious Adrian, to rebuke Irene and her degenerate bishops; and now we must follow him

[1] See Note T'.

to another chapter of his amazing history. We cross the Alps; we watch him as he enters Rome; we seem to see him kneeling before the altar, in the old basilica of St. Peter, on Christmas day, A. D. 800. On a sudden, what happens? Leo III., the patriarch, the pontiff, the nondescript whom Pepin had made a temporal satrap by giving his predecessors the exarchate of Ravenna, — lo! he comes forward and places an imperial crown upon the head of the Frank sovereign, and salutes him as Emperor. "Long live the Cæsar!" "Long live Augustus!" "Long live the Emperor of the Romans!" Such were the shouts that rent the air; such was the stupendous drama of that eventful day. O what a contrast with that first Christmas, that brought peace on earth and good will to men!

21. WHAT IT MEANT.

Well! what had been done? "He had revived the Empire of the West," is the common reply. Nothing of the kind was in his thought. He had mentally deposed Irene, and succeeded to her place, remanding the woman to her distaff. He had hopes of reversing the work of Constantine, and reducing Constantinople down again to Byzantium. It was no more to be "New Rome," nor any kind of Rome; Old Rome was restored to herself, and Charles was the successor of all the Cæsars in their ancient Capitol. Such seems to have been his vast, far-reaching, and almost superhuman thought. It looks hard to doubt his assertion that Leo surprised him. But all appears preconcerted, and I imagine the "surprise" was as to Leo's manner, not as to the act. The shouts of the multitude, echoing through the cathedral, were no doubt unexpected.

22. WIDELY DIFFERENT EFFECTS.

Recall the fact that Southern Italy was at this time theoretically under Irene, and Leo III. was her subject. It was the first instance of the sceptre of the Empire passing into the hands of a woman, and much talk there had been of her own scheme of marrying the King of the Franks, so cementing by new bonds the East and West. Happily, this did not take place, for such statecraft would doubtless have defeated its purpose and made everything worse. The *coup d'état* by which this all-powerful Frank wrenched the West from Irene proved a success then only in part. It failed in so far as the Cæsars of the East were able to continue the Byzantine line for more than seven centuries in New Rome. But things were altogether ripe for a fresh start in the West with Old Rome for the capital, and, if by a mere fiction Charles and his successors considered themselves Cæsars of the West, he was in fact the founder of a new imperial throne, without parallel or paragon. The act of Leo in giving him his crown, though it was possibly a mere *coup de théatre*, of which he was himself the author, committed the patriarchate to the new *œcumene*, and Leo became "œcumenical bishop" in a new sense, because in this new empire he was sole and single. There was no other patriarch, no other "Apostolic See," for the Westerns. The Bishop of Rome became at once identified with the new Cæsar. Thenceforth, the twain were one body and one spirit, though not always of one mind, but quite the reverse. The "Holy Roman Empire," as it was called, by virtue of this religious union, was an ellipse, the one *focus* being at Rome and the other at Aachen or at Frankfort. Thus the Alps were a wall between rival powers, each asserting supremacy in the same empire. The inevitable consequence was the conflict of the two sceptres, and the history of the Middle Ages in the West is the history of fierce collisions between Emperor and Pope; sometimes farcical poetry, "all see-saw between this and that"; but generally one long perpetual tragedy, — a monstrous degradation alike of religion and government, which trampled humanity under foot, and made Europe to resound with its groans and outcries.

23. THE HOLY ROMAN EMPIRE.

And so the patriarchate of Rome became more and more a worldly power, and surrounded itself with a worldly court, and moved on to fulfil its mysterious destiny. The states of Europe were virtually provinces of the Empire, and made up one vast system, under a mixed suzerainty, Imperial and Papal, ever swinging backward or forward between the two *foci*. They maintained a fruitless struggle for independence one of the other, and all for independence of the twin potentates, whose coalition perpetuated their despotism. The student of Dante comprehends what "the Empire" meant in the Middle Ages. For just one thousand years, apart from England, such was Europe; and, as I have said, the *Arc de l'Étoile* in Paris stands where it does, a monument of the recent ignominious fall of this "Holy Roman Empire." Since the defeat of Austria by Napoleon, nothing remains of it save its elements. The new Empire of Germany and the Kingdom of Italy are but expressions of a new order of things; and though popes and princes may still coquet one with another to enslave the minds and bodies of men, the time is past, thank God, when Guelphs and Ghibellines can compose their strifes with the certainty by so doing of overawing and beating down all antagonism.[1]

24. INSULATION OF ENGLAND.

"Except England," I said, in a parenthesis, but emphatically. For England, blessed with insularity, never permitted herself to be absorbed into this system of the Empire. France too asserted her rightful independence, and her crown was always surmounted by an arch, or bow, to signify its imperial character. But over and over again was she made to feel her serfdom and feudal subjection. Not so with the imperial crown of England; poor King John might surrender it for the moment, but it was only to provoke the revolt of an indignant

[1] See Note U'.

people and the thunders of their ability to defend themselves. They were heard in *Magna Charta*, and in the noble watchword of their sons, "*Nolumus leges Angliæ mutari.*"

25. DISTINCTIONS.

The court papacy of Phocas became a paparchy; but, note, there was no such thing as "the Roman Catholic Church." That is the product of Luther's revolution, and of Loyola's reactionary society, which avenged itself on Northern Europe as Rehoboam did upon the old men who advised reform in Israel,— turning whips of thongs into a scourge of scorpions. This is all-important to be understood: there never was a "Roman Catholic Church" till it was created by the Council of Trent. The Papacy and the Paparchy are old, but not the modern Church so called. Of this by and by. What, then, was the condition of Western Christendom while this "Holy Roman Empire" was its master under the two powers that made it? Simply this: the ancient Latin churches were still national churches, with the old Nicene traditions underneath them, smothered but not killed. As the different nations had their own kings and laws, though the Emperor was *suzerain*, so the Gallican Church, the Spanish Church, the Church of the Milanese, and others, asserted their old *autonomies* as well as they could, while they were all dominated by the successful ambition of a usurper at Rome. Favoured by her insularity, her independence of the Empire, and by her old

Cypriote traditions, the Church of England was slow to succumb to this usurpation, and we shall learn hereafter how her liberties were subverted gradually and for a time. But here I may recapitulate in conclusion, the steps by which we have thus far seen the Roman Bishop transformed into something like what is now understood by a Pope.

26. FORMATION OF THE PAPARCHY.

We have seen how faithfully the Great Councils maintained the doctrine of Christ when He rebuked the sin of his disciples, inquiring "who should be greatest." We have seen, also, how peevishly the Bishops of Rome showed their jealousy of the "New Rome," how they felt the indignity of being put on a level with the newest of the great sees, and how instinctively they began to assert their apostolic dignity, which so immensely outweighed all pretensions that Byzantium could set up merely as the first of Christian cities and the capital of the regenerated Empire. As generations passed by, the symptoms of a growing insubordination were increased. From time to time some bolder spirit came to the patriarchal throne of Southern Italy. Measures most daring were resorted to occasionally, and not a few inexcusable ones, for which we cannot account.[1] Among such, those of Leo the Great are memorable as grossly inconsistent with his otherwise dignified character. The Council of Chalcedon sufficiently exposed and abased the

[1] See Note V'.

subterfuges and pretensions of his envoys, and he himself succumbed; but in him the earliest Petrine hyperboles became audible, and the spirit of a nascent Papacy is discerned. We reach the age of Gregory the Great, however, without any practical or definite enlargement of such claims, and providentially we are enabled, by his own earnest and reiterated statements of fact and of doctrine, to prove that he himself knew nothing of what is now meant by a "Pope," even in the lowest Gallican ideas of such a dignitary. For when the Bishop of New Rome, — probably with no other than an assumption of importance based on the obsolete imperialism of Old Rome, called himself the "Œcumenical," that is, the Imperial Bishop, — we find Gregory remonstrating, on the grounds that such an assumption violated the equality of all bishops, was a profane and impious arrogance, and as such a "forerunner of Antichrist." Never does it occur to him to say, "I am the only Œcumenical Bishop; I am, by divine right, the superior of all bishops; such a claim affronts St. Peter in me, and the Lord himself, who established a world-wide sovereignty in that apostle." Not a word like this, but, on the contrary, he rejects the very thought as worthy of Lucifer; he abjures it for himself and his see.[1] At the beginning of the seventh century, therefore, there was no Papacy; nor was there any foreshadowing of a papal predominance, unless it were in Constantinople, in the instance which Gregory stigmatized. Yet, before he had been two years in his grave, Phocas, one of

[1] See Note W'.

the most flagitious wretches that ever reigned, gave the profane title to Boniface III., A. D. 606. It was a worldly court title, as we have seen, and the Church had no responsibility for it whatever. Keep this in view. It was a court distinction merely, but the bishop assumed it. So we must assign to Boniface the disgrace of doing what Gregory had anathematized, and in him a Papacy began to be visible.

27. CONDITIONS PRECEDENT.

A "Papacy," but not a Paparchy. It had no definite character; it invested the pretender with no real power; he was still obliged to respect the councils, and their canons; he pretended to be their defender and executive-in-chief. Nor, while the patriarchs of the East were watching him and forcing him to obey what councils had decreed, could he magnify himself in any dangerous degree. So long as the *œcumene* included the more cultured and learned East, it was impossible for the Bishop of Rome to overshadow the older patriarchates, and to make himself autocratic. When a new *œcumene* had risen, whose master asserted all that Constantine had ever claimed, and who had reversed Constantine's work and policy, Old Rome became, for the first time, independent of the East. While Charlemagne lived, it is true, he was his own pontiff in so large a degree that the new conditions did not permit such advantages to appear in favour of the one "Apostolic See," which had now become all-important to the whole West. But when the founder of "the Holy Roman Empire" came to his end, even a temporal umpire of the West was found only at Rome, and as the East was very soon forgotten, all the spiritual power of its great patriarchs was absorbed by him. It wanted only some man of genius, alike ambitious and unscrupulous, pushing his way to the throne of Leo and Gregory, to find all things prepared for an entire revolution in Western Christendom. He had but to put his foot on the canons, to ignore the East, and to assert himself the Bishop of Bishops, to find support in the necessities of the new Empire, in those of subordinate kings, and in those of the churches now cut off in all practical affairs from their Eastern brethren. Such a man was Nicholas (A. D. 858), and he made himself the first practical Pope.

28. MY POSITION.

The facts I maintain as to the formation of the Papacy are conceded by recent and by older historians of repute. But they fail to state the irresistible conclusion: there was no "pope," strictly speaking, before Nicholas. (1.) Leo the Great was not a pope when he was rebuked and overruled at Chalcedon. (2.) Agatho was not a pope when the last Œcumenical Council anathematized Honorius; when he, like his successors, accepted it. (3.) Gregory was not a pope when he called the asserter of an œcumenical bishopric a robber of the rights of all bishops, and a forerunner of Antichrist. (4.) Adrian was not a pope when Charlemagne called the Council of Frankfort, overruled his decisions, and, sustained by the entire West, convicted him of heresy in accepting a false dogma from a woman and her pseudo council. (5.) Nor, to come to the times of him who crowned Charlemagne, and made a new era for East and West on that memorable Christmas day, — nor was Leo III. a pope when he pleaded before Charles as his subject and his judge; when he offered him personal "adoration"; when he lived and died his subject, and saw him, without remonstrance, exercising pontifical powers, compared with which the *Regale*, as afterwards understood by Henry VIII. or Louis XIV., shrinks to insignificance.[1] (6.) Finally, there could be no pope while this mighty patriarchate was still nominally subject to the canons, and in full communion with the East, which knew him only as an equal.

29. NICHOLAS AND THE DECRETALS.

"Since the days of Gregory I. to our time," says one of his contemporaries, smitten with admiration for the truly imperial genius of Nicholas, "sat no high-priest on the throne of St. Peter to be compared to him. He tamed kings and tyrants, and ruled the world like a sovereign." We have seen that Gregory, noble and pre-eminent as he was, was not a "pope"; and here we have the fact, dropping from the pen of one who knew all about intermediate Bishops of Rome, including Hadrian and Leo, that Nicholas was *something which they*

[1] See Note X'.

were not. All writers allow that he left the Roman see something *essentially different* from what he found it. All acknowledge that he effected a revolution in the churches of the West, and carried his conduct to such a pitch towards the East that they cried out against him for arrogating to himself and his see what was *never heard of before.* For the first time the Roman Bishop made himself the *sine qua non* of all thought and action in Christendom ; the centre and criterion not only of unity, but of communion with Christ himself. As such he excommunicated the Easterns; they returned the compliment, and excommunicated him. These relations were not absolutely final, but they were never repaired by any permanent restorations. There was now a new power in the Church of Christ. The Easterns never accepted it for an hour. But it was fastened on Western Christendom, not as a theory, but as a fact. It was no more a dignity, but a despotism; not a titular papacy, but the Paparchy. There was a Pope in the West, and his power was thenceforth a reality, developing into a supremacy like God's.

The "Pope" now existed in one who swept away antiquity, and all councils and canons which he did not fancy. The instrument by which this prodigious revolution was effected was "the forged Decretals." All men now acknowledge that they are forgeries, but, by whomsoever made, Nicholas brought them forth, appealed to them as authentic, and proved by them that all the Bishops of Rome, from St. Peter down to him, had ruled the Church absolutely by their decrees. The age was unlearned: the Decretals were not subjected to the tests by which learning even in its elements might have refuted them. They vanished like smoke when the art of printing showed what they really were.

But all through the Middle Ages they overawed the West, kings, bishops, monks, saints and sinners alike, and this fact is the apology for St. Bernard and others, who at heart were reformers, but could not refute such testimony. For they passed into history as genuine; they became parts of the canon law; they practically abrogated all the œcumenical canons, they created the pseudo œcumenical canons and the pseudo councils that enacted them; they enabled successive pontiffs to raise their pretensions higher and higher, "deceivers" no doubt, but yet "being deceived"; they made an honest fanatic of Hildebrand, who never doubted his right to speak for God and as God, and who in the eleventh century made the name of "Pope" peculiar to himself, forbidding its application to the patriarchs of the East; and after him they made Innocent III., who turned the fanaticism of the Crusades against Christian men. In a word, they are responsible for all that has made havoc of the churches, East and West, and that perpetuates their schisms at this hour. Every one of these positions rests on irrefragable evidence; on facts not denied, but, alas! not kept before men's minds.[1]

[1] See Note Y'.

30. AN ILLUSTRATION.

And if you ask how it comes that, after such frauds are once exposed to the scorn of the universe, the Papacy still survives and even enlarges its pretensions in our own enlightened day, the answer is sufficiently plain. Did you ever see stone-masons turn an arch? They make a framework out of refuse wood, of laths and scantlings, anything that comes to hand; a few nails suffice to hold them together; they set it in place on abutments well prepared, and then they begin to work in stone. They soon erect the arch and set the key-stone and build upon it, — a bridge, or a castle, or a tower that reaches to heaven. Then no longer any need of the framework; a beggar may kick it out and turn it into fuel to boil his soup; but — the arch remains for ages. So the Decretals have disappeared, but that arch of pride, the Papacy, stands the firmer because of all that has been built upon it. The laws and usages of Europe, the manners of nations, the superstitions of the ignorant, the piety of the devout, the diplomacy of monarchs, the thrones of empires, and empire itself, all must fall together, if the arch be suddenly destroyed. And then the arch itself is old and interesting; it is ivy-clad and green, with associations of poesy and romance. A thousand motives conspire to make men sustain it; and stand it will and must, till nations discover that truth and right are the only supports for what humanity requires, — for what law and equity and order must find indispensable. So long as those old abutments of imperial despotism and popular ignorance remain, the old arch will hold. But thank God, His Providence is contriving reforms, and providing resources, against changes that must come. They are working gradually, but surely, to their glorious result; let us be faithful to duty and love truth in our generation, and leave the rest to Him who has promised, and who is Faithful and True.[1]

[1] Rev. xix. 11.

LECTURE V.

THE MIDDLE AGES.

1. DARK AGES.

THE Middle Ages, as I reminded you, extend from that memorable Christmas, A. D. 800, to the year 1500, when Charles-Quint was born. This period was not all dark, by any means; but what we may fairly call the Dark Ages are here included, and may justly be considered as extending from A. D. 900 to A. D. 1400; from the pontificate of Benedict IV. to that of Benedict XIII., Antipope at Avignon. You observe these convenient "dates of anchorage," and the economy of using the names of two Benedicts as terminal figures. And these names stand for facts that may well stigmatize the included period as dark. For the first Benedict marks an epoch when the crime of Nicholas, with his decretals, was bearing its natural fruit, and the see of Rome was given over to the sway of impiety the most frightful, while the other Benedict denotes the schism consequent upon the removal of the Popes to Avignon, and all the scandals involved in one series of popes at Rome and another in France, mutually excommunicating and anathematizing one another, and, what is worse, damning the unhappy people who respectively adhered to this pope or that, because in their utter bewilderment and consternation they were unable to know which of the two rivals was God's vicegerent, without communion with whom no flesh could be saved. During this period, remember, a large portion of Spain was in the possession of the Arabs, and science fled to their Universities for a season. If these ages are not justly denominated the "Dark Ages," I know not what to call them.

2. MAITLAND'S ELUCIDATION.

We owe to the learned Dr. Maitland a very discriminating work on these ages, which he would confine to the period between A. D. 800 and A. D. 1200, and which, he shows, were not altogether so dark as some have allowed themselves to assert.[1] Hence a reaction. Many, disgusted with Robertson and Mosheim, rush to the other extreme, and pronounce those very ages the most commendable in history. Let us accept Dr. Maitland's just and discriminating view, and with gratitude to God confess that He has shown His mercy and multiplied His saints in the darkest periods of human history. But this fact would not be worth stating unless such periods have been. A rapid glance at the ages I have noted may enable you to judge for yourselves whether or not they were ages of illumination.

3. A GLANCE AT THE EAST.

The predominance of the Institutions of Charlemagne is the characteristic of the Middle Ages:

[1] See Note Z'.

the Dark Ages are those in which the Institutions of Nicholas grew and overgrew the whole state of society in Western Europe, culminating in evils intolerable to the Paparchy itself. But, as we must now pursue our inquiries in the outline of Western history chiefly, it may be well to glance for a moment at the corresponding history of the East.

My plan does not permit me to pursue this almost unexplored field, commonly called Byzantine History. It may be dated from A. D. 800, when the Eastern Cæsars lost their hold on the West, to A. D. 1453, when Constantinople was extinguished as a Christian capital. " From the foundation of the New Rome," says a recent writer,[1] " down to A. D. 1057, the machine of government had worked steadily, with few violent changes. There had been a general accumulation of wealth, with security for life and property, under a system of jurisprudence the most complete ever formulated; a system copied by the whole of modern Europe, and indeed by the civilized world. *The same city had developed and formulated the religion of Christendom.* . . . Under the influence of Orthodox Christianity, Roman law, and the Greek spirit of individualism, a steady progress had been made. No other government has ever existed in Europe which has secured for so long a period the like advantages to its people." This is historic truth. Writers who delight to chronicle only the crimes and disgraces of a period have dwelt so exclusively on their favourite themes as to leave a

[1] See Note A″.

widely different impression upon many intelligent minds.

This period must be divided as follows: — 1. From Irene to the end of the Basilian dynasty, A. D. 1057. 2. Then a period of gradual decline, till Constantinople was taken by the Latins, in A. D. 1203. 3. Then the melancholy period of Turkish advance upon the Eastern Empire, until the West abandoned it to its fate, in 1453. To this epoch we shall have occasion to return.

4. THE DECRETALS IN OPERATION.

Just when the Basilian dynasty established itself in the East, the erection of the Paparchy threw the Eastern churches out of open communion with the patriarchate of Rome. In the Orient no harm followed. The Basilian era was prosperous in proportion as it had nothing to do with the Popes.

But, to confine ourselves now to the Latins, we must note the significant fact that the triumph of the Decretals over the ancient Catholic Constitutions was followed by a period of unparalleled infamy in the Roman patriarchate and of consequent corruption wherever its influence was felt. Here then is a dilemma: either the work of Nicholas was a genuine and just advance of the see of Rome to the position which God designed for the development of His Church, or it was a wicked apostasy from apostolic order and organization. If it was the former, — if Nicholas had placed himself and his successors where Christ meant that they should stand, — the most blessed results should follow.

But precisely the reverse is the case. The evils that were immediately bred of the new order of things, — of the system, that is, which was based on the forged decretals, — these evils were so enormous and so lasting, that even the most besotted defenders of Ultramontane Romanism give up all apologies.[1]

Take the epoch of the Dark Ages which I have denoted. Says an eminent Italian chronicler, "The throne of humility and chastity (i. e. the throne of St. Peter) became the object of all ambition, the recompense of all crimes, the refuge of all abominations." Even Cardinal Baronius (A. D. 1588) is forced to speak of the tenth century in such words as these: "The Holy Roman Church was as foul as could be. Harlots, superlative alike in profligacy and in power, *governed at Rome*, appointed bishops, and intruded their paramours into the see of St. Peter." To escape the awful conclusions he can only invent a theory, in which De Maistre has followed him, that the Popes made by Theodora and Marozia must be discarded from the catalogue. If so, by parity of argument, thirteen Popes are to be stricken out of the succession, and so for sixty years there must have been no one legitimately in St. Peter's chair — so called. The period of these two generations Baronius thus characterizes: "Who can venture to affirm that persons thus basely intruded by prostitutes were lawful Roman pontiffs?" He says: "The canons were buried in oblivion; . . . the ancient traditions under the ban; old customs, sacred rites,

[1] See Note B".

and usages of election, quite abolished. Mad lust, relying on worldly power, and incited by the spur of ambition, claimed everything for its own. Christ was then in a deep sleep in the ship; . . . and what seemed worse, there were no disciples to wake him, . . . for all were snoring. You may imagine what sort of presbyters and deacons were chosen as cardinals by these monsters." Let me mention here, that Roman cardinals were the product of this same period when " the ancient traditions were under the ban," and when "the canons were buried in oblivion." They are the creatures of a worldly court, and often are not even nominally in Holy Orders; yet they pose as " princes," and presume to direct the conduct of the most venerable bishops.

A recent writer, Dr. Littledale, has quoted Genebrard, Bishop of Aix (A. D. 1597), as most justly extending this era of infamy much further than Baronius does. According to him, it reached over a hundred and fifty years, during which, he says, " about fifty Popes . . . have been apostatical rather than apostolical." If we reckon one hundred and sixty Popes after Nicholas, then nearly *one third* of the whole succession have been such apostates. By their own reckoning from St. Peter, nearly *one fifth* of those who have been the infallible oracles of the Most High, and communion with whom is requisite to salvation, are thus painted and described by writers of the Papal communion. No one can wonder that the effigy of Pope Joan sits portress at the gate of this Nicolaitan period.[1]

[1] See Note C".

Account for the strange history as you will, it betokens the abominations of the period of which she is a landmark: it coincides with the apocalyptic prophecy, "I saw a woman sit upon a scarlet-coloured beast."

5. HOW IT LOOKED IN ENGLISH EYES.

All this was imported into England, where Dunstan, alas! was introducing many things unknown to Bede and Alcuin. Even King Edgar, who, though not a severe moralist, was a saint if compared with the pontiffs of his time, has recorded his testimony against them.[1] "We see in Rome," he says, "only debauchery, licentiousness, and drunkenness; the houses of priests are the shameful abodes of harlots, and of worse than these. In the dwelling of the Pope, they gamble by day and by night. Instead of fastings and prayers, they give place to bacchanalian songs, lascivious dances, and the debauchery of Messalina." God knows how I hate even to name these things afresh; but when, in our own times, a pontiff has decreed, and made it dogma, that Popes like these were all *infallible* in setting forth the oracles of Divine truth, I ask, with sorrow of heart, "Is there not a cause?"

6. THE LATIN CHURCHES.

But amid all these horrors, the Latin churches, in spite of the despotism that dominated them, were yet, as such, a portion of the one Holy Catholic Church, and God's Spirit lived in thousands of

[1] See Note D".

saints, who, as best they could, still walked with God and kept His way. Remember, there was no "Roman Catholic Church" at this period, substituting itself for the Church of the Creed and of the old Councils. Hence, these Latin churches were Catholic churches, and the Paparchy including "the Court of Rome," a mere worldly machine, was an artificial system, superimposed by the Decretals, defiling them as by a leprosy, but not destroying organic life, nor yet healthful functions of grace, which were fruitful of good works. Let me for a moment illustrate this by a reference to "Gallicanism."

7. GALLICANISM.

As I have hinted, the spirit of Irenæus ruled at Frankfort, and manifested itself as the spirit of the Anglican Church, in Alcuin. The Decretal system was introduced too soon afterwards, not to awaken the strong impression that it must be spurious. Clearly, Frankfort would have been impossible had Charlemagne known such a code, or had Adrian, who only ventured to hint at its existence, presumed to maintain it. To the honour of Hincmar, Archbishop of Rheims,[1] he resisted Nicholas and his Decretals as soon as they were imposed upon the bishops of Gaul. His conduct and protestations perpetuated the influence of Frankfort, and created the "Gallicanism" which has preserved the semblance of nationality to the Church of France down to our own times. Under Louis IX. (St.

[1] See Note E".

Louis) its essence became formulated and known as the "Pragmatic Sanction" of A. D. 1268. By this instrument, St. Louis asserted (1) his own position as (*Evêque au dehors*) the temporal head of the Gallican Church ; (2) defended the rights of the metropolitans and other bishops; (3) secured the national Church against many pretended powers and privileges of the Popes; (4) re-vindicated the canon law and ancient usages as to elections to bishoprics and the like; (5) reserved the imperial rights of his crown; and (6) forbade the papal emissaries to tax the Gallican Church without its own consent or the royal permission. Such was elemental "Gallicanism," which, in bolder forms, was not less the spirit of the Anglican Church, under the Decretalist usurpation. Ultramontane writers recognize the Church of England as only acting logically under Elizabeth, while the French Church shrank back from the inexorable conclusions.[1] So late as 1688 the Gallicans endeavoured to save themselves from the inconsistencies in which they had become entangled by submitting to absorption in "the Roman Catholic Church," created at the Council of Trent on purpose to supersede national churches. Poor Bossuet! terribly did he feel his chains, when he struggled to save what he could of "Gallican liberties." Feeble, but most significant and instructive to us, was his exclamation, "Let us preserve the massive maxims of our forefathers, — the precious words of St. Louis, — which the Gallican Church has derived from the traditions of

[1] See Note F''.

the Church Universal." Poor Bossuet, indeed! He felt the grip of pontifical imposture when he thus pleaded for limitations: "The ocean itself has bounds to its plenitude; let it overpass them, it becomes a deluge which would make havoc of the universe." Again I sigh, Poor Bossuet! In vain, having let Trent in, does he try to keep this deluge out. What would he have said had he lived, like Dupanloup, to see Pius IX. call himself "infallible," and spurn the venerable bishops of France from the foot of his throne in a nominal council which reduced them all to "sacristans."[1]

8. ST. BERNARD.

Marking the futile heroism of Hincmar, let us come now to the age of St. Bernard. It was the period of the Crusades, and he, alas! was carried away by them. His agency in stimulating the second Crusade is a blot on his memory. He could not be wiser than his times; he lived (A. D. 1090–1153) at a period when the system of the Decretals had culminated under Gregory VII. (Hildebrand), but while as yet it had not exhibited all the fury and flame of its arrogance under Innocent III.[2] Just at the epoch of the first Christian chiliad, when the impression prevailed that Christ was about to make his second advent, and bring the crimes of popes and princes to an end, stands the noble figure of Gerbert, who strove to reform, and so strengthened, the Papacy. The name he assumed, as Sylvester II., goes back to

[1] See Note G". [2] A. D. 1198–1216.

the Nicene epoch, and indicates his desire to restore the piety of the first Bishop of Rome, who bore it. Remember, that with all the Latins down to the epoch of Trent we Anglicans are in full communion; and just so far as theirs was the spirit of Vincent, they were witnesses with us against the iniquity of the Paparchy. Even St. Bernard was, in spirit, one of us; he was a reformer, so far as he knew how to be. It was not his fault that he imagined the decretals to be genuine monuments of the primitive ages. If the Pope favoured a crusade, he inferred "God wills it." Yet, like Hincmar, he did his best to resist the evils that were bred of Decretalism. He loved Eugenius III. as his pupil, yet he remonstrates with him like a prophet, and denounces the profligacy of his court. " Who will give me, before I die," he exclaims, " to see the Church as it was in the ancient days."[1] He was nurtured in the extravagant Mariolatry of his age, but he shrank from any increase of it. In his terrible assault upon innovators who had just begun to talk about " the immaculate conception " of St. Mary, he shows where he must have stood in a more enlightened day.[2] He denounces the nascent fable as an idea " of which the Church's rite knows nothing, which right reason sustains not, which primitive tradition does not favour." He calls it " a novelty rashly admitted against the religious use of the Church; born of levity, the sister of superstition, the mother of temerity, . . . the invention of a few inexperienced simpletons." After nearly eight hundred

[1] See Note H″.   [2] See Note I″.

years, we have seen a Roman pontiff making this
fable into a dogma, and its acceptance a condition
of eternal salvation.

9. THE PATRISTIC PERIOD.

But now a most important point, of which St.
Bernard is the index. He is known to Latin theologians as the " last of the Fathers." He deserves
this name, not because a doctor of the twelfth age
can possibly be reckoned a " Father," but because
he closes the long line of Western worthies who
maintained the patristic principle theoretically, and,
as far as their times would permit, practically also.
I should note Alcuin as the last of the Fathers,
for that would be a parallel to the Greek idea:
they make Alcuin's contemporary, John Damascene, the last. Anselm is rather a forerunner of
the Schoolmen. St. Bernard was the last of those
Latin theologians who professed to be guided by
"the Scriptures and ancient authors,"—by the rule
of Vincent, in short. "What I have received from
the Church, that in all confidence I hold, and that
I teach; what is otherwise, I confess, I am very
scrupulous about admitting." He puts his finger
on the very essence of the new theology, of which
Abelard was forerunner, when in memorable words
he accuses him of doing in the domain of Holy
Scripture what men had been taught by dialectics:
thus becoming a "censor of the faith, not a disciple,
— an emendator, not an imitator." We reach the
epoch when, by the introduction of syllogistic manipulations, truths professed in the Creeds because

contained in Holy Scripture were made the base of indefinite exaggerations. The Fathers were hostile to codes of belief; the Nicene creed bears witness to their tender regard for what is written, while framing liturgic formulas in childlike response to apostles and evangelists. Beyond these simple formulas they would not presume: they felt afraid of applying logic to mysterious realities, and venturing into conclusions which subjected the mysteries of God to the infirmities of human reason not only, but of human speech as well. Hence the Council of Constantinople forbade the framing of any new creed, or the dictation of any other to converts from heresy or schism. What Bernard foresaw was a disposition to break through all this.[1]

10. THE SCHOLASTICS.

Not content with "the faith once delivered to the saints," men were about to erect upon it a fabric of trestle-work, employing Aristotle's syllogisms to build their tower of Babel and scale the heavens. Expounders of Scripture and stewards of the grand deposit of truth were no longer to be accounted theologians. The new plan was this: Human wit must exert itself to find a major and a minor premise in admitted truths. Draw the conclusion, and discover a novel truth. Try it again, and you find another novelty. Make premises of these, and draw a new inference. You have progressive theology, and the process can be extended *ad infinitum*. Such is Scholasticism.

[1] See Note J".

Peter Lombard was Bernard's *protégé*, but he seems to have been fascinated by Abelard, whose pupil he had been. The genius of Augustine had pointed in this direction, and Anselm had followed his indications. Abelard himself was only sparingly acquainted with Aristotle, whose works were imperfectly known in Europe till the Saracens, who had obtained them from the Nestorians, handed them back to the Latins, many of them in very bad retranslations. Lombard became Archbishop of Paris, and is known as the "Master of the Sentences." The "Schoolmen" properly so called became commentators upon these Sentences, and, by logical methods, enlarged their import and their domain. In the middle of the thirteenth century St. Thomas Aquinas became the great Scholastic, but before the end of that age Duns Scotus, the "Subtle Doctor," had founded an antagonist system; and now these rival authorities divided the schools between them. The interminable disputes of the Thomists and Scotists, Nominalists and Realists, became embittered beyond all conception, owing largely to the partisan feelings of the Dominicans and Franciscans, these rival orders each following its own doctor, perhaps very naturally.

11. RELATIONS WITH MODERN THOUGHT.

You will not ask me to go into an elucidation of these disputes; and I am very glad of it, because I confess my inability to appreciate refinements and distinctions —

"which divide
A hair 'twixt south and southwest side,"

and the more I have looked into them the less I feel that I know about them. Pius IX. has forbidden men to look into modern discoveries. Men may think, but not for themselves. Leo XIII., with solemn irony, professing himself a friend of scientific thought, commends the study of St. Thomas Aquinas to inquiring minds of the Roman Obedience. He thus accomplishes two important objects: (1) he shows just where Science ought to stop, in his judgment; and (2) he reminds his people that the natural philosophy of Aristotle has been identified with Trent dogmas, as well as with its moral and intellectual sequels, the new decrees; so that there is an end of all controversy. So far he permits his schools to go in America, but no farther. The fact comes in here as a landmark.

12. THE CRUSADES.

And the Crusades, which lie on the highest table-land of Papal development, between the epochs of Gregory VIII. and Innocent III., must be noted here for a like purpose. Like the Scholasticism to which the Crusades lent new arms from the schools of the Saracens, these are landmarks not merely, but mighty elements as well, in overturning and new-creating, — in evolving out of chaos a new world of thought and action for humanity. What sublime folly! what superlative crime! what tokens of God's way among nations,—

" From seeming evil still educing good " !

Here a word about the ennobling theory and the painful practical history of chivalry. It appears best in allegory like Spenser's, or in epic song like Tasso's. Alas! in history, the Crusaders, whose lives were vowed to the service of Christian womanhood, the defence of maiden modesty and of conjugal chastity, gave themselves over to unbridled excesses of debauchery, under banners on which was portrayed the symbol of the Lamb; and the hosts, who knelt on the holy ground and kissed it when they came in sight of Jerusalem, made its streets run with blood when they took it from the Infidels. The moderation of the Paynim when Omar captured it, presents a contrast which must ever crimson Christian cheeks with shame. Yet if the age of chivalry is extinct, the glorious ideas which it degraded must live forever in the new sentiment of Christian nations. Born of the Gospel, the Gospel is their sure support; and woman, if no longer the inspirer of quixotic lists and tournaments, finds true knighthood in the hearts and the homage of the father, the brother, and the husband, in every Christian home.

When we come to the convulsions of which Wiclif and John Huss were the pioneers, we shall be forced to recognize that nations had been massed and unified by the Crusades to necessitate great transformations; and that the Scholastics were the intellectual gymnasts, who, better than they knew, were preparing minds and consciences for nobler conflicts, and for the emancipation of Europe from the bondage of theory into the freedom of experimental philosophy. Not less did the Crusades set men to thinking, enlarge their knowledge of mankind, awaken just views of the superior culture of the Greeks, and provide for the Revival of Learning.

13. BARBARISM.

If it startles us to find the Dark Ages settling down upon Christian civilization just when it had begun a glorious career of Truth and Life among the nations, we shall find our surprise reversed when we look into the world movements of those times. It is rather astonishing that Christianity itself survived.[1] For take any map of Europe at the close of the fifth century, and what do we behold? The inundations of barbarism had deluged the fairest seats of Christendom; and all those earliest sources of Latin illumination in Northern Africa, where Tertullian and Cyprian and Augustine had glorified their successive ages, are included in the desolations. Where Carthage and Hippo had nurtured saints and scholars, we find the kingdom of the Vandals. From the Pillars of Hercules northward to the Loire stretches the dominion of the Visigoths. The Salian and Riparian Franks spread over the North, from Brittany to the sources of the Weser. The Ostrogoths occupy all Italy, and nearly the whole Eastern shore of the Adriatic, sweeping round by the Danube to the Rhineland. To deal with these rude races, and give them the law of Christ, was a

[1] See Note K".

work to which the Church addressed herself with fidelity. But look again at the map of Europe and the Mediterranean in the age of Charlemagne. The movements of the barbarians had been like the waves of the sea. From beyond the Danube the Lombards had poured into Subalpine Italy, and Teutonized the fair plains watered by the Po. But far more terrible is the condition of North Africa and Spain; the Mohammedans have taken them for a prey: nearly all of Spain is the Caliphate of Cordova. And now the Northmen are pouncing upon the Franks, penetrating all their harbours and navigable rivers; under the name of Danes spreading themselves in England; and waxing more and more terrible, till the Litany itself receives a new suffrage, for Christians in their churches cried unto heaven, "From Rollo and the Northmen, good Lord, deliver us."

14. EXPIRY OF THE DARK AGES.

I have not named the Huns and the Magyars swarming in from the Tartar hives of Asia, but perhaps I have said enough to remind you what a field for research is here opened to the student; and quite enough to explain the intervention of the "Dark Ages." What a dilution of all good, what an infusion of all evil, we have here! For a time, the Arabians, who had stolen Christian learning,[1] became its conservators in their own East, —

"Where science with the good Al-Maimon dwelt," —

and in Spain, where Christians went to them for

[1] See Note L".

knowledge. We retain the Arabic numerals, and most useful they are; and algebra is the most charming of mathematical processes; but while the Infidel kept the magazine of science till Christians once more could bring out its stores, the increase of knowledge among men owed little or nothing to the schools of Islam. Quickened to active exertions of mind by the Scholastics, and enlarged by the Crusades in every faculty that is nurtured by observation, Christendom awakes at the close of the fourteenth age "like a giant refreshed with wine." Here we greet the Revival of Learning. Bajazet was now menacing Constantinople, but God checked him, for Tamerlane had invaded Syria. In Europe the shameless Papal schism perpetuated the scandals of the Dark Ages, but was a help to the great awakening. In England the Plantagenets came to an end by the murder of Richard the Second, never to be forgotten while Shakespeare's genius reduces English history to incomparable painting in words. The accession of the House of Lancaster reminds us that the crusading spirit is not yet extinct, when King Henry the Fourth is made to say, —

> " Therefore, friends,
> As far as to the sepulchre of Christ . . .
> Forthwith a power of English shall we levy . . .
> To chase these pagans in those holy fields
> Over whose acres walked those blessed feet
> Which fourteen hundred years ago were nailed
> For our advantage on the bitter cross."

With commendable license, though with apocryphal history and a gross anachronism, the incomparable poet manages to wind up the play with a rhythmical flourish, in which the whole spirit of the preceding centuries is epitomized. The language, slightly changed, might well describe St. Louis, with whom the Crusades in fact expired:—

> " Many a time hath banished Norfolk fought
> For Jesu Christ in glorious Christian field,
> Streaming the ensign of the Christian cross
> Against black pagans, Turks, and Saracens;
> And, toiled with works of war, retired himself
> To Italy, and there at Venice gave
> His body to that pleasant country's earth,
> And his pure soul unto his captain Christ,
> Under whose colours he had fought so long."

But when the Crusades were turned against Christians, who were massacred by whole races in the South of France, under the bloody Innocent III., it was time to stop. And when Henry dies in the Jerusalem chamber at Westminster, crusading is extinct forever, and the new period is well advanced. I always note the death of Richard and of Chaucer, in A. D. 1400, as the limit of the dark period. One century more of the Middle Ages remains; it is the thrilling, charming, marvellous *Cinque-Cento*, the fifteenth century.

15. THE CINQUE-CENTO.

We magnify the *Cinque-Cento*, and use this term with reference to the fine arts too exclusively. I borrow this convenient term for the age that brought with it the elements of all we now enjoy, in letters and arts, in civilization, in freedom, in the restoration of truth to the nations, and in a genuine Reformation to our English forefathers. In a rapid review of this century of wonders, I hasten to a close of this Lecture.[1]

At the opening of this age, we find John Huss confessor to the Queen of Bohemia. Note that; and this also: the infamous statute for burning heretics is enacted in England, under which Sawtré perishes as a Wiclifite. Jerome of Prague is studying in Oxford. Tamerlane enters Bagdad and Damascus, and prepares to invade Asia Minor. In A. D. 1409 there are not less than three Popes, cursing and excommunicating one another, and men in nations for their respective adhesions. In A. D. 1412, Huss burns a papal indulgence, and he and Jerome denounce the traffic in such things. This was a century before Luther imitated them. Shortly after, Huss himself is burned at Constance, and Sigismund earns infamy by betraying him. The Council of Constance revives the traditions of Frankfort, and deposes the Pope. It has its glory and its shame. It burned Jerome of Prague after Huss, and ordered Wiclif's bones to be cremated and scattered. This Council closes in A. D. 1418. We soon reach the romantic episode of Joan of Arc; the Papal schism is closed by the heroic action of the Council of Basle, which continues the traditions of Frankfort, and deposes another Pope.

And here we may turn to the more gratifying field of Art and Literature. We have seen that in England the death of Chaucer marks the limit

[1] See Note M".

of a long period of night watches. To him and to Wiclif, who greeted the day dawn, and reflected it as from mountain tops, we owe the English language and the glorious beginnings of its literature, in prose and poetry. But on the greater scale of Continental progress, Dante had already created the Italian language, and from him and his brilliant successors, Petrarch and Boccacio, Chaucer's genius had caught the spark that soon burst into flame in his Canterbury Tales. John Gower, his contemporary, lived a few years in the age we are reviewing.

16. THE MEDICI.

The illustrious family of the Medici had been growing up in Florence, in the preceding century, and now Cosmo enters on his great career; making merchandise tributary to letters, founding a university, and ransacking the East for manuscripts, which came with spices and taffetas from the Levant in every argosy that enriched his coffers.[1] His grandson, Lorenzo the Magnificent, succeeds to his great power and influence in the Florentine republic, and largely augments his work, as the patron of scholars and of artists. Cimabue and Giotto had created pictorial art in Italy; but now the invention of oil colours by the brothers Van Eyck, at Ghent, proves that the fogs of Flanders as well as the sunbeams of the South presaged the wonderful development of painting about to be realized. This art reached its acme at a bound.

[1] See Note N".

Leonardo, Michael Angelo, and Perugino's great pupil, Raffaelle, all start up in this century, though they lived also into the next, and they have never been surpassed. Exploring the treasures of the Pitti Palace, in Florence, I saw an insignificant bit of marble, which I recognized at once as a link in a great history. Michael Angelo, a mere youth, was carving that head of an old faun, in the Medicean gardens, when Lorenzo observed its merits. He casually criticised it, "You must not give an old faun such fair teeth," and he walked on. Soon, after, however, he encountered the young man again, and saw that his hint had been taken. Michael had, with admirable skill, contrived to give the mouth and teeth an appearance of age, without disfiguring what was attractive in those features. This secured Lorenzo as his patron; and so grew up that unrivalled master of the three domains of sculpture, painting, and architecture, who moreover was no contemptible poet. He lived to embellishish Florence with his Titanic statues; to paint "The Last Judgment" on the walls of the Sistine Chapel, and to lift the Pantheon to the clouds in the dome of St. Peter's. The Middle Ages expired in glory, if only for this outburst of the fine arts; but in the nobler realms of intellect, of the useful arts, and of faith, it saw greater things than these.

17. GOTHIC ARCHITECTURE.

The link between the fine arts and those too often scorned as merely utilitarian is Architecture.

If we go back to the Middle Ages and trace the rise and development of the pointed architecture (to which Wren applied the nickname of "Gothic"), we cannot but acknowledge that even the Dark Ages brought some goodly things to light. We may justly call it the "Christian Architecture," and, while admitting its great defects, we must admire some of its characteristic ideas. Whether designedly or not, it imitates nature: the forest has naves, and aisles, and arches, with which its spirit strikingly coincides. Again, its aspiring vaults and lofty spires, its clustered columns uplifting its aerial clere-stories, and its abounding vertical lines, all spring heavenward, and lift the eye and the mind, if not the heart, to God. In the decorated examples at Lincoln we see its perfection; but even the "Academic Gothic," as I prefer to call "the perpendicular," retains these features, and in its Tudor debasement we find much that harmonizes with the faith. How notable, too, its reality! It adorns what other styles of the art, with awkward makeshifts, strive to conceal; it turns every prop, every stay, every beam and joint, into an augmentation of beauty. It does not hide its very crutches, for such are the flying buttresses which it so triumphantly elevates into graces; and down in its crypts, and where only the eye of the Omniscient penetrates, it covers no deformity; it builds for the Master-builder above. I fear "the dim religious light" that so fascinates us is nevertheless a striking symbol of the ages in which this architecture was created.

It is not enlightened art in any practical sense.

Michelet[1] has severely remarked upon its feebleness; it is ever crumbling and needing repairs; it is clamped and tied together by corroding bands of iron; it calls in a thousand artifices and expedients to supply its lack of strength; its very buttresses announce the inadequate massiveness of the walls; and when, as in the chapter-house, it erects a central pillar, like the handle of an umbrella, to uphold a canopy of stone, it proclaims its inability to erect a vaulted dome that shall stand by itself.

18. THE NEW CHRISTIAN ARCHITECTURE.

This was the humiliating defect exposed by Brunelleschi when he "broke the egg"; a feat which has no force as told of Columbus.[2] The Florentines were ambitious of erecting a cathedral with an unrivalled dome. The Teutonic architects came over the Alps to do the work, and proposed to uphold it by the central pillar, which is but the symbol of decrepitude, the old man bowed upon his staff. "I would make it stand by itself," said Brunelleschi. "But how?" was the inquiry. "Like that egg," said he; and there, indeed, like an egg-shell, light and perfect in its own fabric, it stands to this day, and may stand forever. It is the only perfect dome in Christendom. Michael Angelo would not consent to imitate it, but confessed his inability to rival it, when he designed the dome of St. Peter's. The Italians would have no more of Gothic art. It melts away, south of the

[1] See Note O".   [2] See Note P".

Alps, in the fairy decorations of that Milanese cathedral of snow. The recent façade of Santa Croce at Florence proves that such art belongs not to the sunny South; it is feeble beyond expression. But the works of Brunelleschi and of Bramante and of Angelo will last, and may supply to practical ages a more enduring Christian architecture.

19. NAVIGATION.

We may well look on in breathless wonder as we follow this age of miracles in its fertility of invention, and its arts of progress. Under John I., who founds a new line of kings, and under the patronage of his son Henry, Portugal takes the lead in maritime adventure. The Azores are discovered in A. D. 1432, and Cape Verde about ten years later. In 1460, they have discovered the isles off the coast of Guinea; the next year an expedition is sent, overland, to India; in 1486, Diaz reaches the southern extremity of Africa; in 1496, Vasco de Gama doubles the Cape; the next year he arrives at Calcutta; he founds the Portuguese empire in India; the highways of commerce are revolutionized, and Venice declines.

But, more and better, in 1442 is born, at Genoa, Christopher Columbus. In 1484, he pleads in vain with John II. of Portugal to give him the means of exploring the Atlantic. It is not till 1492 that he sails from Palos, with his wretched little fleet, for regions unknown; but (October 12) he sights the first shore of a new world; he presses on to Cuba and Hayti, and in 1493 introduces the savages of Transatlantic regions at the court of Ferdinand and Ysabel. After pushing his adventures with continuous success, he is brought to the same court in chains, as the century comes to an end. What an end for such an age, and for its noblest hero!

At this date the discovery of Newfoundland by the Cabots (A. D. 1498) opens the grand history of the English race in America. Vespucci robs Columbus of his just rights, by giving his second-rate name to the continent. Copernicus, born at Thorn, in A. D. 1473, was now pursuing his studies of the universe. Surely the ages of light were returning —

"To warm the nations with redoubled ray."

20. PRINTING.

The Crusades had introduced the cotton paper of the Arabs into Europe, and its manufacture with the stronger fibre of linen was established in Germany in the preceding age. But now comes the art of printing, the discovery of which must be regarded as not half so great a wonder as the fact that God had held back the mind and hand of man from the most simple of all conclusions until now. Every impression of a seal, every footmark in the sand or clay of the soil, every stamp upon coins, ought to have suggested it, ages beforehand. God willed it to wait till now, when the grandest moral and civil revolutions were needed to introduce the last ages of the world. Strange to say, stereotyping came first; for such were the

wooden tables of Koster in 1430, though it took
the sluggish wit of mankind nearly four centuries
more to return to the hint. Gutenberg (A. D. 1442)
had taught the utility of moveable types, and
Faust had brought the art to a practical degree of
perfection (A. D. 1450) by an improvement of the
press and the manufacture of printers' ink. In
A. D. 1455, the glory of the art was reached, when
the final sheets of the first printed Bible were
folded and bound at Mentz, by Gutenberg, Faust,
and Schäffer. Caxton, in a chapel of Westminster Abbey, about ten years later, was working
the first press in England. He died before he
knew that a new world had just been discovered,
where in our day the art in all its beauty and perfection is exercised in Chicago and in the great
port of the Pacific, — cities which fifty years ago
were but hamlets, amid the wigwams of savages.
Yet it deserves to be noted that the art reached
wellnigh the acme of its beauty in the age of its
birth, when Aldus (A. D. 1494), set up his press at
Venice, and introduced the delicate Italic letter, —
a refinement upon that of manuscript.

21. GREAT MOVEMENTS.

Now, also, was wood engraving introduced, and
musical notes were cut in type-metal. Watches
were made at Nuremberg and world-maps were sent
forth from the same city. But while these arts of
peace were in progress, the "Wars of the Roses"
were doing a useful work of another sort in England, and the expedition of Charles VIII. into

Italy, with his invasion of Rome on the last day of the year 1494, marks a new era in the art of war.[1] His invention of a comparatively light and moveable artillery, and the improvement of fire-arms for soldiery, with his passage of the Alps and audacious treatment of the pontiff, were a foreshadowing of the French campaigns in Italy four hundred years later. Napoleon's "flying artillery" was but another stage of progress; the idea of batteries not only possible on the field, but transferable from point to point, belongs to this age of modern warfare.

But the glory and the shame of the century remains to be told. Providentially the art of printing and all the progress of the age circle round its noontide; a crisis which proved a blessing to mankind, as it created the revival of learning and insured the reformation of religion, the exposure of the Decretalist and other Papal frauds, the study of Holy Scripture in the originals, the abasement of the Papacy, the advance of freedom and of constitutional law, and the illumination of the world. Again the Gospel came forth from the East. All these blessings were wrought out of an evil, in itself most disgraceful and menacing to Christendom: the fall of Constantinople in A. D. 1453, and the planting of that cancer in the breast of civilization, the unspeakably abominable Turkey in Europe.

[1] See Note Q".

22. THE FALL OF CONSTANTINOPLE.

The Council of Florence, in A. D. 1439, grew out of the impending horrors which the Greeks foresaw must soon overwhelm them. For ten years had they repelled the arms of Bajazet, when God sent Timour the Tartar to their aid; but now the Turks were at their very doors. Scutari was in the hands of the Ottomans, and, reinforced by siege-guns with balls of granite, were preparing for a final assault. Every motive appealed to the Christian universe for a crusade, which reason and righteousness would have justified. The cause of the Greeks was the common cause of Europe and of humanity; but the Popes saw their opportunity, at last, and would give no aid to the Easterns save at the price of their submission. Their delegates at Florence were starved and menaced into a patched-up compliance,[1] and the "Uniat" compromises were agreed on. But they were received on their return with a howl of execration, and the Greeks, true to the ancient Nicene constitutions, once more rejected the Popes. The Turks might massacre them, but the fraudulent Decretals should not enslave them. As the consequence, on the 29th of May, Constantine Palæologus, the last of the Cæsars, perished on the walls of New Rome, which for more than a thousand years had been the metropolis of Christendom. Under the dome of Justinian, in the solemn night before, he had received the holy sacrament of the altar. That day the streets ran with blood, and, after the brutal

[1] See Note R".

example of Mohammed II., their chief women were given over to unmentionable outrage; twelve thousand houses and churches were burned; thousands were put to the sword. Gibbon, with levity, tells of the horrors to which virgins were delivered, of sixty thousand sold into slavery, and of the Hippodrome streaming with blood. He shares not our sense of shame, when he tells how the imam ascended the pulpit, and the muezzin cried from its turrets, "Great is Allah, and Mohammed is his prophet!" To the disgrace of our mother England, this goes on still; and twelve million Christians writhe under the heels of three million Turks, because Turkish bonds are held in London. O Lord, how long? If England will not hear their cries, then Godspeed to Russia!

23. LIGHT OUT OF DARKNESS.

The Greeks were driven out of their capital, but they brought learning to Florence and to Rome. Now were the Greek Scriptures read once more, and the Fathers began to be printed and studied. Luther's great gift of the Bible to Germany must rank as second to the restoration of the Greek Testament by Erasmus. Aristotle's alloy in Christian theology began to be deprecated, as Plato began to be loved. The Greeks who had fled to Italy before the downfall had enabled Nicholas V. to found the Vatican Library, and now libraries began to be multiplied. It was well; for, as the century came to its end, the Papacy had returned to its vomit and to its wallowing in the mire. The age of Theodosia and

Marozia was revived again under the infamous Borgia (Alexander VI.), and Rome continued to be the hot-bed of ecclesiastical crime and debauchery, when a young Augustinian monk came, and saw, and went away to conquer. Michael Angelo was painting the Sistine Chapel with a parable which the Papal Court was too stupid to comprehend.[1] He wrote *Tekel* on their walls, and reminded them that prophets and sibyls alike foretold the Last Judgment. He portrayed its awful menace before their eyes, and scrupled not to put popes and cardinals among the damned. Some whined when they saw their own portraits in the terrible caricature, but they were too torpid to comprehend the length and breadth of such a prophecy. A day of retribution was close at hand. God was arising to shake terribly the earth.

[1] See Note S".

LECTURE VI.

THE CHURCH OF OUR FOREFATHERS.

1. IDENTITY AND CONTINUITY.

LET me now invite you to a survey of the history of the Anglican Church, its origin, its subjection to the Paparchy in the Middle Ages, and, finally, of its restoration in the sixteenth century. We shall see that from its origin until now it is the same identical Church, — no more another now than the man who has been a prodigal, and who has regained his home and his patrimony, is other than the embryo that was once in the womb, the babe that once drew nurture from its mother's breast, the youth who declined from his parental example and teachings, and the sufferer who, amid the filth and the starvation of the swineyard, came to himself, and said, "I will arise and go to my father." The Anglican Church was primitive and pure; she became enslaved and defiled; she regained her liberties, she washed and is clean. But she is none other to-day, as to individuality and identity, than she was when Italians were sent to put chains upon her; when she shook her chains, in defiance, as she chafed under them; when she lay down and slept awhile, baffled and degraded; or when, at last, she woke and broke from her fetters, and began to be herself again; until now God has given her to many nations and set her footsteps in the seas, and enabled us to say, "Her sound is gone out into all lands, and her words into the ends of the world." Such is the outline of her history, which I propose to make clear and readily recognized by the illumination of truths which have been too little understood.

2. ORIGIN OF THE CHURCH IN BRITAIN.

There are many evidences that the Gospel was preached in Britain by disciples of St. Paul. Three names in his latest catalogue of Roman saints [1] may not have secured your close attention: "Pudens, Linus, Claudia," — that is, Lin and Gladys. These twain were Britons, probably, and their names are thus Latinized, as Saul is also called Paul. Pudens, who had served in Britain as a soldier, married this British lady, as we know from Martial's epigram. Caradoc, whose sister or daughter she may have been, had doubtless become a Christian when he moralized on the Coliseum, as it rose before his eyes, in language which only Christians understood, and which he borrowed from common sayings of early Christians.[2] The return of Caradoc to his distant home, accompanied by Christian missionaries, who were afterwards the evangelists of Wales, is a theory supported by striking probabilities, while it accounts, as nothing else can, for inscriptions and ancient monuments

[1] 2 Tim. iv. 21.   [2] See Ante-Nicene Fathers, vol. iii. p. 108.

at Chichester. The names of ancient sees in Wales, such as St. Asaph's and St. David's, suggest that Jewish converts of St. Paul were their founders, and learned antiquarians have detected Welsh forms of several other saintly names in the Pauline calendar, among the ancient titles of their villages and towns. The history of "Lesser Britain," or Armorica, confirms all this; for the two Britains were inhabited by the same race. The Greek Menology retains the old tradition that Aristobulus, mentioned by St. Paul, was one of the Seventy, and became a British evangelist.

3. PERIODS.

Three periods should here be primarily noted: that of (1) the Primitive British Church, that of (2) the Early English Church, and (3) that of the Later English Church. The Norman epoch (A. D. 1066) is the turning point in Anglican history in its relations with Rome. Thereafter, we note three periods again: that of (1) the Transition to Papal Subjection, that of (2) the Paparchy Established, and (3) that of the Restoration. As to the Primitive British, a few additional words must suffice.

4. THE PRIMITIVE PERIOD.

Lucius, one of the British chiefs, is said to have been the first Christian king; but the legends of Edessa,[1] if they are to be credited, would deprive us of this glory. He lived in the time of Aurelius,

[1] See Ante-Nicene Fathers, vol. viii. p. 647.

when, had he been known to the Romans, he could hardly have escaped the crown of martyrdom. St. Alban, who suffered in Diocletian's world-wide massacre, is reputed the first British martyr. In A. D. 314, before the Nicene era, we noted the presence of three British bishops at the Council of Arles, a fact which seems to me to account for the Easter usages to which the British Church so tenaciously adhered. These bishops found them corresponding with their own traditions in the churches of Pothinus and Irenæus. But of this by and by. It is not pleasant to add, as we must, that Morgan, better known as Pelagius, was also a Briton. His heresy caused great evils, not only in the unlearned and isolated church of his birth and baptism, but ever since among Christians. On the other hand, as St. Paul has said,[1] "there must be also heresies among you, that they which are approved may be made manifest"; and we owe to this principle of the divine economy that masterly exposition of the doctrines of grace in which the faith of primitive Christians is witnessed against Pelagius by St. Augustine.

5. GROANS OF THE BRITONS.

In A. D. 446, "the groans of the Britons" attest their inveterate sufferings from barbarous Picts and Scots; and in A. D. 449, the arrival of the Saxons enables us to date the Early English period from the middle of the fifth century. Invited to come in and drive out the Picts, our forefathers, the

[1] 1 Cor. xi. 19.

Angles and Saxons, took their pay by settling in the delightful lands they had defended. In the Isle of Wight and the opposite coasts settled the Jutes. Essex, Wessex, and Sussex tell the story of the Saxon immigration, and the Angles took the rest of the eastern coast into custody northward and far above the Humber. Such are our Anglo-Saxon forefathers, and I am not very proud of their conduct. But if they proved treacherous allies of the native Christians, they were pagans, who knew no better; and, feeble as were the Christians, they turned upon them at times and gave them a terrible threshing. Gildas, their own British chronicler, reproaches them as believers for not preaching to the Saxons, whom we may now for the first time call "the English," the Gospel of peace and love. The Saxons continued heathen till converted by the missionaries of Gregory.

6. CONVERSION OF THE ENGLISH.

His interest had been excited by the appearance of fair-haired boys from England in the Roman slave-market. "If only they were Christians," said the holy man, "not Angles, but Angels, they might be called." When he became bishop, as if remembering where Pelagius came from, he sent to convert them Augustine, a namesake of the great Bishop of Hippo. Now, though Gregory dealt with his missionaries and their converts in Britain very much as we deal with ours in China and Japan, his conduct, even as related by Bede at a later period, with the disadvantage of his less primitive conceptions, is altogether in keeping with Gregory's primitive assertion of his adhesion to Nicene canons. He was not "the Universal Bishop"; he dictated no deference to his see, but advised Augustine to adopt improvements, if he saw any, among the churches of Gaul; and we cannot doubt that, had he known of their continued existence, he would have advised a generous and brotherly course in dealing with the ancient Christians of the land. These had retreated westward, and were now hemmed in among the mountains of Wales, and by the Southern seas in what we know as Cornwall, perhaps "the Horn of Wales."

7. THE EARLY ENGLISH.

Thus the Early English [1] period opens with the seventh century, say A. D. 601. Augustine repaired to France to be consecrated by the Bishop of Arles (Virgilius), who was assisted, according to the Nicene canons, by two other bishops, of whom the name of one only has come down to us; that of Ætherius, Bishop of Lyons. He succeeded from St. John, through Polycarp, Pothinus, and Irenæus, as the thirty-second bishop of that most primitive and illustrious see. Thus Augustine became the first Bishop of Canterbury, deriving his apostolic office from the churches of Ephesus and Smyrna, both mentioned in the Apocalypse, and saluted by an epistle from our ascended Lord himself with exceptional tokens of approbation.

[1] Not to be understood of architecture.

8. CONSEQUENCES.

Great gratitude is due to Gregory for his nursing care and faithfulness in planting the Church of England; but we must not think it strange that the relations thus established between England and the great Apostolic See of the West led to consequences not in themselves happy, nor even canonical. Our own missionary bishops naturally write to their brethren here for instructions, and the English missionaries write personally to the Archbishop of Canterbury from the ends of the earth. It was much more necessary for similar relations to be kept up, in those days, with the great metropolis of Western Christendom, because books were few and all sources of information rare.[1] Let us imagine how the new primate of England would naturally regard the great patriarch of Rome.

9. RELATIONS TO THE APOSTOLIC SEE.

Not as in any sense "Universal Bishop"; that Gregory abhorred. Not as having any powers or authority superior to his own as a bishop; that also Gregory had expressly and vehemently disclaimed.[2] Yet the Church had established certain great patriarchs, among whom Gregory had a primacy of honour, but no "supremacy" of any kind. Beyond his own limited patriarchate, he might exert a watchful care to see that the Nicene and other œcumenical canons were obeyed; he could enforce them, however, only by the action of councils,

[1] See Lecture III. § 16, page 95.   [2] See Note T".

each subject to its own president, or metropolitan, and not to him. In a mission created by himself, he seems to have, naturally, expected a degree of deference growing out of such circumstances. All this Augustine would justifiably recognize. We must not be surprised to find that the great patriarch was invested in his eyes with an exceptional importance, as succeeding to the apostles St. Paul and St. Peter in the ancient world-centre. All the patriarchs were called *Papa* by way of eminence, and each in his own jurisdiction was "*the* Papa"; just as we call the nearest post-office "*the* post-office," or the chief magistrate of our own city "*the* Mayor." This by no means implies that there are no other post-offices or mayors; and so, when Augustine speaks of "*the* Apostolic See," he detracts nothing from Antioch or Ephesus; and when he speaks of "*the* Pope," he by no means implies that the other patriarchs are any less "popes" than Gregory. Bear in mind that, as I have shown, what we understand by that term was not then imagined; and not till the close of the eleventh century did even a Roman pontiff presume to decree that this title should be peculiar to himself. For, not bearing all this continually in mind, the most erroneous impressions are derived from books that use such expressions unguardedly in the sense current in the times of their authors, as now among the vulgar.

10. A DISCOVERY.

When Robinson Crusoe discovered a human foot-print in the sand, his sensations were serious.

When Augustine first learned that there were already Christians in Britain does not appear; but his first impressions of them were doubtless not very favourable. He learned that they were an unlettered race, who still kept Easter by the ancient, but now uncanonical, uses of Smyrna and Ephesus. For these had been overruled at Nicæa, by universal consent. Were the Britons deliberate schismatics? He doubtless imagined they were, but this was a mistake. The Britons had been so long cut off from commerce with other churches, that they had never received from Alexandria the annual computation. Gregory himself did not know of their existence, and it seems to me probable, as I have said before, that they kept on in the way received by Irenæus from Polycarp, and which Eborius and his companions had learned from Lyons and Arles to regard as lawful.[1] Especially would they be likely to adhere to their old customs, so long as the Patriarch of Alexandria failed to communicate with them, as the canons prescribed. This was their misfortune, not their fault.

11. THE OTHER SIDE OF THE CASE.

Augustine would look at it very differently: they were ignorant barbarians, at best, and it was now time for them to obey the canons. Besides, though he had been expressly counselled by Gregory not to expect every national church to conform to the Italian usages, he felt sure, no doubt, that they were the best usages; just as some of us are quite sure

[1] See *supra*, § 4.

that the Mexican Church and Père Hyacinthe in Paris ought to accept every usage and every rubric of our "incomparable prayer-book." We find some disposed to withhold aid from the "old Catholics," because they prefer, in many respects, their national rites to ours. Human nature does not change.

12. A CONFERENCE.

Augustine obtained a conference with some of the British bishops, and it was held under a tree which remained till comparatively recent times, and was known as "Augustine's oak." What a meeting! What but Christianity could have afforded any common ground for such a conference! There were the aborigines of the soil, and here the robber Saxons; there the ancient Church of Caradoc and Pudens, of Claudia and of St. Paul's own missionaries, and here was a new-comer, who called himself Bishop of the English, and seemed to them in league with their old enemies against them. In answer to prayer, Augustine was thought to have wrought a miracle, which excited their fraternal respect; but they answered, with dignity, that "they could not depart from their ancient customs without the consent of their own churches."

13. AND ANOTHER.

At a second conference, Augustine's bearing and conduct were offensive to these very primitive people. Yet he proposed no terms of union other than such as we should approve. They were to adopt, "not as our custom, but as that of the Universal Church," certain compliances with the local Roman and Apostolic Church, (1) in the administering of baptism, and (2) in the keeping of Easter. Further, (3) they were to act jointly with him in preaching to the English nation the word of God. They refused consent, chiefly because of his overbearing manner. And here he seems to have forgotten what was due to himself and them, for he threatened them with the divine displeasure. When, some ten years later, King Ethelfrid with a great army fell upon them and massacred them in great numbers, the Saxons looked upon this terrible event in one way and the Britons in a very different one.

An ancient Welsh document relates that the answer of the British clergy was made on one occasion in the following words, by Dinoth, an abbot : —

"The British churches owe the deference of brotherly kindness and charity to the Church of God, to the Roman *Papa*, and to all Christians. But other obedience they do not know to be due to him whom you call the *Papa*. As for ourselves, we are under the jurisdiction of the Bishop of Caerleon upon Uske, who, under God, is our spiritual overseer and guide."

Ethelfrid's vengeance fell upon Chester in the North, the ancient name of which resembles that of Caerleon in South Wales. This may have led some to imagine that the massacre was inspired by Augustine's threat, of which he probably had never heard; but it shows how intense was the Saxon prejudice of Bede himself against the Britons, when this holy man can see nothing in the event but a just judgment from the Lord. We must acknowledge with grief, that a like uncharitable comment might be made upon the failure of missions and bishoprics which Augustine founded. There were terrible relapses; some of the bishops retired to France; the old idolatry returned in divers places. The Anglican Church had shrunk to the dimensions of the single county of Kent, when once again it revived, and for a time spread over the northeastern counties, under good King Edwin. But again there came a relapse. In Lincolnshire, where a great work seemed begun, the churches went to decay, and so continued for years. It became manifest that Augustine's work must all be done over again.

14. IONA AND ITS MISSIONS.

But for thirty years (A. D. 633-664) a more primitive and a more successful work had been carried on among the Northern English, by Scots and Picts, the old enemy, now Christianized by the zeal of Columba and his missions that went forth from Iona. King Oswald restored the cathedral at York. Aidan, a saintly bishop, fixed his missionary see at another Iona, Lindisfarne, on the coast of Northumbria, which was long known as the Holy Isle. This bishopric was afterwards enlarged, and settled as the see of Durham. Finan, who succeeded to Aidan, recovered very much people to Christ. A bishop was set over Lichfield, and another was restored to London. Nobody can read the beautiful tributes which Bede pays to the Northern bishops, with whom he differed on so many points, without the conviction that to Iona and to Lindisfarne, and to the meek and loving spirit of their missionaries, the ultimate conversion of all England is chiefly due. At one time only one bishop of the Latin rite was left in the island. And so it came about that this rite was observed only in Kent and a small part of the South, while the converted North adhered to the Gallican rites, or others of very primitive use, brought into the Pictish churches from Ireland. To heal the differences occasioned by such diversity, a synod was summoned (A. D. 664) at Whitby, in Yorkshire.

15. COUNSELS OF UNITY.

And very interesting and truly Christian in spirit were the discussions. Bede attributes the Easter rules of the Northern Britons to the causes I have already instanced, and excuses their non-conformity in this respect, acknowledging their true faith and piety in the spirit of their observance of rules they had received from primitive times. Though the immediate results were not unanimously adopted, this synod unified the churches in a good degree; and soon after (A. D. 667), such a desire for the settlement of affairs was reached that the Northerns came to an agreement with their Kentish brethren, and elected Wighart Archbishop of

Canterbury, desiring him to go to Rome and receive consecration there. This measure was very wisely conceived. The English Church exercised its own rights of election; but the failure of Gregory's mission having become a scandal, it was fitting that "the Pope of the *city of Rome*," as Bede and Alcuin call him, should be informed of the better state of things now existing, — of the growing unity of the Church in Britain, and of their desire to be in unity with the Apostolic See. Unhappily, as we might think, Wighart died at Rome in a pestilence before he could receive consecration; and, very pardonably perhaps, Vitalian, the patriarch of the city, resolved to find a proper person to be the English metropolitan, and send him out as his missionary. This was an unfortunate precedent, interfering as it did with the elective franchise of the English Church, and tending to impair its autonomy. But God overruled all for good.

16. THE MISSION OF THEODORE.

He chose Theodore, a native of St. Paul's own city, Tarsus, and consecrated him Bishop on the feast of the Annunciation, A. D. 668. It was, perhaps, a concession to the North British churches to send them an Eastern bishop, who could best persuade them to adopt the Nicene rules of Easter. But, as a restraint upon him, and to keep up the Latin side of the controversies, Vitalian gave him a sort of archdeacon in Adrian who accompanied him. It was in A. D. 669 that he arrived in England, to reconstruct and to "set in order the things that were wanting." He was cordially accepted, and became, in fact, the second founder of the Church of England. No one of his predecessors is to be compared with this truly great and holy man. Nevertheless, he had marked faults and infirmities, and was not always considerate in dealing with what, no doubt, he considered as yet a mere mission among a rude and half-Christianized people, " wellnigh severed from the whole world."

17. PERILOUS INNOVATIONS.

It has been necessary for me to go thus largely into the character of the Primitive British and the Early English Churches, in order to free later questions from the difficulties with which profound and unpardonable ignorance has encumbered the matter. We are now nearly at the end of the seventh century. The island has been Christianized from the Apostles' times. Its ultimate conversion and the Anglican Church, as a unit, result not from the Latin mission, but from Nicene churches, coming southward in their simplicity and purity from Iona and Lindisfarne. During this whole period the churches have enjoyed the insular privileges secured by the Cypriote canon to all churches so situated. The coming of Theodore was marked by one circumstance which shows how jealous were the native churches of all foreign intrusion. Augustine and his successors had leaned too much on Rome as their natural base of supplies, and this had doubtless increased their difficulties. A thorough and immediate identification of themselves

with the native Christians would have worked
better. Grace had been given to others to repair
the breach, and to heal the old wounds. But Theodore's consecration with an implication that he
was to be their "metropolitan," when they had
elected Wighart, and without waiting for their action in the choice of another, was an infraction of discipline; more especially as the Church of England
had never recognized as yet any metropolitical
power whatever in the see of Canterbury. Wilfrid,
now Bishop of York, had proved this, by going into
France to be consecrated, which would have been
resented by the then Bishop of Canterbury had he
possessed any canonical right to consecrate the
bishops of England. This same Wilfrid had seen
the importance of accepting the Easter usages enjoined by Nicæa, and had favoured unity with the
Latins of Kent and Surrey; but in the circumstances he showed, perhaps, only a proper self-respect
by refusing attendance at Theodore's synods.

18. COMPROMISES.

However, by the humility of St. Chad, who represented the Northern churches, things were so far
harmonized that he became Bishop of Lichfield,
and Wilfrid was appeased, so that all things were
ready for harmonious action. A synod was called
at Hertford by the authority of the Saxon princes,
where the old canons were examined and local
canons passed. By these Theodore was virtually
accepted as the first Metropolitan of the Church
of England; according to the canons, that is, and

not by any authority of a foreign bishop. To show Theodore's own convictions on the subject, in which the churches and the local princes sustained him, he refused all recognition of Agatho, Bishop of Rome, when he presumed to interfere in the matter of a bishop deprived of his see. He did much more, and in a more important matter: for whereas Honorius, Pope of the city of Rome, fell into the Monothelite heresy, and was subsequently condemned as a heretic,[1] Theodore summoned a council (A. D. 680) at Hatfield, just at the time when the sixth and last general council was held at Constantinople, for the same purpose, in which this heresy was condemned. This council of Hatfield marks a great point in the Anglican history; for it thoroughly recognized the Nicene Councils and Constitutions, and all the councils œcumenical, placing the united Church of the Britons and Saxons on the unequivocal base of Holy Scripture and primitive antiquity.

19. WHAT ITS FIRST ARCHBISHOP HAD MADE OF THE ANGLICAN CHURCH.

In this happy estate Theodore the Great, as he may justly be called, left the Church of England, when (A. D. 690) he rested from his labours. He was nearly ninety years of age, and had sat in his see two-and-twenty years. He founded schools, increased learning, and left scholars who were masters of the Latin tongue not only, but of the Greek also, the native tongue of Theodore himself.

[1] See Lecture III. § 27, page 107.

To such schools we owe the precious life and labours of Bede, and of the great Alcuin, of whom we have heard before. So stood the Church of our forefathers at the close of the seventh century.

20. THE VENERABLE BEDE.

We enter the new century at the date of Bede's ordination in the thirtieth year of his age. He loved the Latin churches and the see of Rome, to which he felt that the Saxons owed their Christianity, and his fidelity to this sentiment amounted in him wellnigh to a passion. But it was to the *canonical* dignity and character of the Apostolic See that he was attached. He owed it no subscription. In the year after his ordination to the presbyterate, an English council took occasion to declare that "No decree of English archbishops and bishops should ever be altered by any decrees of the Apostolic See." This was precisely the position of Dinoth and the British bishops in their answer to Augustine. The greatest men of this age, and those most attached to the Latin rites and usages, reaffirmed this position two years later at a conference in Yorkshire; adding a strong defiance of any foreign power presuming to interfere with what the synods of the national Church had decreed.

21. FIRST ENGLISH MISSIONS.

Now went forth Winfrid (or Boniface) on his great mission to the Franks, and the light of England began to illuminate the world. But many things in England itself began to awaken the anxiety of Bede, who reflects upon them with prudent reserve, and says, "Time will show." Egbert, the patron of Alcuin, was now Bishop of York, and Bede complains to him of the great ignorance of the peasantry, sending him copies of the Lord's Prayer and the Creed in the vulgar tongue, which he entreats may be used by the clergy in teaching the people. Here was in rudiments our own Catechism begun. And, indeed, now were the seeds of a subsequent restoration planted; for, in reproving the corruptions of the monasteries and other evils which afterwards arose, he writes like a reformer. He was one of the greatest doctors of the age, and he met his death on Ascension day, May 25, A. D. 735, with his pen in hand, translating the Gospel of St. John into English. In the cathedral of Durham you may see his tomb and his epitaph: —

> "Hic jacent in fossa
> Bedæ Venerabilis ossa."

> "Here lie 'neath these stones
> Bede the Venerable's bones.

22. THE LATER PERIOD.

Of Alcuin and his transcendent merits you have been so fully reminded that I add no more about him. Thus we reach the epoch which closes the history of the early English period, at the memorable date of Charlemagne, A. D. 800. In that same year Egbert began his reign. He nominally was the first King of England; but we may practically reserve that title for Alfred the Great.

Between this date and the Norman invasion, A. D. 1066, which was the epoch of Hildebrand, lies the later English period, during which England itself began to be created, in its constitutions and laws, by the action of the Church. The bishops established the State, "as bees make the honey-comb"; but the State never established the Church of England. She was the precedent condition of the State itself. In the preceding age, Ina, king of Wessex, speaks of the nascent Parliament as having concurred, in its three estates, in enacting the laws. He enumerates: " My bishops, and all my eldermen, and the *eldest witan* of my people, with a great gathering of God's servants." Such was the "Witenagemot," or assembly of the Wise.

23. ALFRED, THE HEAD OF OUR RACE.

Alfred revised and collected the laws of his predecessors, rejecting, with the advice and consent of his *witan*, what he could not approve, but modestly inserting nothing of his own, because "he could not foresee what might be good for such as should come after him." The incursions of the Northmen kept this great prince busy, all his days, resisting their ravages. They made a "dark age" for England; but, at all his intervals of respite, he was not less active in his literary pursuits, promoting learning, encouraging piety and study among the clergy, and with his own hands translating Holy Scriptures and good books for his people. He lived through the ninth century, and expired in the first year of the tenth. I have quoted a saying of King Edgar's about this horrible century.[1] In his reign, Dunstan became Archbishop, and brought in many Italian monks, by whom the sorest evils were soon inflicted on the Church. The ascendency of the Danes and the reign of Canute deserve careful study; they promoted somewhat, at a dangerous period, the influence of Rome, where the Paparchy was now growing to enormous proportions, amid not less enormous corruptions. Edward the Confessor is revered as a Saxon saint and a true Englishman; but Earl Godwin ruled the land, and his son Harold succeeded. All things had prepared the way for a new era; and, after a brief reign of forty weeks, the battle of Hastings gave the realm to William the Norman.

24. TAKING OUR BEARINGS.

Let us see where the Anglican Church stood on the eve of its enslavement to an alien aggression. The idea of a "Papacy" was familiarized; but it was the indefinite conception of a great Canonical Patriarchate, in the apostolic city of Rome, to which filial deference was due. It was a Papacy, but not a Paparchy. Elsewhere the Decretals had done their work more effectually, but England was Nicene, and not Roman. It was free in spirit, and, as yet, in form.

Observe that the canon of Holy Scripture, the Creeds, the Episcopate, were identical with those

[1] See Lecture V., page 151.

we have now. There was no doctrine of Transubstantiation; the communicant received in both kinds; there was no forced confessional. The clergy were mostly married men. The whole scholastic system of theology was non-existent. There were gross superstitions, but no false dogmas. Avoid reading into these times any ideas distinctively more modern, and bear always in mind that the Catholic Church still meant what it means in the Nicene Constitutions. It took five centuries more to produce such a monstrous conception as that of "the Roman Catholic Church,"— a local church that is claiming to be identical with the whole Church Universal.

25. THE ANGLO-NORMAN PERIOD.

The new period is that of the Anglo-Normans, but it includes the century of transition, which was not complete when the Angevine dynasty came in. We shall only note the great changes it created in the Anglican Church, and the debasement of its Nicene position.

It introduced an entirely new class of ideas, for with French and Italian priests came a Latinizing process which, by and by, subjected the Anglican Church to the Roman pontiff; never so, however, as to rob it of its identity as the Church of England, or to absorb it into the Italian, or Ultramontane, system of passive subjection. The terribly sincere Hildebrand was now carrying the assumptions of the Decretals to their logical consequences, and in him the fraudulent decrees of

Nicholas reached their highest mark. Gregory endeavoured to establish a universal Paparchy. This level of culmination was maintained by the ferocious Innocent III.[1] (A. D. 1198), and subsequently till we reach the fourteenth century under Boniface VIII., the last of those despotic pontiffs who successfully enforced the Decretals. The reaction was then begun. But it was precisely when the Hildebrandine epoch was successfully transforming the Latin churches into a system of ecclesiastical satrapies, that England was Normanized. Hildebrand sanctioned the invasion of William. His purpose and policy are evident. This remnant of the Nicene Constitutions must be absorbed. He who forced Henry, the Emperor, to kneel at his gate amid the snows of Canossa, and whose new position was marked by an edict claiming the title of " Pope " as no longer to be applied to other patriarchs or bishops, now proposed to subject England to the Paparchy.

26. THE NEW *EPISCOPUS AB EXTRA*.

I have not called William " the Conqueror," for our forefathers were not conquered when Harold was overcome. It was a duel between two claimants of the English throne, neither of whom had a well-defined right. But William was the nominee of Edward the Confessor, and came in as his regular successor, swearing to maintain the laws and institutions of the English, which, with all his rude and cruel ideas, he did in many respects quite effectu-

[1] See Note U″.

ally. I do not wholly share the feeling of those who see in him only the brutal "Bastard" and despot. Happily, he was bred in the Gallican school of ecclesiasticism, and had imbibed some ideas from Charlemagne, as we shall soon see. What St. Louis did for France in a later age, William allowed the Church of England to do, promptly and vigorously, at this crisis. In fact, when Henry VIII. was called upon by the estates of his realm to "reassume" the ancient rights and privileges of his crown, he did little more than revive the laws of the Church and the land, as they were maintained at this time, even under the pontificate of Hildebrand. This will soon appear from the facts I shall note.

27. THE FOREIGN ARCHBISHOPS.

During the four Anglo-Norman reigns, there were five Archbishops of Canterbury. The first two were Italians; the other three were Frenchmen. By education and in habits of life the Italian primates were, of course, more or less Normanized; for Lanfranc and Anselm were taken from the monastery of Bec. To make way for the former, Stigand, in heart a *non-juror*, after four years, was deposed. William would not be crowned by him, but gave that honour to another. He belonged to the Anglo-Saxons, and did not fancy the invasion; but he was not, apparently, what an English primate should have been at such a moment. It is important, and very creditable to William, to note that, besides Stigand, only two or three of the Anglo-Saxon bishops were deprived.

28. THE GREAT LANFRANC.

For Lanfranc I feel a tender and almost affectionate respect. He was a humble-minded, but, all the more, a great bishop. Born in Pavia, he had been nurtured in Ghibelline ideas; he was therefore, naturally, of Hincmar's school, and accepted the traditions of Frankfort. The Decretals, it is true, had now during two centuries been transforming the Latin canons, and he no more doubted their authority than he did that of the Gospels. He was a personal friend of Hildebrand, and loved him. All the more may we wonder that he successfully opposed that gigantic creator of pontifical despotism, and stood in the eleventh century under William I. just about where, in the sixteenth, we shall find Archbishop Warham with his convocation under Henry VIII. Let us note some of the landmarks which Lanfranc would not suffer even Gregory to remove.

29. OLD LANDMARKS.

Hardly had William seated himself on his throne when Gregory made his first move of aggression. William was in debt to him for encouraging his invasion, and he had invited Gregory to accept his reward. Consequently two Roman cardinals appear on the scene as Legates, and were bold enough to introduce an unprecedented assault upon Anglican liberties, summoning the bishops and clergy to a council at Winchester. Here Stigand was deposed, most uncanonically.[1] However, Lanfranc waited

[1] Like Sancroft, under William III.

for no bulls from Gregory, but was duly consecrated by eight of his comprovincials, thus perpetuating the ancient succession. Nor did he wait for a pall from Rome to assume his authority as a metropolitan. Note, therefore, that even under Hildebrand no such formalities were of any account in England. Palls had been sent since Augustine's time, but with no other apparent motive than that of patriarchal recognition. But if William had paid off Gregory in a matter which suited his own convenience, when he wanted to get rid of Stigand, he was now inclined to show himself an English king, and to resist further aggression. The papal legate, Hubert, in the name of the pontiff, demanded two things,— (1) the payment of Peter-pence, said to be in arrears, and (2) homage, as from a vassal to his suzerain. William, perhaps, did not know that Peter-pence, as such, had not been paid by former kings. Under them the tribute was paid for the support of their own English college at Rome. Nevertheless, he was willing to settle the cash account without dispute. As to the homage, he growled out a reply worthy of the bluff Harry Tudor: "Homage to thee I do not choose to do; I never promised it, nor do I find that it was ever done by my predecessors to thine."

30. AN ANGLICAN PRIMATE.

Gregory had relied on Lanfranc to support this claim, and he now reproached his friend, as forgetting the feelings he had formerly professed, of devotion to him and the Roman see. If William was an English king, Lanfranc now rose to his position as an English primate, and replied, " I am ready to yield to your commands in everything *according to the canons.*" Here was the noteworthy difference between the *Papacy*, as interpreted by Gallicans and Anglicans, and that *Paparchy* which Gregory was trying to stretch over all the churches, but of which England as yet knew nothing. This latter could not be, even nominally, reconciled with Nicene canons. Lanfranc further said, that he had advised William to do as the Pope desired, adding, however, curtly and tartly, in the true Anglican spirit: " The reason why he utterly rejects your proposal he has himself made known to your legate orally, and to yourself by letter." This was not what the tamer of kings and superiors could put up with from an Anglican primate. Thank God, he found in Lanfranc one who would not go to Canossa. It is most important as a landmark to note the pontifical assumptions and the Anglican position at this juncture. Thus then wrote Hildebrand to Lanfranc: " Take care to make your appearance at Rome, within four months from this date. . . . Thus may you make amends for a disobedience we have so long overlooked. If these apostolic mandates are unheeded, . . . know this for certain, *you shall be severed from the grace of St. Peter*, and utterly stricken by his authority; . . . in other words, you shall be wholly suspended from your episcopal office." What happened? Here was the Paparchy (A. D. 1081), and where was Anglicanism at that date? Dean Hook tells the whole story in a line: "The Archbishop of Canterbury did not go, and Lanfranc was not suspended."

31. CYPRIOTE AUTONOMY.

In other words, the Church of England was still a Nicene church, and stood upon the ancient canons. It was just at this time that the Emperor had called a council at Brixen, in the Tyrol, which, in the spirit of Frankfort, had deposed Gregory and elected an antipope calling himself Clement III. Note, then, another proof that neither the Church in England, nor its primate, imagined that communion with the Pope was requisite to Catholic communion; for in this great matter Lanfranc took no pains to be in communion with Gregory, nor was he even influenced by Gregory's threat of excommunication "from the grace of Peter" to seek relief under the rival pontiff. To foreign inquiries upon the subject he returned this cool and truly English reply, as if with the Cypriote canon in his mind: "*Our island has not yet rejected Gregory, but it has not decided upon tendering obedience to Clement: when both sides have been heard, we shall be better qualified to come to a resolution in the case.*" He speaks with calm indifference, but rather as an umpire than as a subject. There are abundant proofs that, even at this date, the Anglican Church was everywhere recognized as maintaining an exceptional position, other than that of the Latin churches connected with "the Holy Roman Empire." Seventeen years later, at the Council of

Bari, A. D. 1098, when Anselm's spare and modest figure was hidden from Urban II., at a humble distance from his throne, he cried out, "Anselm, father and master, where art thou?" When he very meekly advanced, the pontiff gave him a privileged seat, and added, "We include him indeed in our *œcumene*,[1] but as the pope of another *œcumene*." Whatever meaning he may have attached to his almost prophetic words, it is evident that he regarded him as a patriarch, and as somewhat which others were not. Lanfranc, I suppose, speaks of "our island" in that very sense: *orbis alter*, another *œcumene*, no part of the Roman Empire.

32. ANGLICAN LIBERTIES ASSERTED.

Under William and this great primate what were called Gallican maxims two centuries later were thus laid down as Anglican liberties: — (1.) The Carolingian position of the royal supremacy was maintained; the king, like Charles and Constantine, was *evêque au dehors*, the principle afterwards restored under Warham, and less practically reaffirmed under Louis XIV. just six hundred years from the times we are now considering. Yet fools and knaves affirm perpetually that this was an invention of Henry VIII. (2.) If two or more popes were claimants of St. Peter's throne, *the right of choosing his pope* was vested in the king. This defeats all such ideas as were formulated at Trent,

---

[1] "Orbis" seems here to have this significance. See William of Malmesbury (ed. Migne), p. 1493.

or decreed by the late pontiff. (3.) When the true Pope had been thus ascertained, none of his briefs or bulls were to be published in England till approved by the king. (4.) No ecclesiastic, if summoned to Rome, should be permitted to obey without the king's permission. We have seen by Lanfranc's conduct that he may have dictated this safeguard against papal aggression. (5.) The Church of England, in council under the primate, might make no canons without the royal consent. (6.) The Anglican Church in council, with such consent, might regulate her own officers and prescribe her own liturgy. Under this ancient immunity the "Use of Salisbury" was now set forth as a model, and to this the Church of England *reverted* at the Restoration under Elizabeth. Note the essential identity of the Church under William I. and under the later Tudors.

33. THE GREAT ANSELM.

Anselm, who succeeded Lanfranc, was more of an Italian, and, though a great theologian and a holy man, he was a mischievous primate. Nobody makes more mischief than a saint at heart, who is practically wrong-headed. The new king enforced the Anglican liberties, but the primate compromised them as far as he could, though he had received his investiture from the sovereign in contempt of the Roman court. Moreover, he had received his consecration from bishops not then in communion with the pontiff, whom he at the time, and the king afterward, called "the true Pope."

In Anselm this is most noteworthy. When, at a later date, he compromised himself in concessions to the pontiff, the bishops and clergy of England, in the true spirit of A. D. 1530, declared that, rather than concede the temporal supremacy to the Pope, they would expel Anselm and "break off all connection with the Roman see."[1] To the Pope himself the king wrote a letter, deprecating any assumption on his part "which would drive him to the extreme measure of renouncing all intercourse with the see of Rome." It is clear that the Paparchy had not quite clutched England into its grip. For this no thanks to Anselm, who induced William Rufus to give up more than was due, in the matter of investiture, though not by any means all that Rome claimed. Still, when a Roman legate landed at Dover, to exercise legatine powers over England, arousing a universal outcry against such an unheard of papal aggression, Anselm maintained the Anglican liberties, and packed the legate off to Calais in summary disgrace.

34. INTRUSION OF LEGATES.

After the decease of this holy man, whose mistakes were honest convictions, derived from his training and from the times in which he lived, the see was kept vacant for five years, though administered by Ralph d'Escures, Bishop of Rochester, who was then elected to the primacy, after an extraordinary contest, in A. D. 1114. We are now

[1] Anselm (ed. Migne), iv. 4. p. 203. See also Hook's Archbishops of Canterbury, vol. ii. p. 239.

in the twelfth century, and this action is most significant of contempt for the popedom, for which two claimants, if not three, were struggling. The Anglican bishops would not have another Anselm; the king enabled them to choose one who was resolved to maintain the Anglican liberties. Soon after, he asserted his prerogative, and recognized Calixtus II., a Frenchman, who proved as treacherous to England as any Italian could have been. Ralph lived to crown the next Norman king, and William of Corbeuil succeeded to the primacy. A contemporary says, " Of his merits nothing can be said, for he had none." The state of Europe was frightful: Pope and Antipope, between whom all Europe was under an anathema, were now literally in arms, and one of them in person was contending as a soldier. Then came a melancholy concession. The new archbishop permitted himself to be appointed the papal legate over England and Scotland, for he was weak enough not to see that, while this seemed to place him under no legatine superior, it was placing the Church of England in new relations to the Papacy. He crowned Stephen, and was soon after succeeded by Theobald, the third Abbot of Bec, who had been called to the English primacy. This primate also accepted a legatine position, thus letting into England the Paparchy by the thin end of a wedge that was destined to be driven deeper and deeper by sledge-hammers. In the next reign we shall see the consequences. The next legate, as might have been foreseen, was not the primate.

35. WHERE WE STAND.

Our period includes the reign of the first Plantagenet, when the Decretalist system became dominant in England under the new code of Gratian. The reign of Stephen had been inglorious, but he sustained the principle of his predecessors, when he refused to permit his bishops to leave the kingdom on the summons of Eugenius III. to his council at Rheims. Theobald disobeyed him, and was punished; but, good man though he was, he shows what peril there is in trusting great and sacred interests to pious imbecility. The Anglo-Norman dynasty ends in an ignominious surrender of principles which were soon found to have subjected it to all the fraudulent impositions of Nicholas. These were just now framed into the canon law by Gratian, and what were claims before were henceforth canons, overriding all that Anglicans had known by that name. The landmarks, however, had been providentially set up, and the Anglican liberties were recognized by Pope Paschal himself, when (A. D. 1118) he complained to the bishops and clergy of England of their independent spirit in the following words: "Without advising us, you determine all ecclesiastical affairs within yourselves; call councils by your own authority; without our consent give sees to bishops by translation, and suffer no appeals to be made to us." Yes, precisely so, thank God! And so stood the Anglican Church in the second half of the twelfth century, and all this she regained in the sixteenth; which proves that the Paparchy held its usurped sway over the

Church of England only for four hundred years, more or less, — years in which it was never undisputed nor even unambiguously received. Leave out these four centuries, and we have fourteen of Nicene freedom, and, in good degree, of Nicene truth and purity. Which, then, is the church of our forefathers, and which the old religion?

LECTURE VII.

THE ELEMENTS OF RESTORATION.

1. THE TRANSITION YET INCOMPLETE.

OUT of Lake Leman comes the "arrowy Rhone," beautiful as light from the clear blue sky. You may have stood on the little promontory where the Arve issues forth to meet it,— a red torrent from the Alps, once the crystal of melted snows but now arrayed like a papal legate. How the purer river writhes and refuses to be tainted! how the red ruffian presses and pushes it to the wall! Still the Rhone keeps up the contest as best he may. For a time he holds his own, but, alas! the red wins, and the sapphire disappears. What is visible to the common eye is no longer the blue Rhone, but only the blood-coloured Arve. Is the nobler river lost? By no means. It becomes the Rhone again, and rolls on superbly, through the broad lands where Irenæus planted the Gospel, under the walls of Lyons and Arles, and so to the sea. Behold a parable, that illustrates the Nicene Church in England, in her original glory and in her restored identity.

We have not yet reached the point where the stream runs red, precisely. To drop the figure, we must give a full century to the mischief done by the Norman primate who became a nominal "legate," and so let in the foreign element.[1] As yet the struggle is kept up. The Normans are pushing the English aside, and they give way little by little. Here comes the first Plantagenet.

2. THE PLANTAGENETS.

But it was still the Normans under another name. When Henry II. has reigned twelve years, the Norman century is complete, and so is the Transition Period. Its landmark is found in the date of the "Constitutions of Clarendon"; not their acceptance in A. D. 1163, but their arrogant rejection in behalf of the Papacy two years later. Let us see how things stand, just here.

The moment of Henry's accession is marked by an event till then without example, and never duplicated since. An Englishman is made Pope, — Nicholas Breakspear his honest Saxon name, but he is known as Adrian IV. Such an event was enough to turn the head of every ambitious priest in England. What might not happen next? The son of a London merchant, who had mingled his blood with that of a Saracen wife in the veins of his boy, proved just the character to be fired by such an event. The lad was sent to Italy for his education, where he had for his tutor that Gratian who compounded the Decretals with the Canon Law. This remarkable youth had become the Primate of all England when he subscribed the Constitutions; but in two years he not only recanted, but excom-

[1] *Supra*, page 208.

municated everybody that maintained them. But England did not recant. The Constitutions were destined to grow with her growth, and strengthen with her strength. There was in them a principle of life; they proved that native liberties died hard, — nay, were not doomed to die. The Constitutions were not pillars of the Church, but they were buttresses, and shored up her holy walls from outside. In the conflicts that followed, we cannot wholly sympathize with either party. Henry had prescribed the Constitutions, because they strengthened his powers to control the Church, under colour of the old Anglo-Saxon constitutions. Becket resisted his encroachments on the Anglican liberties; and so far, so good. But he did so to transfer us, hand and foot, to the Papacy, which was now a Paparchy also, wherever the new Canon Law was received. Such was the crisis, and thus the Constitutions of Clarendon become a landmark of vast significance. Feeble in themselves, they yet embodied the free principles of Frankfort and of Alcuin, capable though they were of abuse under a bad king. Enough, Becket detested them. With papal approval, he mounted the pulpit on Whit-Sunday at Vezelay, in France, and with dramatic pomp pronounced his anathemas. He read the Constitutions, and excommunicated the King's ministry who had framed them. The bells were rung backward, crosses turned upside down, and torches extinguished. King Henry was called upon to repent, or to expect a like anathema upon his own head.

3. THE SUBMISSION.

The Hildebrandine policy had triumphed, and the Anglican Church was under the Paparchy. No need to follow out the tragedy of the personal conflict between prince and primate. Every schoolboy knows how Henry at last compassed the murder of Becket, and with what heroic fortitude he fell. Our pictured primers of history made even childhood familiar with the penitent Henry, prostrate at Becket's tomb, and flogged on his bare back by grinning monks and acolytes. No doubt he deserved it, and possibly kings were not made any worse by finding that there was a power on earth that could "lay their honour in the dust." Hence the fallacy that enables a certain class of writers to eulogize the Popes. They miss the point. The horse, to be revenged on the stag, in Æsop, was delighted to call in a man and to submit to the saddle, while the man punished his enemy. This done, the horse was greatly obliged to his rider, and wished him farewell. But no, he was saddled for life, and stalled besides, a slave to his deliverer. So, at this period, whoever called in the Pope to punish a tyrant soon found that he had a rider on his back whose little finger was heavier than a prince's loins.

Before this long reign came to a close, one incident is a token of vitality. The primate Baldwin was arrogantly overruled by the pontiff, so sudden was his assumption of power over the metropolitan. The good primate took no notice of the aggression, but legates were sent from Rome with mandates, inhibitions, and excommunications. The parochial clergy rose to uphold their primate, and fearlessly proclaimed to their flocks that such a sentence from foreign parts had no force in England. Yet the yoke of the Decretals was upon her. Not by any action of hers, not by any definition of pontifical powers or rights, but passively, she became as the strong ass of Issachar, " couching down between two burdens,"— the burden of the Norman invaders and the far heavier pack of the papal usurpation.

4. TWO FORCES.

Henceforth we have two organized forces in conflict, more or less, without rest, for four centuries. I cannot affect neutrality in such a quarrel. When, in all the light of what followed, I find the foreign usurpation uniformly labouring to destroy the Nicene Constitutions, the ancient liberties of the Anglican Church, the purity of the Holy Gospels, and the dearest rights of humanity in the household and in the state, I take my stand without a doubt as to the right. These conflicts are my conflicts. My forefathers fought them out in my behalf. In the long struggles of the Anglican Church I read the history of our own Church, and my spiritual and intellectual origin. I am identified with past generations, and with all who frame their thought. Here are my own antecedents. If I had lived in those times, I should have been involved in all the difficulties of my sires. I should have shared their ignorance, their honest credulity, their enslavement to the Decretals, their gross superstitions. How should I have acted? Where should I have been found? Thanks to God, I lived not then.

5. THREE CLASSES INVOLVED.

Here comes in room for humility, charity, and large consideration. I see three classes of characters: (1) honest, faithful men, no wiser than their age, doing their best in the gross darkness, and feeling after light; (2) men, apparently bad, and working for worldly ends to make night darker and bad worse; and (3) elect spirits, called of God to be witnesses for Him, according to their ability, and to work out deliverance for his people. Here, then, I must "judge righteous judgment," or "judge nothing before the time." I must hesitate to condemn my brother man; but I must not restrain my sympathy with all that has contributed to my precious inheritance of light and freedom, and all spiritual riches in Christ and His Gospel. I hate lies; I hate power based upon imposture; I hate the corrosions and corruptions which divested the Latin churches of their Nicene character and their ancient liberties. This is the spirit which inspires me to speak, and in sympathy with which I ask you to trace the Anglican Restoration to its sources, and to follow me thence till it is crowned, by the marked providence of God, not merely with success, but with such developments of strength and of fruitfulness as have made our restored estate a blessing to mankind.

6. INNOCENT III.

After the Lion-hearted Richard comes the great crisis of the West. Lothaire had just mounted the papal throne as Innocent III. By him what Nicholas created and Hildebrand's credulity developed with logical force into Titanic proportions was rendered yet more practical, and was augmented by theological decrees more corrosive than had yet been imagined. Provincial canons were elevated into dogmas of the faith; subtleties of Aristotle, coloured by Averroes, were made the base of his new theology. Even Gregory VII. had not accepted transubstantiation, but now it was to be identified with worship and enforced as doctrine. Worse than all as an instrument of papal despotism came the torture of confession, no longer voluntary, but bound upon conscience by penalties of excommunication and the refusal of Christian burial. The "ear of Dionysius" was appropriated by a Christian pontiff, and he proclaimed it to be the ear of Him "to whom all hearts are open, and from whom no secrets are hid." Kings and queens, princes and peasants, must obey. Every soul in Western Christendom was now brought into personal relations with the power to which the Decretals had led them to believe all power was given. The keys of life and death, of heaven and hell, were in his hand; he could dispense the divine rewards and chastisements with arbitrary sovereignty. Western Europe was thus reduced to one great parish, in which he alone was rector; all bishops and priests were but his curates; he was universal bishop and lord paramount over the souls and bodies of men. To fulminate cruel excommunications and to lay national churches under interdict was his pastime. He assumed all the responsibility for devastating whole races when he turned the crusades against Christians, and devoured by fire and sword the unhappy Vaudois and Albigenses.[1] Under an imbecile and unprincipled king, England was now to share in the blessings of such "another gospel."

7. THE EBB OF THE NORMANS.

But one happy event gave things a better cast for the future. Normandy fell to the French kings; troops of Normans went to look after their estates and this foreign influence began to wane. I remember well when Hanover, by the operation of the Salic law, fell away from the English sovereign by the death of William the Fourth. The crown of Hanover was borne in pomp at his funeral, and then the wicked Duke of Cumberland carried it with him to his petty dominion. It was the symbol of departing Hanoverianism, that nightmare of our Church. When Charles I. packed off "his Mounseers," — the French priests who had tormented his life by meddling with everything in his house, from the scullery to his queen's bed-chamber, — he closed his despatch with the words, "And so the Devil go with them." I cannot adopt such language in the imperative mood; but indicatively, I think much evil went with the Normans, though, as they left

[1] See Note V".

King John, there was sure to be no particular need of any other personal attention to mischief-making. By strong reaction, the Anglican spirit revived; and what Shakespeare puts into the mouth of the King to illustrate his lucid intervals, began to be indeed the rising spirit of the Church and people. To the papal legate, he is made to say: —

> " Thou canst not, Cardinal, devise a name
> So slight, unworthy, and ridiculous
> To charge me to an answer, as the Pope.
> Tell him this tale; and from the mouth of England
> Add thus much more, — that no Italian priest
> Shall tithe or toll in our dominions. . . .
> Though you and all the kings of Christendom
> Are led so grossly by this meddling priest,
> Dreading the curse that money may buy out,
> And by the merit of vile gold, dross, dust, . . .
> Purchase corrupted pardon of a man,
> Who in that sale sells pardon from himself,
> Yet I alone, alone do me oppose
> Against the Pope, and count his friends my foes."

Shakespeare makes no mistake in putting this ambiguously into the mouth of "England," at the crisis which, in spite of the Pope and the King together, gave us the *Magna Charta.*

8. ARCHBISHOP LANGTON.

The best thing Innocent ever did was done by mistake; for he made Stephen Langton Archbishop of Canterbury. To do this he set aside all laws, human and divine, annulling the King's appointment and the election at Canterbury; so that this best gift to the Church of England came by one of his worst acts of iniquity. He had known Lang-

ton in Paris, where they were youths together, and
hoped his old friend would prove the tool of his
further aggressions. In this, happily, he was mistaken.
However, for a time the mischief makes
head. John would not accept Langton, and the
whole kingdom wakes up to a sense of its enslavement,
when it finds itself subjected to a papal interdict.
"As for sermons," says the witty Fuller,
"laziness and ignorance had long before interdicted
them; but now no prayers, no mass, no singing of
service." Millions of simple souls were thus made
to suffer loss of all the means of grace; no church
bells rung, church doors were shut: no sacraments
could be ministered save in special cases to
the dying; none could be married; none could
have Christian burial. Corpses were thrown into
ditches without prayers, nor could Langton's intercession
for his people prevail with the pontiff to
have service once a week in parish churches. Even
"the tender mercies of the wicked are cruel," but
here was the sole shepherd of Christ's sheep on
earth far more cruel than they. The King had
offended him: he takes from a whole unoffending
people the means of salvation. For a whole year
this reign of terror went on. The English nation,
panic-stricken, began to feel where they were, and
"from what height fallen." But Innocent had
lately excommunicated the Roman Emperor, and
now he absolved all subjects from allegiance to
King John, excommunicated him by name, and
gave to any invader, with absolution from all his
sins, a license to conquer England and make it a
dependency of some foreign crown. Five years

such a state of things continued, when the scenes so wonderfully dramatized by Shakespeare became history. He had received his crown on the Feast of the Ascension; and now a hermit of Yorkshire broached the terrible prophecy,

> ". . . in rude harsh-sounding rhymes,
> That, ere the next Ascension day at noon,
> His highness should deliver up his crown."

9. ENGLAND A FIEF OF ROME.

Anselm had opened the door to the next step, and Pandulph appears on the scene, — an Italian legate, as the consequence of an English one. On Ascension day, King John on his knees resigns his crown into the hands of the legate, "granting to God and the Church of Rome, the Apostles Peter and Paul, and to Pope Innocent III. and his successors, the whole kingdom of England and Ireland." For five whole days Innocent was sole king of England, Pandulph holding the crown for him. Then, in consideration of immense promises of tribute, John received it back, to be held by him, but only as the Pope's vassal. This was enough. The spirit of the early English revived. The barons demanded of John a restoration of Edward the Confessor's laws, and the liberties of Church and State which he had sworn to observe. But when he had promised to do better, he refused of course to keep his promise. This just suited Innocent, and so the Pope took his vassal under his protection, and sent another legate, who with bell, book, and candle excommunicated the nobility not only, but the primate himself. He was with them, and in fact at their head. The interdict had been removed; but curses and excommunications were the blessings which Rome still showered on the land.

10. MAGNA CHARTA.

It is amid these scenes, and under the worst of princes and the most cruel of popes, that liberty begins to reappear. Stephen Langton drafts *Magna Charta*, and its first sentence reads thus: "The Church of England shall be free." Mark that, — "the Church of England," her identity not forfeited. Her ancient liberties are reaffirmed, and, with other immortal principles of right, the primate and the barons, at Runnymede, in sight of Windsor Castle, force the wretched King to accept and confirm them. Of course he complies, and of course he retracts. The Pope sustains his vassal, and annuls the Great Charter. Just so; but, all the more, it lives; it grows and strengthens; it makes *terra firma* for the English Constitution to this day; the eventual rejection of the Paparchy is involved in it, and we in America, under the common law and our own constitutions, are the inheritors of its blessings.

11. HENRY THE THIRD.

Henry III. accepted his crown under conditions made by John, somewhat modified indeed, but with promise of tribute. But he afterwards confirmed *Magna Charta*, and Stephen Langton made him keep his promise for a time. He tries to evade his pledges, but over and over again he is brought to book. He invites a legate into England to "reform the Church"; that is, to make it more subservient to the pontiffs. Groans and grumblings are heard, and the legate withdraws. From this reign we receive that sturdy expression of attachment to "the common law," as we now call it, *Nolumus leges Angliæ mutari.* So spoke our forefathers to King and Pope alike. Even Henry remonstrates against papal exactions; but when the threats of the pontiff extort eleven thousand marks from the clergy, his avarice is satisfied for a season. Langton dies, but the great Bishop Grossetête survives to perpetuate his spirit. He exposes the fact, that foreign priests sent into English benefices by the Pope gorge themselves with church revenues more than three times as great as those of the Crown.

The Plantagenets produced two or three of the worst kings that England ever knew; but the others were all great in their several ways, and the dynasty, as such, has bequeathed inestimable blessings to our race. Under the feeble kings, the people grew strong; the nobler Plantagenets, for one reason or another, worked with the people in a long, determined resistance to the Paparchy. Thus, with momentary intermissions, was kept alive a continuous assertion of the ancient liberties, summed up in the first sentence of the charter,— "*Ecclesia Anglicana libera sit.*"

12. TWO EDWARDS.

In Edward the First we come back to the name of the Confessor, so dear to Anglo-Saxons, as one of themselves. And Edward himself, with all his Angevine faults, reflects in some particulars the spirit of his people. He is inclined to be more than half an Englishman. In subduing Wales and humbling Scotland, he is not merely wielding the hammer of the despotic aggressor, but is making England out of Saxons and Britons, welding all into unity, and, as the remote effect, creating Great Britain. In his day the Paparchy passes into the "privy paw" of Boniface VIII., who "came in like a fox, ruled like a lion, and died like a dog." His was the memorable bull *Unam Sanctam*, which defined as "necessary to salvation that every human soul should be subject to the Pope of Rome," — of which more by and by. He was hateful to the French king, whose creature, Clement V., consigned his memory to infamy, and strove to abolish his very name. The Lord took the affair into his own hand, and thereafter the power of the pontiffs began to decline. Boniface had found Edward too stout for him even in his pitch of pride. When he claimed Scotland as his own fief, and ordered Edward to sink his claims and withdraw his troops, the heroic sovereign disdained his pretensions. More than that, Edward's Statute of *Mortmain*, limiting the accumulation of property by the "dead-hand" of corporations, was perhaps the first practical retaliatory blow that the Paparchy felt from England. His poor son was sent to Wales to be born, and became the first Prince of Wales by this cunning stratagem: for Edward had promised the Welsh a "faultless prince, and a native of their own soil." See the portraits of father and son in the matchless "Bard" of the poet Gray, which every student of English history should learn by heart: —

> "Mark the year and mark the night
> When Severn shall re-echo with affright
> The shrieks of death, through Berkeley's roof that ring,
> Shrieks of an agonizing king."

Such the end of the second Edward's ignominy. His reign is marked, however, by the rise of a brilliant star in the horizon of darkness, for now was born John Wiclif.

13. THE THIRD EDWARD.

Of the papal usurpation says quaint old Thomas Fuller,[1] "It went forward until the Statute of Mortmain. It went backward slowly when the Statute of *Provisors* was made under Edward III.; swiftly when his Statute of *Præmunire* was made. It fell down when the Papacy was abolished, in the reign of Henry VIII." Thus he refers to the times of the third Edward two of the great moves which were fatal to the Paparchy. The stout Tudor could have done nothing without them: so that the Reformation did not actually begin when he fell in love with Anne Boleyn.[2]

---

[1] Quoting, "Habent imperia suos terminos, huc cum venerint, sistunt, retrocedunt, ruunt." — Vol. ii. p. 296.
[2] See Note W".

Grossetête — but as the Normans have gone home, we will now talk English, and call him by his honest Saxon name of Greathead — was a century before his time when he exposed the enormous abuse of Papal "Provisions." By this artifice, the Pope provided for his favourites, Italians or Frenchmen, and named them for bishoprics and the like before they fell vacant. As soon as the incumbent died, in marched the intruder and claimed the place for its revenues, neglecting souls and corrupting the clergy by bad example. Greathead protested, and strove to reassert Anglican principles of autonomy. He thus maintained the principle, and what could not be done then was practicable now. To the blow against Mortmain came next the staunch Anglo-Saxon thrust at the foreign usurper, called the "Statute of Provisors." Three years later came the *Præmunire*, forbidding appeals to Rome under heavy penalties. In temporalities, the Reformation was begun already. From an eminent English jurist [1] I quote as follows: —

"The nation entertained violent antipathies against the papal power. The Parliament pretended that the usurpations of the Pope were the causes of all the plagues, injuries, famine, and poverty of the realm, were more destructive to it than all the wars, and were the reason why it contained not a third of the inhabitants and commodities which it formerly possessed; that the taxes levied by him exceeded five times those which were paid to the King; that everything was venal in that sinful city of Rome. . . . The King was even petitioned by Parliament to

[1] Stevens, editor of De Lolme.

employ no churchman (i. e. no ecclesiastic) in any office of state, and they threatened to repel by force the papal authority, which they could not, nor would, any longer endure."

The clergy had been largely involved in the papal invasions, and under kings who favoured them often sided with the pontiffs. So it had been under the former Edwards. Just now the commons were incensed against the Pope, and the King courted his favour to balance himself against the rising spirit of popular independence. We must note all these things if we would understand how thoroughly the progress of Reformation in England was original with England; how it began and was making headway nearly two centuries before Martin Luther was heard of. In temporals, as I said, the work was begun already. Now let us observe its spiritual history.

14. SPIRITUAL PROGRESS.

I have called Alcuin the last of the Fathers, and Anselm the forerunner of the Schoolmen. I have traced Scholasticism to Abelard and Arnold of Brescia, and another side of it to Peter Lombard. I know too little about him to speak of Erigena, whom Alfred invited into England so long before their day; and I am equally unable to express an opinion of Albertus Magnus, to whom some assign the chief glory after them. This premised, I must add, that, for its good and for its evil, England must bear the palm and share the blame. "In England and by Englishmen," says an old

Latin writer,[1] "the scholastic theology had its origin, made its progress, and reached its zenith." Alexander Hales (A. D. 1244) writes his "Body of School Divinity" at the command of Innocent IV. Aquinas and Bonaventure were his disciples. To him succeeds the illustrious Roger Bacon, philosopher, naturalist, and divine, whose foresight of chemistry and other sciences made him a magician in the eyes of his fellow Franciscans. The Pope shut him up in prison. John Duns Scotus comes next: truly an imperial genius, belied by his name in two ways, for Scotus means an Irishman, and *Duns* means that he was no *dunce*. He was born at a place so called, and his great wisdom and learning led men to call a fool ironically a "Duns," — that is to say, a Duns in his own conceit. The Thomists and the Scotists became two schools after his day. Baconthorpe is to be noted (A. D. 1346), because he maintained at Rome, in spite of derision and insult, the great principle that was long after to reach its practical application in England,[2] that "the Pope has no right to give dispensations for marriages unlawful in Scripture." Here rises up the bold figure of William Occam,[3] who defended the Emperor against the Pope, saying, " Protect me with thy sword, and I will defend thee with my words." All that was needed by the Crown of England to protect itself two centuries later, when the Paparchy was expelled, is laid down by this great divine. The armory of the Anglican Restoration was be-

---

[1] Alex. Minutianus. See Fuller, ii. 250.
[2] See Note X". [3] A. D. 1327.

coming formidable to Rome already. But, last of all, let me name the holy Bradwardine, Archbishop of Canterbury, in whom Alcuin seems to revive, and Bede the Venerable as well. If Pelagius was of British origin, now in this great man ample amends were made by the later Church of Britain; for he not only maintained the doctrines of grace against the Semi-Pelagianism that Rome has more recently made into dogma, but his life was an illustration of divine grace from first to last. He was the mediæval glory of the Anglican primacy, and was called the *Doctor Profundus*, from his great learning and deep thinking. Chaucer, forty years later, ranks him with Boethius and with St. Augustine.

15. OXFORD MEN.

All these were Oxford men, and all of that old Merton College which every visitor beholds with reverence as he walks in Christ-Church meadows. But it is important to note how boldly and freely they disputed on points which Rome itself had not yet presumed to crystallize into her enormous "Code of Belief," the product of her Trent Council. Thus Scotus founded the Realist, and Occam the Nominalist school; both were Franciscans. But after the great Dominican, Aquinas, who was a liberal Realist, we ordinarily find the Dominicans of that persuasion. I only note, in passing, how the position which Alcuin gave to the Anglican Church was maintained by great Anglicans even in these ages. Note also how strongly the influence of English Schoolmen was exerted for a better future. Occam seems to have foreseen it; he says of his works, "By means of our preludes men of future times, zealous for truth, righteousness, and the common weal, may have their attention drawn to many truths upon these matters, which, at the present day, remain hidden from rulers, councillors, and teachers, to the common loss."

16. GREATHEAD.

Observe the continuity of spiritual and truly Anglican life in the Church of England. In such an age as that of Henry III. and Innocent IV., see Greathead contending alike against prince and pontiff, not as a proud ecclesiastic like Becket, but as a spiritually-minded lover of souls, and of Christ, their Saviour. He might even better have been named Greatheart. Poet, man of letters, intrepid pastor, and defender of the faith,—conceding a Gallican primacy, but resisting pontifical supremacy,—he is the very ideal of a Catholic, as far as in his day it was possible to be. Books were rare; learning was fettered; the canon law was based on fables which none could confute. But there he stood, a figure monumental. Bulls from Rome fell harmless at his feet. The University of Oxford bore witness concerning him, after he began to be called St. Robert: "Never for the fear of any man had he forborne to do any good action which pertained to his office and duty. If the sword had been unsheathed against him, he stood prepared to die the death of a martyr." To such a man, standing up for truth and right while pontiffs were "making havoc of the Church," and while kings were surrendering England in vassalage to their remorseless grip, how much we owe under God. Truly, what the Lord said of old of "Jonadab the son of Rechab," he seems to have said for the Church of England: "She shall not want a man to stand before me forever."

17. WICLIF.

We come to Wiclif. He was the first mover for Restoration in England, who, as Occam had prophesied, saw something of the length and breadth of its meaning. To him we owe it, under God, that the Anglican Church took care of herself, as a continuous church, in continuous reforms, and made no sudden break even with Rome. To him, the Continent owes its "Reformation," so called; for it began with his pupils, and was only directed into the ditch of divisions and of failure by the perverted genius of its great but wrangling doctors. Of this by and by; but I wish you to observe that nothing can be more the reverse of truth than to begin the Reformation with Luther, and to import it into England, as if England borrowed her work from his, or modelled it after any man's ideas, or after any other standard than "Holy Scripture and ancient authors."

18. THE ENGLISH LANGUAGE.

Now (A. D. 1362) the Norman-French ceases in the law courts. Two of the greatest men of genius that England ever knew took up the English in its elements just here, and made it into language. Chaucer created its poetry, and Wiclif its prose. Well has it been noted that in its very origin it was devoted to the Restoration, and identified with its spirit. Chaucer in the court, Wiclif in the university, and honest Piers Plowman from among the people, consecrated its earliest syllables to the revival of the Anglo-Saxon Church; and when Wiclif had given to our race the first English Bible, he had laid the corner-stone of all that has since given us the lead in Christendom. Blessed be God for this baptism of the English tongue. From its beginnings it is wedded to Truth; and it remains, of all the languages on earth, the hardest to yoke with the tug-team of Falsehood, the most incapable of being forged to falsehood or welded with a lasting lie.

19. THE POPES OF AVIGNON.

Go back to Boniface VIII., and his decree that "it is necessary to every human soul to be in communion with the Bishop of Rome." This discovery was not made dogmatic by Rome itself till he formulated it,[1] and immediately the bolt fell. God reduced it to the absurd instantly, by making it for nearly a century impossible for anybody to know who or where the Bishop of Rome might be. He raised up Philip the Fair, king of France, to force the Popes out of Rome into his kingdom. Philip burned one of the bulls of Boniface, refused to recognize him as Pope, and influenced Benedict,

[1] A. D. 1294.

his successor, to reverse many of his decisions. It is hard, therefore, to see how this can be reconciled with any belief in the infallibility of either pope. For nearly seventy years we have rival popes, one at Rome and another at Avignon, and nobody knows, to this day, which was the true pope and which the pretender. The captivity of Avignon ended in A.D. 1377. But things grew worse again instantly; for now intervenes what is called the "Great Schism" of the Papacy, extending from Urban VI., A.D. 1378, to Nicholas V., A.D. 1447. An assortment of popes and antipopes thus divide the allegiance of the Western churches for one hundred and fifty years well-nigh. When poor Joan of Arc was asked, as a test of her orthodoxy and her inspiration, to say which was the true pope, "What!" she answered, " is there more than one?" The innocent peasant heroine did not even know her peril. According to Boniface and Pius IX., the millions who knew not where to find the infallible judge of controversies, and made mistakes in all that period, are inevitably damned. But what is a "judge of controversies" worth, when, in a controversy so vital to human souls, nobody knows where to find him? In view of this dilemma, John Wiclif made up his mind that it was not the will of Christ that "every soul should be in communion with the Bishop of Rome."

20. WICLIF'S ANTECEDENTS.

Reflect who and what this heroic spirit was. The successor of the Schoolmen in Merton Col-

lege, and the glory of the University, he knew all
the scholastics could teach him, and much more
besides. He was a natural philosopher and a canonist. Few knew any Greek till the next century,
but he was an expert in the Latin Fathers. In A.D.
1374 he is a doctor of theology, and about fifty
years of age. He had been already honoured in
the University in other ways. It seems probable
he had been a member of Parliament, and sustained
the remonstrances of the barons and others against
the Papacy. As an ardent patriot, he resisted the
papal nuncio in A.D. 1372, when he came to bleed
the land and the Church of England for his master.
In 1374 he is sent on a diplomatic embassy to
Bruges, with Sudbury, Bishop of London, and
with —

"Old John of Gaunt, time-honoured Lancaster."

Thus Wiclif became a personal friend of a prince
of the blood, and found him a useful protector.

21. THE GOOD PARLIAMENT.

In the King's jubilee year (A.D. 1376), met "the
Good Parliament." Just four hundred years later,
Washington founded a nation; but we may be
sure no such character as Washington could have
sprung up, worthy of Alfred and carrying out his
institutions in a new world, had there not been a
John Wiclif to make the Parliament "Good" by
his genius and by his personal presence. At this
moment he was the pride of his countrymen and
in the zenith of his influence. He soon made enemies, because he undertook the great work for

which God had raised him up. Less popular he became, no doubt; but vastly more mighty with his age, and useful to his country not only, but to the human race.

22. THE FIRST CITATION.

Wiclif was made rector of Lutterworth by gift of the King in A.D. 1374. When the Parliament of A.D. 1377 was opened, we find him summoned before Courtenay, Bishop of London, at St. Paul's. Accordingly there he stands, like another prophet, tall and spare, in a black gown and girded about his loins. Portraits represent Alcuin in just such a costume. He wears a full beard, but his fine forehead and features are enlivened by his clear and searching eye. He is supposed to have borne a staff in his hand. The Duke of Lancaster appeared with him, and certain friars who were bachelors of divinity. He was politely offered a seat, but the Bishop of London insisted that he must stand. Old John of Gaunt fired up, and had so sharp a quarrel with Courtenay that the session was adjourned before Wiclif had uttered a word. The Lord stood by him and comforted him, no doubt; but he could only look on in mute astonishment, equally ashamed of his bishop and of his fiery protector, who had not done him any good.

23. THE SECOND CITATION.

Wiclif was sustained by his University, when Sudbury, his old colleague at Bruges, now Archbishop of Canterbury, was called upon by the Pope to proceed against him. Bulls came thick and fast from Gregory XI., complaining that the Anglican bishops were lukewarm. The Pope complained of Wiclif and the evils of his teaching, and added: "So far as we know, not a single effort has been made to extirpate them. . . . You English prelates, who ought to be defenders of the faith, have winked at them." He was equally polite in his complaint to the University, and he invoked the King to bestir himself. The Mendicants had drawn up nineteen propositions from his voluminous writings, which they made "exceeding sinful," by their way of putting it. Long afterward the Jesuits made out one hundred and one heretical propositions from the harmless pages of the pious Jansenists; and just so any malignant spirit could extract from Massillon himself nineteen propositions to prove that he was the author of the French Revolution. Here let me say, once for all, that Wiclif was as little responsible for the Lollards as Massillon[1] is for the Jacobins. Their founder, Peter Lolhard, suffered death at Cologne two years before Wiclif was born. It would be nearly as just to attribute the Chartists of 1848 to the influence of Canon Kingsley.

24. LAMBETH.

The University resisted the bulls, and complained of their violation of the constitution. When Sudbury mildly replied, that he refused to lay violent hands on their doctor, and merely proposed to institute an inquiry, they acquiesced, and consented

[1] See Note Y".

to co-operate. The offender, though not as a prisoner, was cited before the primate at Lambeth. He obeyed, and one can see him as he stands in that venerable chapel, where our first American bishops knelt to be consecrated four hundred years later. Well do I know the spot, for I was lodged within a few feet of it at the last Lambeth conference, and daily went in and out to worship there. This solemn history (and oh how much beside!) often rose before me in the dead of night, as I lay awake in what is called "the Lollard's Tower." All London was on his side, and anon the crowd clamoured about the doors, when, to the unspeakable relief of Sudbury, came a rescript from the Queen Mother, the widow of the idolized Black Prince, for a stay of proceedings. The primate, with a gentle admonition advising him not to do so again, allowed the doctor to go back to Lutterworth. He is said to have helped this result by modifying some of his expressions. This may have been a mere modifying of what the friars had charged. If he did more, it only proves what I have often insisted upon in behalf of the other party, and what may be urged in behalf of the good Sudbury himself, and of all earnest writers, in times of great movements, viz.: They hardly know where they stand themselves, between practical duty and theoretical views of truth.

25. THE FRIARS.

When the great endowed orders became grossly corrupted, the Friars originated, with the good purpose of imitating the poverty of Christ and reviving religion among the people. Great was the good they seemed to do, when first they came into England. The Popes, who had no taste for poverty, or for primitive preaching, became their enemies, and the pious Bradwardine had to defend them. He bears his unanswerable testimony to their zeal and fidelity to the souls of the masses. The parochial clergy had neglected their duty, and every Franciscan was a sort of Wesley, doing what others had failed to do. But this soon passed away. The friars came into England exempted from all control of its bishops, and able to defy the parish priests. The new system of confessions threw immense gain into their hands. Even great men were glad to confess to strolling mendicants, who passed by and could not daily stare them in the face. Hence the intense hatred between the friars and the rectors, whose canonical functions they usurped. In the end, the Popes used the friars for their own purposes, and the rectors became more decidedly anti-papal. Chaucer takes their part you remember. His portrait of the " Pardoner" is one of the most remarkable word-pictures in all poesy. His hair, yellow and hanging smooth like "a strike of flax," overspreading his shoulders; his voice small as any goat's; no beard; his wallet brim-full of pardons, "from Rome all hot." He had a bit of Our Lady's veil, and a rag of the sail of St. Peter's boat, —

> "And in a glass he had a pigges bones.
> And with these reliques, when that he fand
> A poor person dwelling upon land,

He gat him more money in a day
Than that the parson got in months twaie.
Well could he read a lesson or a story,
But all the best he sang an offertory,
To win silver, as right well he could."

When you visit England, look at the gurgoyles and crockets on the walls and towers of the old churches. If it is a parish church, you will see, perhaps, a friar caricatured in stone as a "wolf in sheep's clothing"; if it is an old chapel of the Minorites, you will find the compliment returned by a grotesque carving of a rector, with ears of an ass, pretending to preach, while he can only bray.

26. WICLIF'S DEATH AND CHARACTER.

Wiclif has been charged with beginning his reforms by attacking the friars. The reverse is the case, and we can only account for it because, as identified with the parochial clergy, or meaning to be so, he was wise enough not to take up a quarrel which had become so degraded. Nevertheless, as time went on, he was forced to expose the Mendicants, and they were his envenomed assailants. A third time Wiclif was cited before his superiors to answer for himself, and on this occasion at the Chapel of the Black Friars, which has been gratuitously imagined a special token that his judges took their part. Again, however, our hero was preserved from harm; again he took his staff and trudged back to Lutterworth, to go on with his translation of the Scriptures. This great work appeared in 1382. In 1384, as he was devoutly worshipping in his parish church, on Innocents' day, and just as the consecrated host was elevated, he fell in a paralysis. On the last day of that year his spirit returned to God who gave it.

Let the great poet, who knew him well, bear his testimony to so great a benefactor of mankind, in his inimitable portrait of a good priest, in the days of Edward III. and Richard, the last Plantagenet. I must slightly modernize it to make it intelligible.

> "A good man was ther of religioun,
> And was a poor Parson of a town,
> But riche he was of holy thought and werk;
> He also was a learned man, a clerk
> That Christ his gospel gladly would he preach;
> His parishens devoutly would he teach.
> Benign he was and wondrous diligent,
> And in adversity full patient.
> He could in little thing have suffisance."

In short, he gave of that little to the poor, he visited his people through sleet and storm; in sickness hasted to the farthest habitation; early and late upon his feet, staff in hand, he showed by his conduct how sheep should live, and it was his saying, "If gold rust, what will iron do? If the shepherd be foul, how shall the sheep be clean?" "A better priest there is none anywhere."

> "Thus Christ his lore, and his apostles twelve,
> He taught, — and first he followed it himself."

Chaucer knew the man, and draws him to the life; but one loves to believe that thus, in the darkest period of our dear mother Church, there were not a few good shepherds of the flock of Christ. It is also a tribute to others of the parochial clergy of the time.

27. AN ESTIMATE OF WICLIF'S WORK.

In estimating this great doctor's work, let us first observe what he did not do. He raised no sect; he set up no school; he obeyed his bishop's citations; he turned his court influence into no private source of profit; he lived and died the faithful parish priest. Nay, he departed not from the law as it then stood in England, and, while he denied the corporal presence,—I might say *because* he had so modified its significance,— carried out conformity to the letter of the law in the ceremony of uplifting the Eucharistic Body and Blood. In all this, his testimony to restoration, not reconstruction, as his principle, is invaluable. He was no hot-headed iconoclast; he was doing God's work, as God gave him light, and he waited God's guidance as to what next. So by slow degrees, patiently, and as by one who cleanses a golden vase that has been defiled and bruised and daubed with vulgar colours, the Anglican Restoration went on from strength to strength.

28. MISTAKES.

Next, as to his mistakes and errors. I grant he made many, as who does not? How could it have been otherwise, emerging from such darkness, stunned by many voices, confused by the quarrels and divisions of Schoolmen, without any help such as our day affords, and in the very nature of his task forced to review his impressions, revise his work, and to change, from time to time, his original conclusions? Let us reflect on the divisions of theologians at Constance and Basle, and, above all, at Trent, when books had been already multiplied by the press. Nay, go back to Augustine himself, to Jerome, to Tertullian, to Origen. Who shall cast the first stone? Who is perfect? Was not St. Peter himself withstood by St. Paul, "because he was to be blamed"? How could so immensely voluminous a writer, whose works came forth during a long life and in a period of transition of unexampled agitations, — how could he fail to have written many things which he himself, at the end of life, could not approve? Two things let us note: (1) some of his worst mistakes came from St. Jerome, St. Augustine, and from Aquinas himself; and (2) among his contemporaries who was so free as Wiclif from all that runs counter to the rule of Vincent and the Holy Scriptures? He no doubt regarded the Episcopate as an ecclesiastical rather than an apostolic institution. So taught the Schoolmen, to depress the bishops and exalt the Popes. Calvin himself learned Presbyterianism from Aquinas; for, stern logician that he was, he inferred that, if bishops were only the Pope's vicars, and not Christ's, they must go with the Pope. When he taught that presbyters are the highest order of divine appointment, that is just what Rome taught him. Afterwards she made this into a dogma at the Council of Trent, and in her Catechism she teaches Presbyterianism at this day.[1]

[1] Part. II. cap. vii. qu. 22.

29. THE GOOD THINGS.

But the great question remains, What is the positive good which we trace to him? I go back to the negatives first cited, and claim them all as an example of moderation, and humility, and godly patience, which furnish an example to all reformers, and which convict those of the Continent, whose course was widely different, of great responsibilities for the failure that ensued. He was a man of genius, as really so as Calvin or Luther; but he raised no sect, he made no Wiclifites. We owe it largely to him that the Anglican Church follows no human lawgiver, is tied to no Schoolman, and has no "Code of Belief."[1] Enough that, with long and patient hopes of a reformed Papacy, he at last was led to the just conclusions which the Church of England reached more slowly, as to its unscriptural and uncatholic character. When to all this, without dwelling on his share in creating our language, one adds his thorough awakening of English consciences, and the stimulus he gave to intellect at such a period, it is enough to demand our homage. But far more is his due. His grand work was the translating of the Bible. Before the art of printing had multiplied books and made such work easy, he gave the Scriptures to every English Christian as his birthright. But hardly second to this was his resting the work of restoration, not on any scholastic system, but on the Holy Scriptures. He stood on the rule of Vincent, in point of fact,

[1] See Note Z".

and he made it, as I shall yet show, the radical and glorious criterion of the Anglican Restoration, when compared with the Reformation on the Continent.

30. A PERIOD OF DELAYS.

Behold the wisdom of Providence in arresting the work just there, till the revival of learning and the deeper convictions of pious men were better prepared for its completion. Now came the Wars of the Roses, so terrible, but so necessary to what was for the common weal. Under the house of Lancaster — usurpers who strove to propitiate the pontiffs — came the infamous statute for burning heretics. It was overruled to make the Paparchy more detestable than ever. Then the clash of arms:

> " Long years of havoc urge their destined course,
> And through the kindred squadrons mow their way."

Yet these were the years when men had time to reflect as well as to fight, and to ask what they were contending for. Dean Hook observes sagaciously of Richard III., that " he had not observed the signs of the times, nor perceived how the spirit of the age was changed. Christianity even in its corruption had been silently doing its work. War was no longer regarded as the only honourable employment, and the hearts of men were softened." Womanhood, too, as he observes, was assuming a new place in society. In short, the Holy Scriptures had begun to be read and loved.

31. OUR GREAT BENEFACTORS.

According to the ennobling principles I am now illustrating, we should be just as truly in sympathy with the Anglican Church of those days as of our own times. We take our stand, it is true, with the progressive churchmen of those days, — with their patient reforms, as well as with their bolder conflicts with evil. With Wykeham, that far-seeing spirit of Edward the Third's day, we may rejoice to claim kindred. This great architect, as founder of schools and colleges, was undermining the monasteries, which had become an anachronism. To him succeed Waynflete and Fox, — the latter in a notable instance illustrating my point under the first Tudor. When he thought of founding a monastery one of his brother bishops remonstrated: "Why build and provide for housing monks, whose end and fall we may live to see? . . . Provide for the increase of learning, and for such (men) as shall do good to the Church and the commonwealth." Fox became the founder of schools accordingly, and especially of that college in Oxford which produced the very model of such men as had been described, the judicious Hooker. Of this sort were not a few when Erasmus came to Oxford to study Greek. Let me name with special reverence Dean Colet, who founded St. Paul's school in London. Surely, the better day was already begun. With the reign of Henry VII. we cannot now concern ourselves; but in him the old Britons come again to power. Gray's genius seizes on their Welsh name, and welcomes the

Tudors as the ancient race coming to their own again : —

"All hail, ye genuine kings, Britannia's issue, hail!"

God had indeed a work for them to do, worthy of Gladys and of Linus; and whether they willed it or not, he made them instruments of the greatest blessings to our race, overruling their very crimes for the good of his Church and for mankind.

32. THE EPOCH OF WOLSEY.

Where Wiclif left the spiritual work we find the whole Anglican Church ready to take it up and complete it in Queen Elizabeth's day. The first prayer-book of Edward VI. would better attest where he stood. Not till then was the Church of England reformed theologically. What happened under Henry VIII. was merely the reassertion of those temporal rights and liberties of which Rome had divested our forefathers. Certain modifications of existing practices and doctrines were indeed attempted, but they amounted to little more than Rome herself has had to tolerate ever since the Council of Trent. Henry himself never ceased to burn those whom Rome accounted heretics. His laws would have sent to the stake every Anglican bishop, priest, and deacon who accepts the Anglican prayer-book. Whatever he was, he was bred in Rome's school; his life was fashioned after that of princes most in her favour; and if he was not a better man than he should be, which of the Popes, his contemporaries, set him a better example? His character I abhor; for it reflected all that Rome had been doing for the corruption of princes for centuries. All that we have to do with him is to note that his quarrel with the Pope reversed the policy of the kings of England, who, since the Plantagenets, had favoured the Paparchy. Not one of them had possessed a strictly legitimate claim to the crown, and they needed the support of Rome to prop up their thrones. Now came one who, whatever his faults, was the most resolute and courageous prince in Christendom. It is of no consequence to our case whether he was right or wrong in his personal quarrel.[1] A conflict arose which, after years of patient waiting, enabled his people and the Church in her convocations to call upon him to "reassume" what the Plantagenets had so often asserted, what even under "the Roses" and the first Tudor the Church had not suffered to be forgotten, and what Henry now enforced by an appeal to the actual law in the old statutes of *Provisors* and *Præmunire*. By these, the legatine position of Wolsey and others was shown to have been illegal and void from the beginning; and, basely as Henry may have treated the Cardinal, whom he tempted into his false position, the crisis had come when the Church had to speak out or perish. Cruel as were the circumstances, her voice came in terrible earnest,—the old refrain, *Nolumus leges Angliæ mutari*,—We will not let our laws be changed.

[1] See *supra*, page 228, and Note X".

33. RESTORED RIGHTS.

As for Wolsey, how beautifully Shakespeare has summed up his good and bad, putting it into the mouth of such a "chronicler as Griffith"! Let us hear what a modern Roman Catholic thinks of him. Mr. Pugin says that he was "a greater instrument in producing the English schism than the arch-heretic Cranmer himself. . . . By his vexatious exercise of his legatine power, he caused the spiritual authority of the Roman pontiff to become an odious and intolerable burden; by dissolving religious houses, he paved the way for the destruction of every great religious establishment." Pugin might have added, that, by persecuting the married clergy, while he himself was raising illegitimate children, he faithfully represented the contemporary Popes, and so made even Henry look respectable. But let us note what that Bluebeard really permitted the Church to do. It is often stupidly said that Henry made himself "Head of the Church," refusing to give that dignity any longer to the Pope. The facts are, that he did nothing of the kind. He asserted the old temporal headship which Adrian had recognized in Charlemagne and the Nicene Fathers in Constantine; nothing but what Gregory the Great had recognized in the miserable Phocas; nothing but what the Popes long afterwards allowed the Gallicans to recognize in Louis XIV.; nothing but what, though just then eclipsed by legatine assumptions, had been steadily kept up and maintained down to these very times by the law of the land. Again, this head-

ship, or "supremacy," was never the Pope's, for
his supremacy had never been recognized in any
way, theologically or legally. It was still maintained that Christ was the only Supreme Head of
the Church, and nothing but temporalities admitted of any earthly supremacy. Accordingly, the
headship of Henry was limited when the whole
convocation voted as follows (*nemine contradicente*):
" Of the English Church and clergy, we recognize
his Majesty as the singular protector and only
supreme governor, and so far as the law of Christ
permits, even the supreme head." How far was
that? No further than had been conceded to Constantine as *episcopus ab extra*. The unreformed
Henry and his daughter Mary used this form;
but when we come to Elizabeth and to the theological restoration, she herself objected to its ambiguity. It then received its true interpretation in
the only form that has been lawful for three centuries: the English sovereign is simply styled
" supreme governor over all persons and in all
causes, ecclesiastical as well as civil." And this
was precisely what, during the entire Paparchy, the
English kings had always legally claimed and been
able to defend against Rome by laws of Church
and State.

34. WHO DID THIS?

And here let us recall the fact, that all this
was done by the unreformed Church of England.
Henry was himself as much a Papist as the late
Victor Emmanuel. But he and many divines had

fallen back on the old idea of a papal primacy, under the ancient canons, and were determined to restrict the Pope to what he had been before the days of Nicholas. So utterly undefined, indeed, had the *chimera* been through all the Middle Ages, that there was now room for all manner of theories as to what the Pope should be. They who restored the King's rights to govern his own kingdom without foreign meddling differed widely as to the position to which the Papacy was now replaced; but Gardyner and Bonner themselves voted for this measure. The Paparchy was at an end, but nobody yet dreamed of detachment from the Papacy. And all this was done under Archbishop Warham, who died in full communion with Rome. To quote a recent writer, himself of that communion: —

"It was done in a solemn convocation, a reverend array of bishops, abbots, and dignitaries, in orphreyed copes and jewelled mitres. Every great cathedral, every diocese, every abbey, was duly represented in that important synod. . . . One venerable prelate (Fisher) protests; his remonstrance is unsupported by his colleagues, and he is speedily brought to trial and execution. Ignorantly do we charge this on the Protestant system, which was not even broached at this time. His accusers, judges, jury, his executioner — all Catholics; the bells are ringing for mass as he ascends the scaffold."

This is all true. I venerate old Bishop Fisher, and Sir Thomas More no less.[1] They would have abhorred the late Vatican Council: they believed in a theoretical papacy, and they were never "Roman Catholics."

[1] See Note A'''.

35. ANOTHER STEP.

The second step, less noted, was a bold stand made by the convocation, under lead of the bishops, for limiting the royal power over their convocations. It ended in compromise, but was a landmark of what the Church understood as her inherent rights, and could not surrender voluntarily. So far under Warham. The next step, however, rose to the position of Frankfort and of Constance as that to which the Papacy was put back. In A. D. 1534, "the old doctrine was affirmed that a general council represented the Church, and was above the Pope and all bishops, the Bishop of Rome having had no greater jurisdiction given him by God, in the Holy Scriptures, within this realm of England, than any other foreign bishop." Cranmer was now primate, and this was progress to full Cypriote independence and to Nicene ideas of the "ancient customs" which ought to prevail. Mark also, all this was done by the Church. No act of Parliament had touched the matter. The "act of Parliament religion" was first seen under Pole and Queen Mary.

36. HOW IT LOOKED IN FRANCE.

When it pleased God to summon King Henry to his own judgment, we must observe how his case was regarded by others. In France, it must have been felt that he had simply carried out Gallican principles to an unprecedented extent; yet without any scruple, and in contempt of Rome, a mass for his pious soul was performed with all ceremony at Notre Dame, in Paris, by order of Francis the First.[1] How things stood before the later sessions of the Council of Trent, in the minds of men of the time, is evidenced by this striking fact. It had hardly opened its work of seventeen years, when Henry died.

37. THE SEQUEL.

In the reign of Edward the Sixth, the theological reformation was undertaken, and too hastily pressed forward. It pleased God to arrest it just when it might have been imperilled by influences from the Continent, and blessings came in disguise to England when the pious and princely youth passed away. It remained for the short-lived reaction under Mary to give England once more a taste of papal usurpation, and the fires of Smithfield and of Oxford burnt out of the souls of Englishmen the last traces of any lingering fealty to the Roman see. Once more a papal legate entered England, and an act of Parliament overruled the deliberate action of the Church. The legate was only a deacon,[2] yet he assumed by papal authority to grant absolution, and that not only from papal censures, but from sins! Thus, a deacon presumed to absolve a whole house of bishops and their priests! Queen Mary adopted and used her father's title of "Head of the Church." In her reign, nothing seems to have been done canonically, if we judge by ancient usages; but Pole

---

[1] See Note B'''.   [2] See Note C'''.

became Archbishop of Canterbury by the royal mandate, which was a confession of her supremacy, and that of her father, too as Catholic and lawful.

38. THE BLOODY QUEEN.

Poor Mary! She will ever be remembered as "the Bloody," yet the blood clings to the skirts of the legate rather than to hers. To him, and to her Spaniard husband, the infamous Don Philip, we must trace the martyrdoms; they reek of Alva's spirit, and of Torquemada's. Vain is the attempt to balance them by Calvin's cruelty to Servetus, — a holocaust by a kid![1] Widely different were the dynastic barbarities of Henry and Elizabeth; the sufferers under the Queen were traitors and assassins, who would have made a St. Bartholomew's massacre in England if they could. Hundreds perished in Mary's reign for offences technically political; but over and above these, hundreds of her victims were martyrs. We except the saintliest of them all, that lovely child of seventeen, the charming, the brilliant Lady Jane. Innocent and holy, she died for treason, — not hers but her father's. The martyrs were "five bishops, twenty-one divines, eight gentlemen, eighty-four skilled artisans, one hundred husbandmen, and twenty-six women." Not a Calvinist in the world but blushes when Servetus is mentioned, not a Puritan but avenges the Quakers, not an Anglican who does not abhor the cruelties of Elizabeth; but Rome glories in the rivers of blood with which she has flooded the

[1] See Note D'''.

nations. She has painted the Paris massacre at the very doors of her pontiff's private chapel as a triumph of the Church; she sung Te Deums and struck medals for the slaughter of the Huguenots. Rome never repents.

39. THE MARTYRS.

Thank God, since he willed it so, that the Anglican restorers died not in their beds, but, like Polycarp, at the stake! Five bishops sealed their witness with their blood, and breathed out their spirits confessing Truth in the flames. To them we owe, under God, all our blessings of freedom in the state, not less than in religion. We are free to breathe, and speak, and write, and cherish our homes, and worship God amid luxuries of devotion, because they counted not their lives dear to them. Not without faults and frailties; they themselves had persecuted perhaps; but in times of unparalleled trial they came to a triumphant end. When they advised others to fly for their lives, they heroically stood by the ship. I should as soon think of reproaching St. Peter for his fall, as Cranmer for his momentary fright. How memorable his confession in St. Mary's! how unflinching the hand he laid upon the flames in the High Street of Oxford! There honest Hugh Latimer, with the faithful Ridley, had lighted the candle that shall never cease to illuminate our race. How gloriously they preached Christ out of their pulpit of fagots! Those sermons were eloquent beyond rhetoric: they shall never cease to thrill the hearts of Christian men, good and true like them. Nor let poor Hooper be forgotten, — a doubting Didymus in some lesser things, but a true confessor at the last, and a hero, confessing Christ in the fire amid his agonizing and praying flock at Gloucester. Much more may we praise the intrepid Ferrar at Caermarthen. Wales had historic claims to this glory, and the Romanized bishop that burned him was the namesake of Pelagius, her only historic shame. But to Ridley, so far as man can judge, belongs the more graceful palm and the more starry crown. To this great spirit we owe what was best and deepest in the fruits of Cranmer's learning. He restored the Catholic doctrine of the Eucharist, the doctrine of Ratramn, and the ancient doctrine of the Anglican Church, as testified in the Saxon homily of Ælfric. That doctrine is the corner-stone of liturgic science, and qualifies all worship. Hence, to this profound divine and holy martyr I ascribe more than to any other our incomparable Book of Common Prayer, the first book of Edward the Sixth, so called, reproduced in our American Liturgy. Who can estimate its value? It came forth with the Bishops' Bible, — next to the Bible the greatest boon to our race. In these gifts the Restoration was already complete, in all that was of its essence. The Marian martyrs sealed it with their blood. Like a precious coffer of gold, subjected to the furnace to purify the last remnant of its dross, the Church of Linus and of Gladys,[1] of Alcuin and of Alfred, came forth from the fiery heat restored to its virgin beauty, a "vessel of honour, fit for the Master's use."

[1] See Note E'''.

LECTURE VIII.

A CATHOLIC VIEW OF CHRISTENDOM.

1. THE ACCESSION OF ELIZABETH.

THE Restoration was complete when Elizabeth succeeded Mary. Complete, not finished. Nothing which the Anglican Church has ever regarded as essential to her restored condition was wanting when King Edward died. Her "Articles of Religion" are not a "Code of Belief," nor have they ever been made terms of communion to her children, or when she has offered her maternal breast to strangers. To us in America she granted the episcopate and full communion, with no stipulation whatever as to the Articles; nor did we ourselves adopt them till the first year of this century. We were without them for twenty years. I am not undervaluing them; they require no apology; they are Catholic doctrine; but as they are popularly represented they are quite another thing.

2. THE MARIAN SCHISM.

The reign of Mary was, of itself, a very important stage in the process of clinching and securing the work that had been done. The legatine intrusion of the deacon, Cardinal Pole, and the undoing by Act of Parliament of what the Church of England had done in synod, was a schism. God is wiser than men. To revise results and to secure them, and once for all to make the heart of England ready to ratify the rejection of the Papacy, no process could have been more effectual than this experiment of reversal. This reign wrought the casting out of devils. It was the last assault of papal usurpation, — the expiring convulsion of the Paparchy in the Church of our forefathers. Poor Mary and her kinsman and primate almost at the same hour gave back to God their kindred spirits:

"Forbear to judge, for we are sinners all.
Close up their eyes and draw the curtain close;
And let us all to meditation."

Like Cardinal Beaufort, in Shakespeare's inimitable portrayal, so perished the delusion of the Decretals in England. Her Church stood, once more, on the old foundations; her metropolitical throne rested on its canonical foothold, the Cypriote Constitution,[1] and the "ancient usages" of Nicæa. Her lawful episcopate survived in full measure; in England sufficiently, in Ireland more largely. How marked the providence that left the Primacy vacant at this solemn moment! It was wisely and opportunely filled by the consecration of the godly and well-learned Matthew Parker.

[1] See Lecture III., page 96.

3. THE RESTORED AUTONOMY.

Go back to our own history, after our episcopate was established, for an illustration of the case as it stood with the new primate. We had a prayer-book to revise; a theological framework to arrange for the education and guidance of the clergy, and many minor matters to set in order by provincial constitutions and canons. None other was the actual situation in England at this crisis. The Second Prayer-Book of Edward had hardly been in use when the Marian schism intervened. Revision and completion were the first requisites. The creeds were an all-sufficient theological base, but they had been so overlaid by scholasticism and by pontifical decrees, that a reform of the received system was necessary. In Henry's time, and subsequently, conflicting experiments had been tried, but they were experiments only. The "Bishops' Bible" was the one all-important and munificent bequest of that transitional reign. It is a monument of the Biblical character imparted to our reforms by Wiclif himself. The Germans, who have only lately awakened to their own obligations to our great Reformer, accuse him truthfully with not understanding "Justification by Faith"; that is, of course, as they understand it. But what they esteem a defect is indeed his glory. The Scriptures, with "reason and authority" for their interpreters, were made by Wiclif the corner stone of Anglican Restoration. The Reformers of the Continent risked all on Scholastic subtilties, beginning with Luther's maxim that "Justification," as he defined it, is "the criterion of a standing or falling church." The consequences are significant as they are immense. A Scriptural reformation was Catholic Restoration; the Scholastic reformation could only end in ecclesiastical suicide, and in the evolution of endless divisions and conflicting sects.

4. THE ARTICLES.

But, at such a moment, when the Latin churches were committing themselves more and more inextricably to school doctrines which had been enlarged and shaped into dogmas and unlimited refinements upon the Faith, and when the Protestant Reformation was given over to like speculations, as yet indeterminate and embroiling its leaders one with another, it was impossible that Scholasticism should not be at work among the profoundly learned and thoughtful scholars and divines of England. When we look at the case as it thus stood under Parker, we may wonder, indeed, at the issue. Revising the draught of Cranmer and Ridley, and reducing their Articles to *thirty-nine*, he gave us, substantially, what we still retain. What are they? Not a "Code of Belief," in any sense, though they include the Creed and the definitions of the Œcumenical Councils. A correction of school doctrine, by Scripture and antiquity, is found in twenty-six articles beginning with the ninth. Viewed apart from these, they amount to a *rejection of Scholasticism* as a system, and a strict limitation of Scholastic teaching to certain theses.

The age was rife with Scholastic discussions. It was impossible that Anglican divines should have no opinions about them. Their public teaching, however, was hereby restrained in a practical manner, within certain bounds, allowing freedom of inquiry and of thought, but setting metes and safeguards to controversy. In this view, I admire the Articles. They practically eliminated Scholasticism from the domain, of conscience and made us free, as Truth only can. After the debates of a century, in which they furnished an escape valve for the spirit of disputation, it was left for our great theologian, Bishop Bull, to secure what Hooker had promoted, a practical end of controversy. In his "Defence of the Nicene Creed," he illustrated our Catholic position so admirably as to win the homage of Bossuet and the whole Gallican Episcopate. In his "Harmonia Apostolica," he refuted the Lutheran and Calvinistic theories, and placed the exposition of our Articles upon a sure foundation. The famous Seventeenth Article[1] ignores the crucial point of Calvinism and Arminianism alike, and leaves the outline of truth indeterminate as to causation. This enables all Scriptural minds to accept it. As diversions and gymnastical exercises, the old discussions will never wholly die out; they exist in the nature and the moral faculties of the human mind. But they no longer ensnare or enslave men's consciences. The results fully justify the wisdom and purpose of the Articles; nor, so long as St. Augustine is remembered and studied, can they ever cease to be useful.

[1] See Note F'''.

5. THEIR CATHOLIC CORE.

In the Sixth Article is embodied the great Nicene principle of our Restoration; and in the Thirty-fourth, to say nothing of others, we have the pith and marrow of the Vincentian Rule practically applied. The Sixth I must quote in full. It is on "The Sufficiency of the Holy Scriptures for Salvation," as follows: —

"Holy Scripture containeth all things necessary to salvation; so that whatsoever is not read therein, nor may be proved thereby, is not to be required of any man, that it should be believed as an article of the Faith, or be thought requisite or necessary to salvation."

This golden Article merely imitates the great Councils, putting the Scriptures on a throne in the midst of the Church, as the oracle of Christ's infallible Vicar, the Holy Ghost. It was accompanied by the golden canon which affirms Vincent's rule, and restricts preachers to the word of God, and what "the Catholic Fathers and old bishops have gathered from its teaching."

6. THE FORMATION OF THE TRENTINE CHURCH.

Thus the English Church was restored before "the Roman Catholic Church" was in existence. I must thank the French *savant*, Quinet,[1] for a suggestive statement of facts which demonstrate what professed historians have too generally overlooked. The spirit which Constance and Basle had striven to eliminate was made at Trent, as he says,

[1] See Note G'''.

"the very Constitution of the Church." In other words, Trent created a new Constitution, organizing what remained of the Latin churches into a Western spiritual and temporal empire, — a provincial church claiming to be the whole Church. Quinet observes, that "the artifice consisted in making this change without anywhere speaking of it. . . . From that moment Popedom usurps all Christendom."

He notes how craftily all the notes of the old Œcumenical Councils were got rid of. The East and the North were almost equally wanting; — Italian prelates, one hundred and eighty-seven; only two German bishops; Spaniards, thirty-two; Frenchmen, twenty-six; and the voting changed from churches to individuals, a vote for every member of the Council personally, so that the Italian bishops swallowed up all the rest. The French were so ill-treated that their ambassadors left the Council. The Spanish bishops were virtually driven out. "*Excant*, Let them go," shouted the Italians. "Laynez, the Jesuit, became the soul of the Council, and, reaction against the North prevailing over every other idea, *the organization of the Church assumed a new form.*" In other words, the modern "Roman Catholic Church"—a gigantic sect, but a sect only — was thus created. It emerged from that portentous conventicle of seventeen years' duration with only a vestige left of the Latin churches, as such. They had been absorbed, or rather they were caged in the iron framework of a new and anomalous union. France, refusing the discipline and accepting only the new creed subject to Gallican interpretations, preserved the Gallican "name to live," while doomed to die. And so a new church emerged from the Trent caldron, (1) with a new Canon of Holy Scripture, including the Apocrypha, as equal with the Prophets; (2) a new Creed, that of Pius IV.; (3) a new "Code of Belief," necessary to salvation, embracing all the interminable definitions of the Trent Council; (4) a new system of church polity, in which a presbyterian theory of the ministry is made dogmatic,[1] and the Episcopate is no longer recognized as one of the Holy Orders; (5) a new main-spring of vitality, wholly sectarian in its character, namely, the consolidation of the Society of Jesuits with the new Constitution, in such manner as to make their General its practical lord and master, and the Pope himself only the mouthpiece of their decisions and decrees. From absorption into this sect, and all the ruin and debasement which have followed in every nation that has accepted it, the Nicene Church of England was saved as "a brand plucked from the burning." Such was "the arrow of the Lord's deliverance," when Queen Mary died, and Don Philip went to found the Inquisition and prosecute his cruelties in Spain and the Low Countries. These he had designed for England when by the Divine Providence Parker became Metropolitan, exclaiming, "Lord, into what times hast thou brought me?"

[1] See Note H'''.

7. RETROSPECT.

Let me now go back to events from which all this came forth, and see whether Germany and Northern Europe owe not all their troubles to half-way measures, and to their blind refusal to proceed as England did in the line of Restoration. Let us note how, by refusing to hear the voice of Wiclif, they incurred the revolutions of Luther and the despotism of Laynez. Wiclif's light had not been hidden under a bushel: it began to illuminate Europe before he died. The Universities of Europe were a great exchange for the commerce of learning and of thought. From the Moldau young scholars came to the Isis; Oxford and Prague were in close relations in Wiclif's day, and when Anne of Luxembourg, "the good Queen Anne," arrived in England to marry King Richard, she was attended by a retinue of learned youth and accomplished men. These found Wiclif and his doctrines the talk of the Court, the Church, and the Universities. The "great Evangelical Doctor" had just published his Bible, and manuscript copies were multiplied. It is known that Queen Anne herself became a Bible reader, and a lover of Wiclif's name and person. She survived him for ten years, and on her death her attendants returned to Prague with Wiclif's books, and impressed with his great idea of giving free circulation to the Holy Scriptures. In A. D. 1397 came back from Oxford that brilliant youth, Jerome of Prague, a Bohemian knight. He brought with him books and parchments, copied by his own hand from Wiclif's writings. He showed them to John Huss, destined to be the Wiclif of Bohemia; but he was no Wiclif then. After reading one of the proscribed books, he advised Jerome to burn it, or to toss it into the Moldau; no doubt a sacrifice to the local saint, St. John Nepomucene, whose bridge spans that river,— the "proud arch" of Campbell's poetry. But from that moment the study of the Evangelical Doctor became more general, and it electified Bohemia. The century of discovery and invention opened with this movement. Huss was now confessor to King Wenzel's second wife, Queen Sophia of Bavaria; he was the most faithful and eloquent of court preachers, and the rising man.

8. THE MISTAKE OF GERSON.

Happy had it been for Germany and for Bohemia too had these master spirits been allowed to open and control the Continental Reformation. It would then have proceeded, probably, as in England, upon the lines of Restoration; for these illustrious men were Catholics, not sectarians, and to the last they prompted no subversive measures. I love them as Anglicans at heart; by which I mean true Catholics, who would have guided their fellow Catholics of Europe into the paths of Nicene revival and orthodoxy. But just here things took a decisive turn in another direction. The justly celebrated Gerson, Chancellor of the Archdiocese of Paris, eminent for his learning and his piety, gained the control of the reforming demands of

Europe. The Popes of Avignon and of the schism that followed, for one hundred and fifty years, had kept the churches and the nations in perpetual broils, demonstrating the folly of pretending that the Paparchy was a bond of unity. Moreover, the vices of these popes and antipopes, with their licentious courts, had become an abomination that " smelled to heaven." No words can do justice to their immoralities, except those of their contemporaries, who not only saw them, but shared them. The groans of the Latin churches were universal; an outcry for a reformation of the Church "in its head and its members." Gerson was in no respect in advance of his age; he was a Gallican, but a Scholastic and a fanatical Nominalist; he was the honest dupe of the canon law, which means of the forged Decretals. He accepted, therefore, an ideal papacy; not at all the Paparchy as it then existed. As a Gallican, he fell back upon the principles of Frankfort, supposing that, if the Popes could be put back to what Charlemagne found them, all would be well. His great scheme was to make Councils supreme; to empower them to depose a bad Pope and elect a new one; and, in general, to recognize no other supreme authority in Christendom. How plausible! Here was the great Nicene doctrine saddled, and, as it proved, rendered abortive, by the Decretalist whim that there must be a Pope of some sort. However, so far and no further could Gerson and the Gallicans proceed. It was progress for the Latin churches in general. It was the old, ill-conceived position of poor, puzzled Hincmar, and the Anglicans had adopted this same idea under Anselm and the Normans. Just here also stood Sir Thomas More and dear old Bishop Fisher, when the tyrant Henry took their heads off for not going further while he was disposed to do so. In other respects Henry and they stood together; they learned this policy of Gerson.

9. SCHOOL GRUDGES.

There was another clog of which we cannot now comprehend the immense significance. Wiclif was a Realist, and Realism was fashionable with all who had learned from him. Gerson was a bigoted Nominalist, and therefore hated the name of Wiclif, attributing to the Realists all the mischief of his writings. Puritans and Cavaliers never hated one another more passionately than did these rival schools, each inspired by the *odium theologicum* to the verge of frenzy against opponents. Gerson's scheme of reform included, therefore, two antagonistic schemes. He drew a line thus: (1.) There must be no reformation of doctrine, and all reproach of "Wiclifism" must be put away by stringent measures. (2.) This point secured, the authority of councils must be asserted, and practically carried out, to any extent found necessary. Such were the ideas that called the Council of Pisa (A. D. 1407), designed for a cleansing of the Augean stables of the Paparchy. There were now two rival popes, and Europe was a very hell between them, everywhere embroiled in quarrels political and religious. Who was Pope and who was Antichrist? One nation was tied to a French pope, another held to his rival. Gregory had Rome in actual possession, and felt that nine points of the law were with him. But such were his oaths and perjuries, his protestations and his subterfuges, that finally his cardinals, all save seven, turned upon him and appealed to a General Council. They professed to fear that he would assassinate them all. They became Gallicans all of a sudden, and said, "We appeal from the Pope to Jesus Christ, of whom he is vicar; from the Pope to a Council, to which it belongs to judge the sovereign pontiff; from the present Pope to a future Pope, authorized to redress what his predecessor has unwarrantably enacted."

10. PISA.

Behold that ancient cathedral hard by the leaning tower in Pisa. There the Council was opened, with august ceremonial, on the Feast of the Annunciation, A. D. 1409. John Gerson was there in person to press his doctrines with admirable force and logic. D'Ailly, Archbishop of Cambrai, was, next to him, the leader; a genius who anticipates Bossuet in the *sobriquet* of "the Eagle" of France. As the result, both popes were deposed, and the Roman See declared vacant. All their bulls, anathemas, and excommunications were declared null and void. They proceeded to an election, and Philargus of Milan, a good old man, was proclaimed Pope, as Alexander V. This was brought about by the legerdemain of Balthasar Cossa, who will soon appear again. Counter councils were called, of course, in favour of the deposed pretenders; but the work at Pisa closed here, and the respectability of the new pontiff stifled for the moment all clamours for reform. John Huss gave his hopeful adhesion to Alexander; but one voice was lifted up for more effectual reforms. The learned and saintly Clemangis, once rector of the Sorbonne, was studying the Scriptures in holy retirement in the vale of Langres. He shared Wiclif's ideas for more thorough work. "The Council of Pisa," said he, " has only trifled with the Church, crying, *Peace, peace*, when there is no peace."

11. SIGISMUND VISITS ENGLAND.

At this time Sigismund, the Emperor elect of Germany, had not been crowned, and his difficulties led him to desire another Council. Chicheley was Archbishop of Canterbury, and was engaged in fierce controversies with the Lollards, when the Emperor arrived in London to persuade England to unite with France for the carrying out of the reforms Pisa had failed to effect. Doubtless he gained very false ideas of Wiclif, at this juncture, confounding the turbulent Lollards with his disciples, and hence all the more readily accepting Gerson's opposition to Wiclif as the only safe course for crowned heads. He was brother to the good Queen Anne, and better things might have been hoped from him had he not been the Emperor and a sensual voluptuary.

12. THE ENGLISH EMBASSY TO CONSTANCE.

Chichcley appointed three bishops to attend the new Council, summoned to meet at Constance. Hallam of Salisbury and Bubwith of Bath, with Mascall of Hereford, made the embassy. Hallam was the leading spirit. The King sent a lay delegation as co-ambassadors, and a vast and splendid retinue attended them. The Emperor received them with special honours, and wore his English decorations of the Garter when he entered Constance. He had been recently crowned at Aix-la-Chapelle, over the sepulchre of Charlemagne. Frankfort was opened again at Constance, as I have said, but only to make itself a monument of Gerson's folly, in his fond attempt to reconcile any theoretical Papacy whatever with Catholic Councils and the old Nicene Constitutions. The Decretals had done their work; men's minds had been chained by them for five centuries, and the "immedicable wound" could only be remedied by eradication and actual cautery.

13. HUSS AS A REFORMER.

Under the impulse given him by Jerome of Prague, Huss was already known as a reformer less fanciful than Gerson, though he by no means saw the impossibility of retaining the Papacy. Wise, holy, and inspired by communion with God in Holy Scripture, he was nevertheless far in advance of his times, and his reputation as a "Wiclifite" insured him the deadly hatred of the

Council. When the Archbishop of Prague had burned Wiclif's books with public ceremony, Huss rebuked the act, and carried with him the heart of Bohemia. Though he committed himself to nothing more than a plea for liberty to read and examine, he was everywhere stigmatized as Wiclif's disciple. He even appealed to Rome,— yes, to that same Balthasar Cossa, now John XXIII. This was in the matter of an episcopal censure vented against him when he opposed the book-burning. This marks where he stood at this time. So far he was with Gerson. Alas! why was not Gerson with him?

14. CONSTANCE.

It is not my purpose to dwell on the history of this great man. Let us come to the Council. The infamies of John XXIII. were unutterable; and this was the pontiff who answered the appeal of Huss by a bull of excommunication, in A. D. 1412. It is noteworthy that, in protesting against it in a most catholic spirit, Huss quoted the well-known example of Greathead, the saintly Robert of Lincoln. The Council was opened at last, and Huss was summoned to be present. The Emperor gave him a safe-conduct to go and *to return*. Jerome kissed him as he left Prague: "Dear master," said he, "be firm." Already the wicked Pope had appeared on the scene, his ambitious splendours and the unblushing shame of his conduct and that of his courtiers adding to the scorn of all decent men. Huss soon found himself a prisoner at Constance, where he had opened his cause with dignity and power. The Emperor ordered his release, but Sigismund had not yet arrived in person, and the Pope had. So the latter kept Huss confined. When Sigismund appeared, the Pope's own case was uppermost, and Huss was left in prison. Jerome too had been cited; he also came and was imprisoned. It was a foregone conclusion that Wiclif and his followers must be condemned, to balance what they meant to do with Pope John. When this pontiff's character and conduct were under examination, his crimes proved so frightful, that our Hallam, Bishop of Salisbury, gave it as his opinion, that "he ought to be burned at the stake." He fled from Constance in terror, and the Council solemnly deposed him on the last day of May, 1415. The arrogant John became the most abject of suppliants. In outward appearance, at least, he accepted his sentence, and ratified it by his own hand.

15. THE MARTYRS OF CONSTANCE.

When, after an extraordinary revival of the old scholastic controversies, John Huss found himself condemned, he stood in the presence of Sigismund, and looked him steadfastly in the face, as he said, "I came here on the safe-conduct of the Emperor." Sigismund crimsoned to his forehead, and that blush saved Luther at Worms. Charles-Quint said, "I should not like to blush like Sigismund." It is said that Huss and Jerome both prophesied a day of other counsels. "You roast a goose to-day," said Huss, punning on his own name; "in a hundred years will come a swan[1] you cannot burn." Why dwell on the heroic martyrdoms of Huss and the brilliant Jerome? Reciting the creeds and praying to Jesus, these intrepid heroes bore witness to the Faith. Æneas Sylvius, afterwards Pope, said: "They went to their punishment as to a feast. Not a word escaped them which betrayed a particle of weakness. In the midst of the flames, without ceasing, they sang hymns to their last breath. No philosopher ever suffered death with such constancy as they endured in the flames." So speaks one who saw it all and shared it all,—an enemy and a subsequent Pope. Who will not say *Amen*, when I devoutly look up to God and add, May my soul be with theirs when we all come to stand before the only just tribunal, at the last day!

16. THE INFAMY OF CONSTANCE.

The martyrdoms were dramatically carried out, with refinements of cruelty and torture too horrible to narrate. Was there ever such work done by Christians in council assembled under invocation of the Holy Ghost? To a calm observer, there were but hair-splitting differences between the burners and the burnt. Good Lord, forgive them, for they knew not what they did! Constance was smitten with impotency from that hour, and Gerson's great learning and virtues perished without

[1] Luther's device was a swan.

any adequate record of success. Ignorantly he had entailed upon France and Germany the convulsions that for a century, after Luther, made Europe an Aceldama. Nay, the French Revolution itself may be traced to the reactionary consequences of Gerson's failure to promote such a Catholic Restoration as was insured in England under wiser counsels. Poor John Gerson! To his fanatical aversions we owe another disgraceful act, which likened this Council to hyænas that prey upon the dead. Wiclif's bones must be dug up and consumed. On such a dismal errand came commissioners to quiet Lutterworth, and there they enacted this mockery. The sacred ashes of the great confessor were thrown into a little brook that murmurs under the old walls of his church. And Fuller quaintly says: "Thus this brook hath conveyed his ashes into Avon, Avon into Severn, Severn into the narrow seas, then into the main ocean; and thus the ashes of Wiclif are the emblem of his doctrine, which now is dispersed all the world over."

17. ONE VOTE AND THE CONSEQUENCES.

The eloquence of Jerome as he pleaded before the Council is said to have left Cicero in the shade. Huss was hardly less eloquent. Both were yet young men. Huss suffered on his birthday, aged forty-five; Jerome was about the same age, and was a layman. With them passed away the hope of Catholic reformation for the Latin churches. One vote cast at Constance by the English Bishop of Bath elected Martin V. in place of John. That vote, says Dean Hook, "delayed the cause of reform for a century." It did far more. It threw the inevitable into the hands of another generation, and of men of another character, who, as I have shown, were not restorers, but Scholastic doctors, — giants who built up nothing in place of what they threw down.

18. THE COUNCIL OF BASLE.

We must regard the Council of Basle as a mere continuation of that of Constance, and it was far more resolute and creditable to its engineers. Pope Martin was forced to convoke it,[1] and severe were its reproaches against his duplicity in trying to postpone. Over and over again had he laboured to convene it in Italy, but they defied him, and insisted on Basle, under Sigismund's protection. Here was something like Frankfort again. He did not live to see it opened, and was succeeded by Eugenius IV. This Pope pronounced the Council dissolved, but they asserted their superiority as a "General Council," and went on. They proved too strong for the Pope, and he was forced to yield and recognize their claims. Gerson was no longer living to control them, but their history is that of a final testimony about the Paparchy. And praiseworthy, so far as they went, were their tokens of better feeling towards the Hussites, to whom they restored the communion in both kinds, reversing what was done at Constance. The chal-

[1] December 14, 1431.

ice thus restored gave the adherents of Huss the reputable name of Calixtines. This was an entire overruling of Martin, who had only preached in the spirit of Innocent III., a crusade of extermination against the Hussites. But all too late! There was no John Huss to guide his friends and to give this Council a truly primitive character. The book of life was shut; the seals were to be broken in another generation, but only to disclose thunderings and voices. A Titanic avenger was to ride on the whirlwind, but he was wholly unable to direct the storm; and they who had burned Huss and Jerome, and strewn the ashes of Wiclif, were chastised by Luther first, and then given over to the oligarchy of Laynez the Jesuit. Either extreme was abhorrent to the doctors of Constance and of Basle; but their fatal compromises were the creators of both alike. Luther's agitations crossed the Alps, and at one time had begun to work under the eaves of the Vatican itself; but when this last menace was disregarded, there was nothing left to Rome but an absolute surrender to the Society of Loyola. These ate the oyster and awarded the shells. They assumed to themselves all the supremacy which Basle had claimed for a General Council, and to the Pope they conceded only the homage of doing everything in his name.

19. TWO POINTS SET RIGHT.

Perhaps I have sufficiently illustrated my points, as to the Anglican Restoration and the "Reformation" of Luther. (1.) The Anglican work begun and was wrought from within,—begun under Wiclif, who only brought to a focus what had been continuously maintained by Anglican witnesses, from the Norman invasion onward, and what was resumed, and brought to the issue of a restored autonomy, under Henry, and Edward, his son. (2.) The German Reformers lighted their candle from England; there could have been no Luther but for Huss and Jerome, the disciples of Wiclif. How absurd and illogical, therefore, is the conventional instruction of our school histories, and even of Church historians, who treat of our Anglican Reformation as if it began with Luther's burning of the Pope's bull! They make it an importation from Germany, if not from the Diet of Spires, where the Lutherans were called Protestants. Let those admire a feeble and impotent name of negation and discord who can possibly do so; but the reader of Kahnis must exclaim,—

"Can aught exult in its deformity?"

20. POLITICAL PROTESTANTISM.

But let us not fall into vulgar mistakes about the Protestants. As a political cause, my sympathies are with the Protestant heroes and sufferers. Theologically, I cannot go with them, although the worst mistakes of Calvin and Luther are venial as compared with the Council of Trent, its monstrous "Code of Belief," and its daring dictation to Christendom of a new Creed, equalizing the mere novelties of Pius IV. with the Nicene symbol, making it more practically *the* Creed, and not less essential to salvation. In the conflicts and wars it generated, my heart is with the lost cause of the Calixtines and the Huguenots. I had rather be with the poor "winter-king" of Bohemia, than with Louis XIV. ravaging the Palatinate, desolating the Rhineland, and revoking the Edict of Nantes. Yes, and who would not choose death with Coligny, rather than share with Catherine de Medicis and the pontiff that awful account with God for the massacre of St. Bartholomew's day? To come nearer to our own times, recall the sorrows and sufferings of the godly Jansenists, the nuns of Port Royal dragged out of their graves, like Wiclif, and their chaste bodies exposed to the worst indignities, while their very roof was torn away from the heads of the survivors, their walls levelled, and their names covered with anathemas. Gracious Lord! that a Church should call itself "Catholic" which was too narrow for a Pascal, an Arnauld, a Nicole, — nay, too narrow for Bossuet and the old Gallicans, whose condemnation at the late Vatican conventicle was as real as that of Wiclif at Constance, and whose bones would just as certainly be exhumed and cremated, were it possible just now to execute such an *auto-da-fé* in Republican France.

21. REFLECTIONS.

Let me pause a moment for a reflection. It has often struck you, perhaps, as I have had to recount the history of events that disgrace our holy religion, to ask, "Where is the religion of

Christ, and what is it doing for the world in times like these?" This anxious inquiry was anticipated and answered by the Holy Ghost, when He said, "Nevertheless the foundation of God standeth sure, having this seal,—*the Lord knoweth them that are His.*" In every age, it is evil that forces itself on the sight; it is the worst of men that make themselves seen and heard. But always, if there are such as Judas, there are such as Stephen; if there are persecutors, there are heroes; if there are murderers, there are martyrs. Meantime, thousands of humble and holy men and women, humble-minded peasants and Christian children, are living the life of faith and love, and dying the death of saints, unnumbered and unknown. The great prophet supposed that he alone was left in Israel, a true worshipper; but the Lord said there were seven thousand besides him that had not "bowed the knee to Baal." Even in the days of Annas and Caiaphas, there were such priests as Zacharias and Simeon; such holy women as Elizabeth and Anna; such "Israelites indeed" as Nathanael. Let us be sure that in the dark places of earth, as now, so always, God has had his hidden saints, who have not been hid from Him, and whose faith overcame the world.

Then, as to the vulgar mistakes about Calvin and Luther. Giants they were indeed in those days; Scholastics even when they quarrelled with Scholastics, and their worst errors came from the Scholastics. Such were Calvin's presbyterianism and the reactionary ideas of Luther, that made Solifidianism. Calvin's predestinarianism had a similar origin, and his terrible logic about infant damnation is Scholasticism, which is now hardened into creed by Rome itself in its Trent theology. I must own that the spirit of Melanchthon is that with which I find my own heart entwined, almost exclusively, when I study the Protestant Reformation. Erasmus might possibly have renewed the influence of Huss, and directed the movement on the Continent, had he been more in earnest, less fond of his jokes, and less afraid of the stake. He had not taken his ideas from Wiclif; he was rather a pupil of Gerson, and the arrogant dictation of that "pope in the bosom" which Luther owned he carried, made Erasmus recoil.

At intervals the influence of this new class of reformers was felt in our affairs. The floods of Continental violence rolled like a tidal wave against the fast-anchored Church and isle of England. Here and there are holes which it gnawed and fissures which it opened, but our rock threw back the broken billow and repelled it as from a fortress of adamant. Had the counsels of Gerson prevailed in England, our fate would have been involved with the Continental Reformation; or else we should have been swallowed up by Trent. See how the Inquisition and the extinction of the old Mozarabic spirit of freedom has brought down what was the greatest of kingdoms, imperial Spain, to the dust. From all this, the Lord delivered us. England was not swamped in the Protestant marsh of sect and schism. She escaped the net of the Jesuits at Trent. She became the most Catholic Church in Christendom.

22. RECENT REACTION.

Our own time has seen a revolt in England alike against reason and Holy Scripture and the Providence of God. Men who owe all that gives them weight and influence with contemporaries to their training in the Church of England, and to the moral nutriment they drew from her maternal breasts, have ungratefully "lifted up their heel against her." It is the greatest scandal of an enlightened age; it is an indictment of human nature itself in its better estate. In the name of common sense, what is it they would have, when they regret the Anglican restoration? Do they regret the death of Mary, and wish the Spanish Armada had restored her reign of blood, set up the Inquisition, and done for England what Alva did in the Netherlands? Do they grieve in their hearts for the failure of the last Stuart to restore the Paparchy? Can they then lament for him whose treachery insured the ruin of the dynasty, from which Charles I. prophetically withdrew his blessing in case it should ever depart from the teachings of Hooker[1] and the catholicity of the Church of England? Again I ask, What would they have instead of the blessings our race has inherited from the Marian martyrs, and which have made us the envy of the world? Had England copied Spain, would that have been wisdom? or France, in her half-reforms? Look at the Spain of to-day and the France of the last hundred years. Is there more of the Gospel in these

[1] See Note I'''.

countries, or in Italy, fast by the Papal throne, than in England, with all her faults? Oh! it is in the "States of the Church," I suppose, blotted out from the map of Europe by an indignant civilization, that we lost the kingdom of heaven, when it "came nigh" unto men! Is it such a Sardis they would make the soul and centre of English Law and Gospel for all generations? But enough! "Let them alone,"—as Scripture said of one joined to his idols. Let us go on to secure to children's children the inestimable blessings they are too besotted to understand, too ungrateful to enjoy.

23. THE CONTRAST.

And if we would estimate aright the difference between a Catholic Restoration and a Protestant Reformation, let us know them by their fruits. The difference was radical, at the outset, as I have shown: Scripture and antiquity inspired the one and governed it; the other risked all upon Scholastic theologies. Now, I do not like to speak unkindly of our Christian brethren in Germany and Switzerland, and therefore I shall merely refer you to authorities for light upon the subject. Ranke will show you how it came to pass that popes regained nearly half of all that they had lost, and Kahnis, that excellent Lutheran of our own times, will tell you more than I care to recall of the history of German Protestantism in its operations upon mind and heart, and in its destructive work upon national churches. On the other hand, look at our mother Church of England! "There she stands," — poor as the second temple compared with the first, if we contrast her with the pattern in the mount, but, in spite of all, "beautiful for situation," and fast making herself "the joy of the whole earth." See what the Lord has done for her, in these latter days! Look at her daughter Church in these States, and at her colonial children. The Romish missions were vigorously prosecuted, in the spirit of the Propaganda: look at them! Look at Mexico, and Hayti, and Brazil! We find a parallel to that which Christ himself rebuked, when he cried woe to those who "compassed sea and land to make one proselyte." To England, in another sense, and for different ends, God has said, "Possess thou the east and the west." Yes, truly, " her sound has gone forth into all lands, her words to the ends of the world." And where does she stand as related to her fellow Christians, alike Protestants and Romanized Latins? I appeal to one of her most persistent adversaries, to the Ultramontanist De Maistre. After all he can say against her, yet he allows, "She is *most precious*." If ever Christendom is to be reunited, he thinks the movement must proceed from her. He recognizes her as the mediatrix who can lay her hands upon both parties; for, as he says, "with one hand she touches us (Roman Catholics), and with the other the Protestants." If this be her mission, as De Maistre supposes, "truly she is most precious." He owns the truth, at last, which Rome has so perversely tried for centuries to gainsay.[1]

[1] See Note J'''.

24. THE FALL OF THE PAPAL THRONE.

Even Laynez could not have conceived of the ultimate results of the mastery he gained for his Society at the Council of Trent. In that Council his manipulations subverted the Latin Episcopate, reducing it to a mere Papal Vicariate: his policy has since reduced the Papacy itself to a mere mask for the "black pope," the General of the Jesuits, the autocrat of the "Roman Catholic" world. The rod of its nominal despot is really held by him; his military forces submit with the "passivity of a corpse," and obey with the activity of Napoleon's flying artillery. The pontiff, be it Pius IV. or be it Pius IX., is merely a voice to send forth the oracles of the Society. But by its fatal blunder, when it bolstered up the feeble *Pio Nono* to issue his late decrees, it committed the Roman system to an irreparable breach with all antiquity, and the end is not yet. It dealt a death-blow to Gallicanism, which can no longer exist in communion with the Papacy, but its sting was like that of the serpent which strikes venom into its victim with a fury that destroys itself.

At that same moment when in his "Synod of Sacristans," amid darkness that might be felt, amid thunders and lightnings that made the foundations shake around him, the pontiff proclaimed himself Infallible, there went forth a voice, "yea, and that a mighty voice," which instantly took effect. His last temporal support perished at Sedan; and the temporal royalties of the Papacy perished with it. The voice said, " Remove the diadem and take off the crown; . . . exalt him that is low, and abase him that is high." Men fail to see the meaning of contemporary events, because they read not history, nor the word of God. But it is a great thing to be alive when so quietly, and by means apparently so insignificant as the red shirt of Garibaldi, is wrought a change that Emperors and nations have struggled for in vain. Since Pepin gave the Exarchate of Ravenna to the Roman patriarch, in A. D. 754, the Bishops of Rome have been "princes of this world." The fall of the "Holy Roman Empire," under Napoleon, carried this logically with it, but "the mills of God grind slowly." We have seen a consummation which may be momentarily defeated by diplomacy, but the thunderbolt has fallen. For the first time in a thousand years, not a single power in Europe is identified with the Papacy. The Syllabus has made it impossible for kings and peoples to submit to its yoke. The "Old Catholics" may seem a feeble folk, but the testimony of Döllinger and his noble allies is as imperishable as that of Wiclif. You, young gentlemen, may live to see fresh struggles for Ultramontane supremacy, but the issue is inevitable. An epoch of prophecy has been signalized: a new era begins with hope.

25. SURVEY OF CHRISTENDOM.

The present aspects of Christendom I venture to suppose are hopeful, and give blessed promise of reconstruction. The signs of the times point to the speedy overthrow of Islam in Europe, and the

Patriarchate of New Rome is rising into importance with the gradual increase of learning and piety in Russia. Such a theologian as Bishop Macarius of Vinnitza assures us that the study of the Greek Fathers must soon bear fruits of reformation throughout the ancient churches of the East. A Russian diplomatist[1] remarked to me not long ago, that the theologians of St. Petersburg, over whom Macarius presides, were now the only Russians who could even appreciate the Anglican doctors; but, said he, "we are educating a new class for the future." He had recently visited England, and he said, "There is no church equal to the Anglicans for learning and character; every parish priest has scholarship enough for a bishop." But the Russian Church is not sterile. She has studded Northern Asia with missions; they stretch to our own Alaska, by the Aleutian Isles. I have had Bishop Nestor of Alaska at my table, as my guest. The Holy Ghost is moving the hearts of fathers to children, and of children to their fathers, everywhere where the Nicene Council and its "ancient usages" are revered and maintained.

26. NICENE CONSTITUTIONS IMPERISHABLE.

For the Nicene Unity of Christendom is imperishable, and God has protected it everywhere among the nations. By its canon of threefold concurrence in ordinations, the historic episcopate is woven into a net-work, instead of drawn out in a chain where one broken link ruins all. It is

[1] Prince Orloff, late Russian Ambassador in Paris, A. D. 1877.

impossible that the Apostolic Succession should fail where this law is observed. So the canon of Holy Scripture and its sacred text have been maintained and preserved. The Nicene Creed is thus perpetuated, and the Christian year is guarded by the Paschal Canons of the Council. Thus, and by other providential contrivances, it is a most striking fact, that *organic* unity has been maintained even where *functional* unity is lost. There is a fundamental Unity, and all men see it, between Greek and Latin and Anglican Christians, , because the Nicene foundations alike underlie them all. Even Trent, though it nearly smothered Nicene vitality beneath accumulated fables, has left the old bases solid underneath. Hence it is, that, in spite of new dogmas and of all the Roman superstitions, many " Roman Catholics" live on the old bases, while they outwardly conform to the new. How I have blessed God, that millions of the peasantry, nominally conformed to Trent, know very little practically of its heresies. Simple folk! They know the Apostles' Creed, and have read the Nicene, and can sing pious hymns; so that, like Goethe's Gretchen before her fall, — yes, and even when they fall, — they love to worship Christ and to trust in him for salvation. Now, what is held alike, and from the beginning, by Greeks and Latins and Anglicans, — that is Catholicity, and in that we all consent. The specialties of each communion are not Catholic, and with them we are not called to communion by Nicene law. Woe to those who erect local and provincial specialties into articles of faith, and cast out brethren for not accepting them. We appeal against Diotrephes to the Common Judge, "but when they curse, we bless." That Church which refrains from narrowing the limits of Catholic communion, and includes all who would have been included at Nicæa, is therefore the most truly Catholic. Where is it found? Judge ye.

27. PRACTICAL UNITIES.

Our Anglican desire for Unity is no ambitious longing for "lordship over God's heritage." It is pure and "unfeigned love of the brethren" for Christ's sake. Leaving Him to be the only umpire and judge, I have enjoyed through a long life the Unity I have illustrated, in practical ways, among foreign churches, "no man forbidding me." The Catholic spirit renders it impossible to wear the fetters of a sect. Only less does it forbid a life virtually sectarian, which is cooped up in one's local or provincial church. The whole Church of the Creed is ours to live in. No pope can hinder us. Often have I knelt at the altar of St. Peter's in Rome, and in almost all the great cathedrals of Europe. On such occasions I have recited the Nicene Creed, and offered our Anglican prayer "for the good estate of the Catholic Church." While they have mumbled their mass in an unknown tongue, I have prayed God to accept what he found acceptable in it, and have read in my prayer-book the service for the day. This I have done in the chapel of the great St. Bernard, as the sunrise gilded the surrounding pinnacles of the Alps; and when my guide over the mountains knelt at a wayside shrine, I bowed myself before the Invisible God of Catholic worship, looking up to the clear blue sky, and begging the Lord to bless my peasant brother, — mysterious symbol of millions of simple souls, who for a thousand years have bowed down to images, because so willed the Empress Irene. Surely He who loved the Samaritans loves and accepts these our brethren, who call upon Him out of a pure heart, though ignorant and once polluted perhaps as Rahab, who was "justified" in spite of her ignorant lie. For " Mercy rejoiceth against judgment." Among Christians of the Greek rite I have enjoyed much closer and sweeter communion; have been received into their chancels, as they have been received into ours, accepting their brotherly recognitions, and uniting in such portions of their Liturgy as are truly ancient and Scriptural. Prematurely, we should not go further. The Holy Spirit will accomplish the rest. Thank God, none of the ancient churches have lost the Truth. They have added to it; but the line is drawn between Truth and modern additions. In the latter we have no part nor lot; in all that is Catholic we are in practical communion with our brethren the Latins and the Greeks.

28. THE PARABLE OF PATMOS.

This principle of Unity is given us in the vision of Patmos, — the Master amid the churches. Observe how corrupt were some of the seven: yet, so long as he did not destroy them, but patiently awaited their return to first faith and first love and first works, he walked amid their golden candlesticks and held their stars in his right hand. So He teaches us to be in communion with Sardis itself, though not with her pollutions. And when we look at home, well may He ask, How are we better than others? Is not our American church a veritable Laodicea? I think it is. Let us "anoint our eyes with eye-salve," that we may see ourselves as the Master sees us. We have no occasion to be proud. Many of our fellow Christians surpass us in good works, and set us an example that ought to make us ashamed. That is a rebuke to us, but it does not alter the facts, nor diminish our privileges. The good Samaritan was a rebuke to priest and Levite; but, none the less, the priests and Levites were God's ordinance and "salvation was of the Jews." It is our own fault, if in this dear Church we fail to learn lessons of piety from all Christians, and to "go and do likewise." But look every man to his own duty, and despise not others. Bearing in mind that the great thing is "love to God and man," give me leave to love also the precious Church of my fathers, in which, emancipated from such trammels as sects impose, I live in all the Christian churches and in all the Christian ages; read the Fathers as my fathers; keep the Christian feasts, and travel through all the Christian year, in sweetest sympathy and ennobling communion with "the past, the distant, and the future." No man can rob a Catholic of this gift of God, this life in the universe, this expansion of heart and mind and soul to the Catholic thought of which God is the author. It is high as heaven, and deep as Hades; it lifts us to the heavenly choir; it unites us with all who "sleep in the Lord Jesus." Oh how blessed the privilege of him who can say with the saintly Bishop Ken, " I live and die in the communion of the Catholic Church, as it was before the disunion of East and West, and as it stands distinguished from all Puritan or Papal innovations"!

29. PERILS OF THE REPUBLIC.

Young gentlemen, your attention has been directed to the solvent operation of sect, and to the corrosive action of the Trent religion, especially as the virulence of its corruptions has been concentrated in the monstrous moral system of Liguori. In our dear country both these classes of peril are terribly active, and the worst of the evil is that practically they work together. Sectarianism makes fuel for Romanism; Loyola triumphed in Germany wherever Luther and Calvin had created sectarian divisions.[1] To the ignorant and the indifferent Rome makes an appeal which Sectarianism knows not how to meet, and to which it lends apparent force. "Look," says the Jesuit, "at these religions of yesterday, all the fragmentary creations of Protestantism, all wrangling among themselves, and all united only in a negative antagonism to Rome, which has no positive character or base. Here, on the other hand, is that

[1] See Note K‴.

which they agree to vilify and disparage, the old Mother of all Christians, the Church of Peter, the one only Church of Scripture and the Creeds." Our popular journalism proceeds on this theory in fawning upon Rome for political purposes, and the popular mind falls into the trap. The trap is constructed by Sectarianism itself, which calls Rome "the Catholic Church," "the old religion," "the oldest of the churches," and so on,—which repeats with relish Rome's insults to Anglicans, calls ours the "Church of Henry VIII., the creature of the English Parliament," and the feeble offspring of Luther's great movement in Germany, or whatever else a Jesuit may dictate against us. Now, in a republic dependent upon popular intelligence and national morality, it is impossible that such elements of mischief should co-operate for the confusion of ideas in religion, without undermining all that rests upon religion and upon truth. The rapid decay of American institutions is threatened from the combined forces of Sectarianism and Ultramontanism, working together as they have been working in Germany and France towards a general downfall into irreligion, unbelief, atheism. The perils assailing us are such as they who framed our Constitution never anticipated. The popular religion, with all its good, is yet a solvent, and operates to destroy. But home-bred evils are aggravated beyond all computation by an ignorant and vicious and pauperized immigration, which pours in upon us like a deluge. If these poor waifs and outcasts of Europe came here as regiments, and were landed daily with bayonets in their hands, we should confront them and repel the invasion. But they come in stealthily, and we ourselves put arms in their hands far more terrible as they use them than would be cold steel or gunpowder. We give them the ballot; they hold the balance of power; and demagogues make them the arbiters of our destinies. They may soon overthrow our schools; they have already thrown out of them the Holy Bible; they grasp our taxes, with insatiable rapacity, to endow their own schools, disguised as protectories and hospitals, or other institutions of charity. In Protestant Upper Canada they are a minority; but by the game of demagogues they have overcome the tax-payers and dictate their own terms to the government.

30. THE CONSTRUCTIVE FORCES OF THE AMERICAN CHURCH.

Now, I must be permitted to express my convictions, resting on no superficial base, that the Church which is entwined with the entire history of our race, with the growth of which is bound up the common law, which reflects the genius of our literature and embodies the principles out of which has risen our national Constitution, — that such a Church has in herself those conservative elements and constructive forces which are just what our national fabric requires. In everything else that is called American, the centrifugal force predominates : what we need is the balancing force that generates an orbit, and holds us to the light and heat of the sun. Macaulay very justly reflects upon Jefferson for introducing into our system an element which gives too much to the passions of the multitude, unrestrained and uneducated to obey the law.[1] Macaulay ought to know, for he did all he could to introduce the same element into England. But he saw from a distance what he could not discover at home: he reproached our system as spreading all sail and providing no ballast. We fly before the wind, but we are wholly unprepared for the gale. Happily, we have resources. The colossal character of Washington, the Alfred of the New World, has provided us with maxims and with examples to which our youth may be profitably pointed. He gave our Constitution a religious character when he took the first oath to support it in the office of President. He reverently bowed down and kissed the Bible, and then, with all the retinue of Congress and officials, he went to St. Paul's, and began his own and the national career in offices of worship and prayer. Now, if we study this great example of the true American, we find in it, whatever his faults, a certain harmony and proportion of qualities which are only rarely developed in the narrowness of sectarian education. A class of Christian laymen has been generated in the Anglican communion, through successive ages, possessing a certain family likeness, which is recognized in all their varieties of station and manner of life. Not to go further back, take the poet Spenser and Sir Philip Sidney, — take Raleigh, and Sir Henry Wotton, and Hyde, and Falkland, and John

[1] See Note L'''.

Evelyn, and Izaak Walton, and Boyle, and Addison, and Burke, and Johnson, and Cowper, and Wilberforce, and others, whose very names are lessons, — such are the characters we need in the Republic. Such were our own John Jay, and many of our most eminent countrymen. It has been, over and over again, asserted by critics and orators, that Washington's character was formed by his mother, by the catechism she taught him, the books she read to him on the day of the Lord, and the habits to which she trained him as a young Christian. It is true in a larger sense that he owed this to his mother, — to his mother's mother, the Anglican Church. Well has De Maistre said, "She is most precious," — most precious to our country, so long as she preserves her salt. If that should "lose its savour," and cease to season our social and civil estate, I doubt not we shall speedily perish.

31. AN APPEAL TO YOUTH.

In such a great and marvellous country, and at a most trying crisis, you, my dear young friends, are about to enter upon life. In former lectures I have invited you to claim for yourselves a noble mission, and to let God mark out for you a career of usefulness and of duty. I reminded you, at the outset,[1] that your mark is to be made upon the beginnings of another century. The era is outgrowing its *teens;* there is solemnity in the very sound of the *Twentieth Century,* with which you

[1] Lecture I., § 4, page 12.

are to be identified. You have yet a few years to prepare for it: avoid American hurry, and give those years to thorough study, that you may enter upon your maturity and your allotted work with the thoroughly furnished mind which is the secret of power and mastery. Beware of shiftless means and irresolute aims. Beware of the sort of life epitomized by Dr. Young: —

> "At thirty man suspects himself a fool;
> Knows it at forty, and reforms his plan;
> At fifty chides his infamous delay;
> Pushes his prudent purpose to resolve;
> Resolves and re-resolves, then dies the same."

If, in directing your attention at this stage of your preparation to the ennobling study of history, I have given you any practical hints for that pursuit, I am largely rewarded already; but far greater will be my reward, when, in later days, you know by experience the value of what I have taught, and in those days perchance may recall these evenings of the "Hobart Guild," —

> "Remembering me, and these my exhortations."

32. CONCLUSION.

Yours will then be no share in the remorse of those who, having lived liked fools, come to "die as the fool dieth." The sickly whine, "Is life worth living?" will have received its answer in a life well spent. You will find at least some fruits of your toils and efforts recognized by your fellow men as wholesome and refreshing. But, far better, in your own conscience will be your sweet reward, in the sense of duty done, and a mission fulfilled through the grace of God. " Is life worth living?" No, gentlemen, if by life is meant the torpid existence of the materialist, or the feverish excitement which is called life by the voluptuary; not if life is but groping in the dark, and refusing to walk in the light of day; not if it means drifting to and fro without ballast, without rudder, without chart and compass, and with no certain haven where one would be; not if it be " without God in the world " and without hope in death. But oh! what a gift is life " that answers life's great end "! that adds another to the noble army of the faithful, by whose testimony truth has been maintained, by whom the blessings of the Gospel have been handed down to successive generations, by whose intercessions the world itself has been upheld! The secret of such a life was found by Saul of Tarsus, when he uttered his first Christian prayer, " Lord, what wilt thou have me to do?" He has left the greatest mark upon the ages ever imprinted by a human mind upon humanity, and let us be sure that, in our humble degree, we shall not fail to find a similar work, and to fulfil it, if we begin, in the same spirit of humility and self-devotion, kneeling before Him who is the Light of the World.

GENERAL NOTE.

To explain the enlightened plan and purpose of the BISHOP of MICHIGAN, in founding the HOBART GUILD and the BALDWIN LECTURES, it seems proper, in this first volume of the proposed series, to publish the " Deed of Trust," almost entire. In each subsequent volume, it is presumed, a much smaller extract will appear, as is usual in such cases.

"This Instrument, made and executed between Samuel Smith Harris, Bishop of the Protestant Episcopal Church in the Diocese of Michigan, of the city of Detroit, Wayne County, Michigan, as party of the first part, and Henry P. Baldwin, Alonzo B. Palmer, Henry A. Hayden, Sidney D. Miller, and Henry P. Baldwin, 2d, of the State of Michigan, Trustees under the trust created by this instrument, as parties of the second part, witnesseth as follows:—

" In the year of Our Lord one thousand eight hundred and eighty-five, the said party of the first part, moved by the importance of bringing all practicable Christian influences to bear upon the great body of students annually assembled at the University of Michigan, undertook to promote and set in operation a plan of Christian work at said University, and collected contributions for that purpose, of which plan the following outline is here given, that is to say:—

"1. To erect a building or hall near the University, in which there should be cheerful parlors, a well-equipped reading-room, and a lecture-room where the lectures hereinafter mentioned might be given;

"2. To endow a lectureship similar to the Bampton Lectureship in England, for the establishment and defence of

Christian truth: the lectures on such foundation to be delivered annually at Ann Arbor by a learned clergyman or other communicant of the Protestant Episcopal Church, to be chosen as hereinafter provided: such lectures to be not less than six nor more than eight in number, and to be published in book form before the income of the fund shall be paid to the lecturer;

"3. To endow two other lectureships, one on Biblical Literature and Learning, and the other on Christian Evidences: the object of such lectureships to be to provide for all the students who may be willing to avail themselves of them a complete course of instruction in sacred learning, and in the philosophy of right thinking and right living, without which no education can justly be considered complete;

"4. To organize a society, to be composed of the students in all classes and departments of the University who may be members of or attached to the Protestant Episcopal Church, of which society the Bishop of the Diocese, the Rector, Wardens, and Vestrymen of St. Andrew's Parish, and all the Professors of the University who are communicants of the Protestant Episcopal Church should be members *ex officio*, which society should have the care and management of the reading-room and lecture-room of the hall, and of all exercises or employments carried on therein, and should moreover annually elect each of the lecturers herein before mentioned, upon the nomination of the Bishop of the Diocese.

"In pursuance of the said plan, the said society of students and others has been duly organized under the name of the 'Hobart Guild of the University of Michigan'; the hall above mentioned has been builded and called Hobart Hall; and Mr. Henry P. Baldwin of Detroit, Michigan, and Sibyl A. Baldwin, his wife, have given to the said party of the first part the sum of ten thousand dollars for the endowment and support of the lectureship first hereinbefore mentioned.

"Now therefore, I, the said Samuel Smith Harris, Bishop as aforesaid, do hereby give, grant, and transfer to the said Henry P. Baldwin, Alonzo B. Palmer, Henry A. Hayden, Sidney D. Miller, and Henry P. Baldwin, 2d, Trustees as aforesaid, the said sum of ten thousand dollars to be invested in good and safe interest-bearing securities, the net income thereof to be paid and applied from time to time as hereinafter provided, the said sum and the income thereof to be held in trust for the following uses : —

"1. The said fund shall be known as the Endowment Fund of the Baldwin Lectures.

"2. There shall be chosen annually by the Hobart Guild of the University of Michigan, upon the nomination of the Bishop of Michigan, a learned clergyman or other communicant of the Protestant Episcopal Church, to deliver at Ann Arbor and under the auspices of the said Hobart Guild, between the Feast of St. Michael and All Angels and the Feast of St. Thomas, in each year, not less than six nor more than eight lectures, for the Establishment and Defence of Christian Truth; the said lectures to be published in book form by Easter of the following year, and to be entitled ' The Baldwin Lectures'; and there shall be paid to the said lecturer the income of the said endowment fund, upon the delivery of fifty copies of said lectures to the said Trustees or their successors; the said printed volumes to contain, as an extract from this instrument, or in condensed form, a statement of the object and conditions of this trust."

Under this trust the Right Reverend Arthur Cleveland Coxe, D. D., LL. D., Bishop of Western New York, was appointed to deliver the Lectures for the year 1886.

DETROIT, *Advent*, 1886.

NOTES.

NOTE A, *page* 21.

Consult Dean Stanley's "Eastern Church" (Lecture III. p. 113) on the continuous application of the title *Papa* to the Bishops of Alexandria, down to our times.

NOTE B, *page* 21.

"The Rise of the Papal Power," etc., by Robert Hussey, B. D. Oxford, 1863. See page 48, on the Sardican Canon, but compare Littledale's "Plain Reasons," etc., (London, 1879,) pp. 120, 121, where the best and most succinct account of the matter is comprehended in a few paragraphs. Philip Smith's "History," etc., is a truly valuable manual, and, if purged from its ambiguities, would be precisely what I could refer to as a manual for my readers. But it falls into the old ruts, gives the "Popes" from St. Peter, and credits St. Jerome, apparently, with making Peter a *pope*, when he only means that Jerome considers him the first bishop of the See of Rome, which is of itself only a partial truth. Then he says: "This title is used as *convenient*, though it was not appropriated to the Bishop of Rome till about A. D. 500." It was not so *appropriated* till a century later: he means that Western writers began to speak of "the Pope" as we speak of "the post-office,"—meaning the nearest one; but in the seventh century the West began to draw away from the East. But why is it "convenient" to mystify the student, and to upset historic truth, in the structure of a work meant to give true history?

Note C, *page* 22.

See Dean Milman's "History of Latin Christianity," vol. i. pp. 24-30, where, mixing up some mere fictions with a great deal of truth, this author lays down facts which revolutionize the entire scheme and structure of his own work. Taking this firm ground of fact, which he should have held impregnable, he comes down from the fortress and drops into that same "Serbonian bog" which has swallowed up, not merely armies, but nations, — I mean the fictions of the Decretals. Of these he speaks, not forcibly, but feebly, when he comes to Nicholas I. See vol. ii. p. 303. On the previous page he recognizes the exceptional character of this pontiff, but fails to note that even the few facts he chronicles define Nicholas as the first of the "Popes," as that term is now understood.

Note D, *page* 23.

See Stanley's "Eastern Church," p. 16, Lecture I. On the Latin or Roman pretences to Catholicity, see some remarks of Coleridge, "Aids to Reflection," Aphorism VIII. p. 165, ed. London, 1859.

Note E, *page* 24.

For lack of a firm grip upon the true origin of the Papacy, and because he fails to note the difference between the *Papacy*, as titular, and the *Paparchy*, as created by the Decretals under Nicholas and the canonist Gratian, I am forced, most reluctantly, to qualify my estimate of this author's valuable work. But it is the best we have on the subject.

Note F, *page* 25.

See "Ante-Nicene Fathers," Am. edition, vol. ii. p. 165. If the history of Alexandria for the first four centuries could have been turned over to Rome, the Decretals would not have been needed by her pontiffs. They would have appeared supreme without them.

Note G, *page* 26.

See "The Idea of God," etc., pp. 83-109, Boston, 1886.

This is a most creditable work, for its author is turning his face, and not his back, to the sun.

NOTE H, *page* 28.

See as above. But note the entire failure of the author to prove what he assumes, namely, that Augustine is antagonistic to Clement and the Greek Fathers; which is only true as to single statements, (chiefly in treating of the Manichæan heresy,) and not as to his system of anthropology, received by the whole Church, in what are called "the doctrines of grace." See the above-mentioned work, pp. 94, 95.

NOTE I, *page* 30.

The present pontiff gives his subjects leave to think, but only in the formulas of Aristotle and the deductions of Aquinas. And even Aquinas is overruled in his Scriptural positions about the Immaculate Conception, etc., by the new dogmas which Leo XIII. accepts from his feeble predecessor. He has thus lost his great opportunity to qualify them by such explanations as are resorted to, in his obedience, by all sensible writers. Without such explanations, the chaos into which they throw the Papal decrees and the theology of Trent is simply " confusion worse confounded."

NOTE J, *page* 31.

Consult Gladstone's "Vatican Decrees," etc., Dr. Schaff's edition, New York, 1875. Also, Mr. Gladstone's "Answer to Replies," etc., New York, Harpers, 1875. Also, " The Vatican Council," (containing the speech of Bishop Kenrick, not spoken, but suppressed and subsequently privately printed by the author,) New York, American Tract Society, 1875. Also, "Janus, Pope and Council," pp. 86-96, Rivingtons, London, 1869.

NOTE K, *page* 32.

See Bacon's Works, vol. viii. p. 76 *et seq.*, and vol. ix. pp. 97-102, ed. Boston, 1864. The utterance of any new creed was *dogmatically* condemned by the Council of Chalcedon. It had been denounced by Canon previously. See this ably demonstrated by Ffoulkes, " Letter to Manning," 1869.

NOTE L, *page* 33.
See Ruskin's "Bible of Amiens," p. 41, ed. London, 1848.

Note M, *page* 36.
See "Ante-Nicene Fathers," vol. viii. pp. 601–644, Am. edition. But here I must enlarge, for my argument in these Lectures turns on the fact that the Decretals, out of a canonical Patriarchate and a merely titular Papacy, created the Paparchy. Thus abolishing the Catholic Constitutions, they mark Nicholas I. as the founder of the Papal System, with the "Holy Roman Empire" as its *Œcumene*. It is a Western fiction and a Western schism; and Nicholas is clearly the first " Pope " in history, as we now use that term. I shall cite the Jesuits themselves in proof.

In their *Études Religieuses* (No. 471. p. 392), as quoted in the original French by Mr. Ffoulkes, in his Letter to Cardinal Manning, written while he was himself a Roman Catholic, they make a candid statement which I translate as follows: " The pseudo-Isidorian *reform* (that of the false Decretals) was good assuredly, for it was adopted by St. Nicholas in A. D. 865, and by the Eighth *Œcumenical* (Roman, or Western *œcumené*) Council in A. D. 870. It was confirmed by the Council of Trent in A. D. 1564, and for nine centuries has been the Common Law of the *Catholic* Church " ; — i. e. the Church which ceased to be *Catholic* by these very acts.

Here then is the origin of the Paparchy in 865, and the foundation of the existing "*Roman* Catholic Church," so called, when, just seven hundred years after Nicholas, adopting the new creed of Pius IV. (subsequently formulated) they made these Decretals *the base of another novel organization.*

But let us see what the Jesuits say further. Here is their comment, recognizing the fact that Nicholas revolutionized the West, and *detached it from the Catholic Constitutions.* They say : " But the ancient discipline (of Nicæa and the great councils) was good also, because for the eight centuries previous — *the Church had known no other.*" Up to that day, then, even the titular " Popes " of the West had professed to be subject to the Nicene Constitutions, and to be bound to enforce and *to obey them.* These Jesuits add, that "the Christian world has been the dupe of a *mistake* for seven hundred years"; that is, the honest mistake of Gratian when he forced into the Canon Law what was originally a "premeditated lie." It took three centuries to turn it from a Papal imposture into Western Law.

Now, if the Church of England succumbed, *functionally* but not *organically*, to such an imposture for four hundred years, what is more evident than the fact that her Restoration to Catholicity was effected, under Warham, when her Convocation with such unanimity rejected the false Canons and reverted to the Nicene?

NOTE N, *page* 36.

See Littledale's "Plain Reasons," pp. 178-180. Bear in mind that *primacy* is not *supremacy*.

NOTE O, *page* 43.

See Renan, "Les Apôtres," etc., Paris, 1883, pp. 216-229, and "St. Paul," pp. 2, 3, *et seq.*

NOTE P, *page* 47.

See Juvenal, Sat. iii. 62-65, and compare Suetonius, "The Twelve Cæsars," under "Nero."

NOTE Q, *page* 48.

Renan, *ut supra*, "Les Apôtres," etc., pp. 224 *et seq.* Even Renan confesses here the beautiful fruits of Christian civilization. Does he understand that the glorified Roman Law comes out of it? Elsewhere I have said (see Ante-Nicene Fathers, vol. vi. p. 4) as follows:—

"Justinian calls Berytus 'the mother and nurse' of the Civil Law. Now Caius, whose *Institutes* were discovered in 1820 by the sagacity of Niebuhr, seems to have been a Syrian. So were Papinian and Ulpian; and, heathen as they were, *they lived under the illumination reflected from Antioch*, and, not less than the Antonines, they were examples of a philosophic regeneration which never could have existed until the Christian era had begun its triumphs. Of this sort of pagan philosophy Julian became afterwards the grand embodiment; and in Julian's grudging confessions of what he had learned from Christianity we have a key to the secret convictions of others, such as I have named, — characters in whom, as in Plutarch and in many retrograde unbelievers of our day, we detect the operation of influences they are unwilling to acknowledge, — of which, possibly, they are blindly unconscious themselves. Roman law, I maintain, therefore, indirectly owes its origin, as it is directly indebted for its completion in the Pandects, to the new powers and processes of thought which came from 'the Light of the World.' It was light from Galilee and Golgotha, answering Pilate's question in the inward convictions of many a heathen sage."

NOTE R, *page* 53.

See "Ante-Nicene Fathers," Am. edition, vol. i. p. 45. Compare Lightfoot's "Apostolic Fathers," vol. ii. sect. ii., *passim*.

NOTE S, *page* 58.

The moth is the enemy of the bee, and, strange to say, a very formidable one. On Pantænus, see "Ante-Nicene Fathers," vol. ii. p. 165, and vol. viii. p. 776.

NOTE T, *page* 59.

See Fiske's "Idea of God," 3d edition, 1886, *ut supra;* and "Ante-Nicene Fathers," vol. vi. p. 303. I am sorry that Mr. Fiske speaks (p. 97) of "the mischief wrought by the Augustinian conception of Deity." It is essentially that of Athanasius.

NOTE U, *page* 61.

See "Ante-Nicene Fathers," vol. vi. p. 495; and Coleridge's strictures, "Notes on English Divines," vol. i. p. 266, ed. London, 1853.

NOTE V, *page* 62.

Professor Allen of Cambridge seems to have prompted John Fiske to such ideas, in his "Continuity of Christian Thought," a "suggestive work," indeed, but terribly involved as to the *Unity* of Christian Thought, which is essential to its "Continuity."

NOTE W, *page* 64.

I have endeavoured to bring this out clearly, to the great credit of the Church in Rome at this early period, in several volumes of the "Ante-Nicene Fathers." See vol. ii. p. 3, and vol. viii. p. 765. The Catacombs confirm such evidences.

NOTE X, *page* 64.

See "Ante-Nicene Fathers," vol. i. p. 309.

NOTE Y, *page* 66.

See "Ante-Nicene Fathers," vol. iii. p. 4. Also, Stanley, "Eastern Church," Lect. V., p. 184.

NOTE Z, *page* 68.

The *suburbicarian* district is explained in "Ante-Nicene Fathers," vol. v. p. 156, and its nature and relations to the Bishop of Rome are illustrated in the succeeding pages to page 162. Note also Ibid., pp. 409–420, and p. 557.

NOTE A', *page* 68.

See Hippolytus, "Ante-Nicene Fathers," vol. iii. p. 3, Am. ed. For those who have no access to this edition of the Ante-Nicene Fathers, let me note that the statue of Hippolytus was discovered in the progress of excavations at Rome in 1551, and was seated in the Vatican just when the new creed of Pius IV. was promulgated. He was greatly glorified as a saint, at Rome, till his works were discovered on Mt. Athos, in 1842. In 1851, when their authenticity and genuineness were established, I saw the statue in the Vatican. But, just then, Providence seems to have warned Pius IX. not to make a new dogma, as, three hundred years before, the unearthing of the statue seems to have warned Pius IV. not to make a new creed. For Hippolytus proves that Zephyrinus and Callistus, two early Bishops of Rome, were not only basely immoral, but rank heretics, whom he and his co-bishops barely saved from delivering over the See of Rome to heresy at this early date. In the face of this warning, Pius IX. declared all the Roman bishops, from the beginning, to have been, like himself, "Infallible."

Note B', page 72.

See "Ante-Nicene Fathers," vol. ii. pp. 295-298. The early martyrs were "multitudes," says Tertullian. Can it be possible that he would use such language to the magistrates, if he knew that such instances were of rare occurrence? The disposition of our times to *minimize* the persecutions of our Christian forefathers calls upon us to note such references, all the more important because occurring *obiter*, and mentioned as notorious. Note also the closing chapter of his Apology, and reference to the outcries of the populace, in cap. xxxv. See admirable remarks on the benefits derived by the Church from the sufferings of Christian martyrs, with direct reference to Tertullian, in Wordsworth, Church History to Council of Nicæa, cap. xxiv. p. 374.

Note C', page 75.

Compare Bossuet on Psalm ii. 10, *Et nunc reges:* "Il les a donc appelés *non point par necessité*, mais par grâce." Opp., vol. iii. p. 83, ed. Paris, 1845.

Note D', page 78.

See "Ante-Nicene Fathers," vol. viii. p. 3, where I note the absence of exultation on the conversion of the Emperor.

Note E', page 79.

Concerning the celibate, I have elsewhere noted, "Ante-Nicene Fathers," vol. iv. p. 115, a remarkable admission from an unexpected quarter, — an admission that the principle of a pure asceticism, like that of the early anchorets. lies deep in our nature, as human. Thus speaks Professor J. P. Cooke, of Harvard: "*It is well to go away at times, that we may see another aspect of human life* which still survives in the East, and to feel that influence which led even the Christ into the wilderness to prepare for the struggle with the animal nature of man. We need something of the experience of the anchorites of Egypt, to impress us with the great truth that the distinction between the spiritual and the material remains broad and clear, even if with the scalpel of our modern philosophy we cannot completely dissect the two; and this experience will give us courage to cherish our aspirations, keep bright our hopes, and hold fast our Christian faith until the consummation comes." See his "Scientific Culture," New York, 1884. Nevertheless, marriage has been the rule, and celibacy the exception, in the Church of Christ.

St. Peter was a married apostle, and the traditions of his wife, which connect her married life with Rome itself, render it most surprising that those who claim to be St. Peter's successors should denounce the marriage of the clergy. Her touching story, borrowed from Clement of Alexandria, is related by Eusebius. "And will they," says Clement, "reject even the apostles? Peter and Philip, indeed, had children; Philip also gave his daughters in marriage to husbands; and Paul does not demur, in a certain Epistle, to mention his own wife, whom, in order to expedite his ministry the better, he did not take about with him." Of St. Peter and his wife, Eusebius subjoins, "Such was the marriage of these blessed ones, and such was their perfect affection."

The Easterns to this day perpetuate the marriage of the clergy, and enjoin it; but unmarried men only are chosen to be bishops. Even Rome relaxes her discipline for the *Uniats*, and hundreds of her priesthood, therefore, live in honourable marriage. Thousands live in secret marriage, but their wives are dishonoured as "concubines," and unchaste living is all but universal. It was not till the twelfth century that the celibate was enforced. In England it was *never* successfully imposed; and, though the "priest's *leman*" was not called his *wife*, to the disgrace of the whole system, she was yet honoured (see Chaucer), and often carried herself too proudly. See "Notes and Queries," vol. i. pp. 147, 148.

The enormous evils of an enforced celibacy need not here be remarked upon. The history of "Sacerdotal Celibacy," by Henry C. Lea, of Philadelphia, (Boston, Houghton, Mifflin, & Co., 2d edition, enlarged, 1884,) is compendious, and can be readily procured. We must not be wiser than God, even in our zeal for His service.

Note F', *page* 79.

A paragraph, good so far as it goes, in Stanley's "Eastern Church," page 230, closes with a most pregnant sentence, thus: "Undoubtedly, if Constantine is to be judged by the place which he occupies among the benefactors of mankind, he would rank, not among the secondary characters of history, but among the very first." The same remark applies to Charlemagne, though less strikingly, all things considered. Compare Döllinger, "Reunion," etc., p. 24, and Stanley, *ut supra*, p. 249. For the *humanity* of the new system, see "Ante-Nicene Fathers," vol. v. p. 563, Elucidation xii. From my own remarks in that series, I cite as follows: —

"Clement was able to remind the heathen, in Nero's time, that Christ had '*already* made the universe an ocean of blessings.' The moral canons of Christianity reflecting the Light of the World operated practically. The first Christian hospital was founded (A.D. 350) by Ephraem Syrus. His example was followed by St. Basil, who also founded another for lepers. The founding of hostels as refuges for travellers was an institution of the Nicene period. 'In the time of Chrysostom,' says Lecky, not too well disposed towards the Gospel, ' the church of Antioch supported three thousand widows and virgins, besides strangers and sick. Legacies for the poor became common; and it was not infrequent for men and women who desired to live a life of especial sanctity, and especially for priests who attained the episcopacy, as a first act, to bestow their properties in charity. A Christian, it was maintained, should devote at least one tenth of his profits to the poor. A priest named Thalasius collected blind beggars in an asylum on the banks of the Euphrates. A merchant named Apollinus founded on Mount Nitria a gratuitous dispensary.'

"So Cyprian's canons, in days of persecution, in lieu of revenge and retaliation, enforce (1) works of mercy; (2) almsdeeds; (3) brotherly love; (4) mutual support; (5) forgiveness of injuries; (6) the example of Christ's holy living; (7) forbearance; (8) suppression of idle talk; (9) love of enemies; (10) abhorrence of usury, (11) of avarice, (12) and of carnal impurity: also, (13) obedience to parents; (14) parental love; (15) consideration of servants; (16) respect for the aged; (17) moderation, even in use of things lawful; (18) control of the tongue; (19) abstinence from detraction; (20) to visit the sick; (21) care of widows and orphans; (22) not to flatter; (23) to practise the Golden Rule; and (24) to abstain from bloodshed. In short, we have here the outgrowth of the Sermon on the Mount, and of St. Paul's epitome, 'Whatsoever things are true,'" etc.

Note G', page 84.

See "Ante-Nicene Fathers," vol. i. p. 52, and vol. v. p. 411, Elucid. iv. Consult Balmes, "Le Protestantisme comparé," etc., cap. xiv. p. 171, ed. Paris, 1851. This author, a Jesuit, takes to the credit of modern *Roman* Catholics all the good done to the world by primitive Christians.

Note H', page 85.

See Cyprian, *passim*, in his Epistles, "Ante-Nicene Fathers," vol. v., and my Introduction, page 263. Also, Ep. xi. p. 292.

Note I', page 85.

Stanley is a thorough Erastian, yet we may well consult his view of the growth of the Imperial influence. See "Eastern Church," p. 230, and elsewhere.

Note J', page 87.

De Maistre is a fanatical assailant of Gallicanism in all its phases, but most instructive are his admissions as to the essential *identity* of the *Regale*, as conceded to France by all the Popes, and denied to England at the Restoration. Henry VIII. in A. D. 1551 went no farther than Louis XIV. in A. D. 1682; that is, the English Convocation was excommunicated under Henry for what was done with *entire unanimity* by the French bishops under the lead of Bossuet. See De Maistre, Opp., vol. iv. p. 326, and the entire treatise " De l'Église Gallicane."

Note K', *page* 91.

Stanley, *ut supra*, Lect. IV. p. 140.

Note L', *page* 91.

"Ante-Nicene Fathers," vol. v. p. 413, Elucid. x., and the "Treatise on Unity," *passim*, but specially see Elucidations, p. 557 *et seq*. As to ecclesiastical regimen, based on the co-equality of bishops, and their *consent* to the priority of certain brethren for the sake of order and convenience, note that in the time of Constantine the Eastern and Western Empires were each divided into seven districts, called *dioceses*, which comprised about one hundred and eighteen *provinces*. Each province contained several cities, with a district attached to it. The ecclesiastical rulers of the dioceses were called *patriarchs*, *exarchs*, or *archbishops*, of whom there were fourteen; the rulers of the provinces were styled *metropolitans*, i. e. governors of the μητρόπολις or mother city, and those of each city and its districts were simply known as *bishops*. So that the division which we now call a *diocese* was in ancient times *a union of dioceses*, and a *parish* was a *combination* of modern parishes.

Note M', *page* 93.

See "Ante-Nicene Fathers," vol. vi. pp. v. and vi., prefatory. Also, Stanley, *ut supra*, Lect. III. p. 113. "The Bishop of Alexandria," says this author, "was known by a title which he alone bore in that assembly (Nicæa). He was *the* Pope. The 'Pope of Rome' was a phrase which had not yet emerged in history, but the 'Pope of Alexandria' was a well-known dignity." Why then stultify history by calling the early Bishops of Rome *Popes?*

That the theology of the great school of Alexandria had a character of its own is most apparent; I should be the last to deny it. As its succession of teachers was like that of hereditary descent in a family, a family likeness is naturally to be found in the school, from the great Clement to the great Athanasius. It is a school that hands on the traditions in which Apollos had been reared; it not less reflects the Greek influences always dominant in the capital of the Macedonian hero; but it is a school in which the Gospel of Christ as the Light of the World was always made *predominant;* and, while a most liberal view of human *knowledge* was inculcated in it, yet *the faith* was always exalted as the mother and mistress of the true *gnosis* and of all science. The wise men of this world were summoned with an imperial voice, from this eldest seat and centre of Christian learning, to cast their crowns and their treasures at the feet of Jesus. With a generous patronage Clement conceded all he could to the philosophy of the Greeks, and yet sublimely rose above it to a sphere it never discovered, and looked down upon all merely human intellect and its achievements like Uriel in the sun.

It was the special, though unconscious, mission of this school to prepare the way, and to shape the thought of Christendom, for the great epoch of the (nominal) conversion of the Empire, and for the all-important synodical period, its logical consequence. It was in this school that the technical formulas of the Church were naturally wrought out. The process was like that of the artist who has first to make his own tools. He does many things, and resorts to many contrivances, never afterwards necessary when once the tools are complete, and his laboratory furnished with all he wants for his work. See "Ante-Nicene Fathers," vol. vi. pp. 257, 303.

Note N', *page* 96.

Under the Cypriote privilege, the Church of England maintained her autonomy till the time of Henry II., and never lost it, altogether, under the succeeding reigns. After about four hundred years of usurpation, the Cypriote Canon took lasting effect again under Henry VIII. By this canon, the eighth of Ephesus, *all insular churches* are exempt from jurisdiction of the Patriarchates. And, apart from this, the second Canon of Constantinople ordains that "churches *among barbarians* must be governed according to the customs prevalent with their ancestors." This meets the case of the Church of England even in the days of Theodore of Tarsus, its second founder. So also Canon XXVIII. of Chalcedon.

Note O', page 97.

The Nicene Creed, so called, ends abruptly, and is closed by the *anathema*, its enacting clause, which is therefore not recited as part thereof. Obviously, however, it was not to stop here, liturgically, when recited in the public worship of the Church; but it was allowed to conclude as we still use in the Apostles' Creed, or in the Creed of Jerusalem. The Council of Constantinople added the Jerusalem formula, slightly varied, and made it the orthodox confession touching the Holy Ghost, the Church, etc. See Stanley's "Eastern Church," Lect. II. pp. 71–74; and the whole subject, in "Ante-Nicene Fathers," vol. vii. p. 524.

Note P', page 103.

See Note K', *supra*, p. 91. Dean Stanley infers that what was thus done to honour the Scriptures in later councils was based on the example of Nicæa. But though this is a reasonable inference, and among Easterns especially, I do not find the recorded statement. See Stanley, "Eastern Church," p. 140, with his references.

Note Q', page 108.

The *Liber Diurnus* obliges every Pope to anathematize (his predecessor) Honorius as a heretic. See Döllinger, "Popes of the Middle Ages," p. 229, ed. 1871; "The Church and the Bishops," by H. St. A. von Liano, London, Rivingtons, 1870.

Note R', page 120.

Alcuin, Opp., vol. i. p. 52, Epist. xxxviii., ed. Ratisbon, 1777. This edition omits the "Caroline Books," on advice from Rome.

Note S', page 121.

Dupin does not decide the question as to the authorship of the "Caroline Books," but suggests no other name with equal probabilities in its favour.

Note T', page 130.

Voltaire exults in details of his ferocity, but Bossuet's

eulogy is extravagant, and makes him a saint. He was canonized by the Antipope Paschal II., A. D. 1165.

NOTE U', *page* 134.

The Guelphs and Ghibellines were also known as the *Bianchi* and *Neri*. The readers of Dante are familiar with these names, which represent the *Welfen* and *Waiblingen* of Germany, in Tramontane forms of the South. See a strange account of them in the work of Aroux, a French Ultramontanist, entitled, "Dante, Hérétique, Révolutionnaire et Socialiste," Paris, 1854. The Guelphs were the Pontifical party, and their antagonists were Imperialists, among whom Dante is chief.

NOTE V', *page* 137.

See Littledale, *ut supra*, pp. 120 *et seq*. I refer frequently to this valuable manual, because it may be had at petty cost in the form of a tract of the London S. P. C. K. It condenses much material and gives useful references. Every student should possess it, as an index to reading on this subject.

NOTE W', *page* 137.

Many of his expressions may be found in Littledale, *ut supra*, pp. 176, 177. Also, S. Gregor. Epist., Lib. V. Ep. xviii., Paris, 1849.

NOTE X', *page* 140.

Thus Charlemagne summoned a council meant to be *œcumenical* in effect. He overruled Adrian and humbled Leo. I am pleased with the terse remarks of Goethe on this period, in a letter to Zelter (Sept. 8, 1828): "As soon as Charles Martel appeared, the chaos which had enveloped Gaul and the rest of the world disappeared. Happily Pepin and Charlemagne follow, but then again a long period of chaos." See "Letters to Zelter," p. 333, ed. Coleridge, London, 1887.

NOTE Y', *page* 143.

It is all-important to bear in mind the unquestioning submission of the West to the Canon Law, with which Gratian identified these forgeries. They knew no better. Since their exposure, however, they have been adopted and reenacted, and made the framework of the modern "Roman Catholic Church." This is shown in the letter of Edward Ffoulkes to Cardinal Manning, heretofore quoted.

Note Z', *page* 146.

The valuable work of Dr. Maitland was a reprint from the "British Magazine," edited by the estimable Hugh James Rose. The third edition appeared in 1853, and I think several have appeared since. It gave a great impulse to the Oxford movement, but was unfortunate in its secondary effects, which were reactionary and extravagant.

Note A", *page* 147.

"The Fall of Constantinople," etc., by Edwin Pears, etc., New York, 1886. See page 4. This is a work on the Latin Conquest; not the final fall of the Christian metropolis, in A. D. 1453. On this subject, I cannot forbear to quote the forcible words of Mr. Ffoulkes in his letter to Cardinal Manning: "It has often been set to the credit of the Popes, that they saved Europe from the Turks. History says that *they opened the door by which the Turks came in*. It is certain that the Latins proved the ruin of the Greek Empire, much more than the Turks. Had the Greek Empire been left to itself, or helped honestly, it would have barred the Turks from Europe *to this day*, and preserved all the civilization, population, and Christianity contained in it for man." This is not only true, but *so very true* that by this fact alone the Paparchy, convicted of a war upon Christendom in the interest of Mohammedanism, is proved an Antichrist.

Note B", *page* 149.

Littledale's chapter on "The Wickedness of the Local Church of Rome," *ut supra*, p. 208 *et seq.*, may well be referred to. And see Ffoulkes's letter to Manning on this head also.

NOTE C", *page* 150.

The history of Pope Joan is given with candor in Bishop Hopkins's "End of Controversy Controverted" (New York, 1854); but see also Döllinger, "Fables respecting the Popes in the Middle Ages," translated by Plummer, London, Rivington, 1871. In the splendid church on the Superga, near Turin, amid pictures of the pontiffs, I saw that of Pope Joan, in 1851. It was pointed out by the *custode* with derision. A similar memorial in the cathedral of Sienna has been removed. Those anxious to look into this very curious matter are also referred to the "Esame critico degli Atti e Documenti relativa alla Favola della Papessa Giovanna, di A. Bianchi-Giovini," Milan, 1844. It was reviewed in the North British Review for February, 1850.

NOTE D", *page* 151.

Edgar's speech, as reported, agrees with authentic documents of the age in all that it includes; but I do not find it in William of Malmesbury.

NOTE E", *page* 152.

Hincmar deserves especial note. See "Church of France," by Jervis, London, 1872, vol. i. pp. 32–38; also "Life and Times of Hincmar," by J. C. Prichard, Oxford, 1849.

NOTE F", *page* 153.

De Maistre complains that Louis XIV. established "la suprématie anglaise dans toute sa perfection." Why then was France not excommunicated, like England? This author devotes to this inquiry a whole chapter of "L'Église Gallicane," p. 341, Paris, 1853.

NOTE G", *page* 154.

Bossuet, according to De Maistre, is indeed to be pitied. See page 334 of that author's "L'Église Gallicane," which impeaches him so severely. This great bishop used to speak of "the Romans," and thus authorizes us to do the same.

NOTE H", *page* 155.

St. Bernard's words are these: "Quis mihi det antequam moriar videre Ecclesiam Dei, sicut in diebus antiquis ; quando apostoli laxabant retia, non in capturam argenti vel auri, sed in capturans animarum." Epist. ccxxxviii. tom. i. p. 499, ed. Paris, 1839.

NOTE I", *page* 155.

This golden letter of St. Bernard to the Canons of Lyons may be found as above, Epist. clxxiv. p. 390. See his strictures on the Papacy, (De Consideratione, iii. 4,) Ibid., p. 1049.

NOTE J", *page* 157.

Of Bernard's conflict with Abelard, see Archbishop Trench's " Mediæval Church," p. 210, New York, 1878.

NOTE K", *page* 161.

Trace the overflow of barbarians upon Western Christendom in any map series like that of Gage, New York, 1869. See Trench, *ut supra*, pp. 24, 25, *et seq*.

NOTE L", *page* 162.

Whewell, in his " Inductive Sciences," makes this clear. See vol. i. pp. 177, 181, ed. New York, 1858.

NOTE M", *page* 165.

The *Renaissance* is powerfully outlined by Michelet, to whose work I shall have occasion to refer. See " Histoire de France au XVIme Siècle," Paris, 1855.

NOTE N", *page* 166.

See Roscoe's Life of Lorenzo, — a fascinating account of this great man's hand in the revival of learning,— chap. i. p. 59, London, Bohn, 1846.

NOTE O", *page* 169.

See Michelet, *ut supra*, p. 83 of his Introduction, on the lack of scientific building in the pointed architecture.

NOTE P", *page* 169.

Michelet, *ut supra*, p. 84 of Introduction. Hogarth has fastened this story on Columbus, but see " Notes and Queries," 1856, p. 72.

NOTE Q", *page* 173.

Michelet (*ut supra*, p. 1) has a brilliant picture of Charles VIII. and his invasion of Italy, A. D. 1494.

NOTE R", *page* 174.

Of the Council of Florence, a recent writer, while a member of the Papal communion, speaks thus forcibly to Cardinal Manning: "Of all Councils that ever were held, I suppose there never was one in which hypocrisy, duplicity, and worldly motives played a more conspicuous or disgraceful part. How the Council of Basle was outwitted, and Florence named as the place to which the Greeks should come; how the galleys of the Pope outstripped the galleys of the Council, and bore the Greeks in triumph from Constantinople to a town in the centre of Italy, where the Pope was all-powerful; how they were treated there; and why they were subsequently removed to Florence, — would reveal a series of intrigues of the lowest order, if I had space to transcribe them; unfortunately, they were too patent at every stage of the Council for the real objects of its promoters to admit of the slightest doubt." He adds, justly: "The Easterns were trampled upon for maintaining their rights, ejected from their churches, . . . and supplanted by a rival hierarchy, wherever the Crusaders conquered."

NOTE S", *page* 176.

This is brilliantly illustrated by Michelet, treating of Angelo " comme prophète " (*ut supra*, pp. 210-228). On the anniversary of the opening of the Sistine chapel, All-Saints' day, 1851, the work of Michael, before the eyes of such a court, greatly impressed me, as I saw Pius IX. pontificate.

NOTE T", *page* 183.

See Note W', *supra*, p. 317. See also Ep. xix. pp. 744, 749, and Lib. vii. Ep. xiii. p. 891.

NOTE U", *page* 199.

Alarmed at the growing fulness of my notes, I have omitted citations in this Lecture, to which I now refer my reader in general terms. My notes are designed to hint, to youthful students, the sources of information ordinarily to be found in college libraries. Consult Soames, "Anglo-Saxon Church," 4th ed., 1856; Innett, "History of the English Church," Oxford, 1855. Collier's great History of the same, in nine volumes, and Bede's works, translated, may be found even more readily perhaps. Fuller's "Church History of Britain" is so witty that young students find it a delightful work to begin with.

NOTE V", *page* 218.

This is shown by Michelet in a frightful note to his Introduction (p. cxli.), where he cites his proof that Innocent accepted with enthusiasm the whole responsibility for the massacres of the Vaudois, etc.

NOTE W", *page* 225.

The divorce of Queen Vashti might almost as well be made the starting-point for a history of Henry VIII. as that of Queen Katherine. But, the beaten track is still plodded over in new books, as well as in journalism.

NOTE X", *pages* 228, 247.

There was no "divorce" of Queen Katherine properly speaking, because there was no marriage. It was a case of incest, licensed by Pope Julius for money. Yet see how Guizot falls into the ruts, and flippantly gives his opinion of the "divorce" against all the contemporary decisions of Universities, scholars, and divines, in the Papal communion itself. See his "History of France," vol. iii. p. 143. He seems to imagine that Henry could have acted arbitrarily in so great a case, instead of seeing that it was only because England was ready to break with the Papacy that he was able to bring it about on such slight provocation. The facts about the divorce are admirably stated by Bishop Hopkins, "End of Controversy," etc., vol. i. pp. 23, 40, 197, 215, ed. New York, 1854.

NOTE Y", *page* 236.

Massillon has been accused of sowing the seeds of revolution, but the age no doubt regarded his expressions as mere flourishes. Yet in the "Petit Carême" are apparent premonitions of the Reign of Terror. He says, for example, that God visits upon princes their accumulated sins, "extinguishes their families, withers at the root the stem of their posterity, causes their titles and their possessions to pass into strange hands, renders them striking examples of the inconstancy of human affairs, and monuments beforehand of his judgments against hearts ungrateful and unfeeling, under the fatherly care of His Providence." He tells them that "they owe their place to the free consent of the people," and adds, that, "in a word, as the prime source of their authority is from us, kings should use it only in our behalf." Such were the views in which the French Revolution began, and, however just, they were a species of Lollardism under Louis XIV.

NOTE Z", *page* 243.

Concerning "Codes of Belief," De Maistre has expatiated eloquently, as follows: "If a people possesses one of these *Codes of Belief*, we may be sure of this, that the religion of such a people is false." This he says because he imagines the *Thirty-nine Articles* to be a creed, — a code required of all men as a condition of salvation. But such is not the case, and so his maxim harms not us; but it is fatal to the creed of his own communion. For the Council of Trent has set forth the most enormous system of scholastic subtleties ever digested into a *Code* by the human mind. And all of this is professed as an article of the Faith in the Creed of Pius the Fourth, as follows: "I embrace and receive all and every one of the things which have been defined and declared in the Holy Council of Trent. This true Catholic Faith, *without which no one can be saved*, I do freely confess and sincerely hold." Here we have a *Code of Belief*, indeed, such as De Maistre pronounces necessarily false. I am forced to adopt this conclusion. Not the Anglican, but the Romanist, puts a code into his creed. And think what this code involves, "without which no one can be saved." Millions who cannot write or read are forced to receive even its infinitesimal definitions, some of which not even the wisest men can understand.

Note A''', *page* 250.

This quotation is from Mr. Pugin. My readers may be glad to know that it is accessible, with much more from the same source, in an invaluable periodical, sustained so many years by that noblest layman of the American Church, the late Hugh Davy Evans, LL. D., of Baltimore. See his "True Catholic," vol. ix. pp. 212, 265. It was originally published in London, by Dolman, in 1851, as an "Earnest Address, etc., by A. Welby Pugin, Esq."

Note B''', *page* 252.

Of the mass at Nôtre Dame, it is enough to say that Francis understood from his Gallican standpoint what More and Fisher should have understood as well from ours. Guizot and other French and German Protestants always, from theirs, fail to comprehend the case. It is therefore noteworthy, when I find in the "Revue des Deux Mondes" so true and clear a statement as the following: "L'Église Anglicane n'a donné au César que cela que lui appartient; la même autorité que tenait l'Empereur aux jours de Grégoire I., le même, en effet, que l'Église Gallicâne a si souvent réclamé pour ses rois dès les jours de St. Louis. Avec la révolution de Luther, *Sa réformation n'a de commun qu'un éclat contemporain.* Le flot du Continent vient battre les rochers de son isolement, mais sans entrer dans la place ; et dela naquit le 'Dissent,' qui est le véritable *protestantisme* de l'Angleterre."

Note C''', *page* 252.

It is surprising that such an act, by a person in *deacon's orders* only, has not excited more remark on the gross ideas about absolution prevailing in the Roman Court. The deacon's functions are "non-sacerdotal"; yet, when put into the College of Cardinals and made a legate, the bishops and all orders of a nation kneel before him for sacramental absolution. The Marian schism exhibits nothing Catholic.

Note D''', *page* 253.

The impertinence of quoting this shameful act against Calvin, as if it balanced the sweeping off of nations by

Innocent III. and the wholesale blood-shedding of Alva, ought to be apparent to common sense. Yet, under colour of the false liberality of our times, how constantly we find journalists and others remarking that, if Rome persecuted, so did the Calvinists and others. In a few detestable instances, such facts, it is true, disgrace the Reformation, and our Restoration also. But (1) they were exceptional and not systematic ; (2) they were the lingering results of cruel laws, which we owe to the pontiffs and to the kings who sustained their persecutions ; (3) and they have been repented of, abjured, and abhorred universally. But the Roman persecutions were as vast as those of the Caliphs ; were accepted and glorified as triumphs of the Church ; and they have never been disclaimed, but, on the contrary, are justified to this day, and the right to renew them is asserted by modern pontiffs.

NOTE E''', *page* 255.

Concerning Linus and Gladys, see " Ante-Nicene Fathers," vol. iii. Elucid. ii. p. 108, and the references there : also, viii. p. 641; and, for a very interesting summary, Lewin's " Life of St. Paul," vol. ii. pp. 394-397.

NOTE F''', *page* 260.

See Faher's masterly treatise on the " Primitive Doctrine of Election," New York, 1840. For popular instruction touching the Scholastics, see " Mediæval Church History," by Archbishop Trench, p. 200; also, for Nominalism and Realism, pp. 268, 328, ed. New York, 1878.

NOTE G''', *page* 261.

In his Third Lecture before students of the College of France, Quinet (a friend and colleague of Michelet) treats of " The Roman Church and the State "; elsewhere of " The Roman Church and Science," of the same " and Law," etc. The whole course of Lectures is vigorous and suggestive, and, coming from a person familiar with French history in its relations with the Popes, a man of the world and not a theologian, the work is worth studying just now, when the conflict with Ultramontanism is beginning in our Republic. An English translation of the Lectures was published in

London in 1845, under the title of "Ultramontanism, or the Roman Church and Modern Society" (John Chapman, Publisher). It is all the more valuable, as showing where things stood in Europe just before the accession of Pius IX.

NOTE H''', *page* 263.

The Schoolmen, writing down the bishops to write up the Pope, (see Aquinas, Opp., tom. iv. p. 1055 *et seq.*, ed. Migne, and Peter Lombard, tom. i. p. 394,) seized upon some passionate expressions of Jerome, which appear to have been copied by Augustine, and theorized, against all antiquity, that the Episcopate, though an order in the hierarchy, was not of itself one of the Holy Orders. The bishop was only a presbyter acting in a given place as a vicar of the one Universal Bishop at Rome. Calvin, educated in Scholasticism, shared this view, and accordingly, in rejecting the Papacy, he supposed the Episcopate must go with it. Yet he deeply felt the value of the *primitive Episcopacy*, and professed himself in favour of it, if only it might be had. See his Institutes, Opp., vol. viii., ed. Amstelod., 1667, p. 60.

NOTE I''', *page* 281.

When King Charles demanded a private interview with his judges in the Painted Chamber, he said, "The child which is unborn may repent it," i.e. a refusal of his request and a hasty judgment. (King Charles's Works, p. 417, London, 1735.) His appeal so touched the court, that, but for the browbeating of Cromwell, a motion would have been made to allow what was asked. Think, then, of all that followed in 1660, in 1688, and down to 1715 and 1745, in fulfilment of the prophecy. But let nobody suppose that the disinheriting of his unworthy son James II. would have been regretted by the King. He made it *a condition of his blessing* to his children, that they should "perform all duty and obedience to their Mother, . . . and to obey the Queen in all things, *except in matter of religion*," commanding the Princess Elizabeth particularly, in that particular, "upon his blessing, never to hearken or consent to her, but to continue firm in the religion she had been instructed and educated in, what discountenance and ruin soever might befall the poor Church under so severe persecution." See Lord Clarendon's "History of the Rebellion," book x. p. 68, and book xi. p. 230, ed. Oxford, 1707. He thus withdrew his blessing from his posterity in case they should lapse; and his charge to his son and successor was the same, in his last letter to him from Newport, November 25, 1648. It was reserved for James to forfeit this blessing, and to reap the penalty. This last of the Stuart kings seems to have been a reproduction of King John.

NOTE J''', *page* 283.

" She is most precious; for, like a chemical *medium*, she possesses the power of harmonizing natures otherwise incapable of union. On the one hand, she reaches to the Protestant; on the other, the Roman Catholic." (See De Maistre, Opp., vol. i. p. 27.)

In amplifying this thought, I have elsewhere expressed myself as follows: "Her charity, indeed, is made her reproach; but she follows apostolic example in this, as in other things. She dictates the creeds, she prescribes a Scriptural liturgy. This she must preserve, as they have come down to her as an inheritance from the purest ages of the Gospel; but she refuses to make more narrow the old Catholic way of salvation. She dares to say, and none but a Catholic Church can say so much, 'Let us, therefore, as many as be perfect, be thus minded, and if in anything ye be otherwise minded, God shall reveal even this unto you; nevertheless, wherein we have already attained, let us walk by the same rule, let us mind the same thing.' Thank God, this was the spirit of her Reformation. In a scholastic age she was reproached by the Calvinists on one side, and the Romanists on the other, because she utterly refused to erect a Code of Belief, as they did, or to split metaphysical hairs and bind humanity, like the giant in the fable, by Liliputian webs, a bond slave to scholastic subtleties. This is the sect spirit; the Catholic spirit has nothing of it." From a sermon preached in Montreal.

NOTE K''', *page* 291.

The work of Ranke gives the melancholy evidence of this. And the court of Louis XIV., in which atheists were tolerated, but not the Huguenots, may sufficiently illustrate the results of such policy in the fate it brought upon Louis XVI. and his unhappy people.

NOTE L''', *page* 294.

A letter of Lord Macaulay's, dated May 23, 1857, addressed to H. S. Randall, Esq., author of a "Life of Jefferson," was published in the "Southern Literary Messenger," some thirty years ago. It is an admirable comment of that visionary man of genius upon the maxims with which he had spent his life in trying to induce Englishmen to destroy their own Constitution, while professing supreme devotion to its spirit, its marvellous vitality, and its vitalizing power. At this crisis, both Englishmen and Americans would do well to recur to that letter for a moral suited to the times.

P. S.—NOTE ON THE TEMPORAL SUPREMACY, *page* 249.

Dupin affirms that the *Evêque au dehors* may be called Head of the Church, in a justifiable sense. Dissert. Histor., D. vii. c. iii. § viii. p. 582, ed. Paris, 1686. Also, that in the time of Clovis, not the Pope, but the King, was esteemed, "after God, the head on earth of the Church in his own realm." See his treatise on the Gallican Liberties, p. 175, ed. 1609. Noailles ("Ambassades en Angleterre," p. 175, Leyden, 1763) relates that Queen Mary the Bloody, after dropping the title "Supreme Head," *resumed* it six days before the date of his letter, April 23, 1554. On the other hand, Queen Elizabeth would not suffer herself to be so styled, whether "in speech or in writing." See Bishop Jewell, Zurich Letters, First Series, p. 33, Cambridge, 1842.

But now compare with *this local and temporal title* (which Henry VIII. and his daughter Mary used, but which has never been permitted since in England) the title of "Universal Bishop," which the Roman Bishop has presumed to wear ever since Gregory I. rejected it, as Antichristian. What said Gregory about it? He said, "To consent in that nefarious phrase is nothing else but to forfeit the Faith." Epistle xix. p. 744, tom. iii., ed. Paris, 1849.

www.ingramcontent.com/pod-product-compliance
Lightning Source LLC
Chambersburg PA
CBHW021150230426
43667CB00006B/335